Assessment Engineering in Test Design

Assessment Engineering in Test Design

Methods and Applications

Richard M. Luecht

Routledge
Taylor & Francis Group
NEW YORK AND LONDON

Designed cover image: Getty Images via olaser

First published 2025
by Routledge
605 Third Avenue, New York, NY 10158

and by Routledge
4 Park Square, Milton Park, Abingdon, Oxon, OX14 4RN

Routledge is an imprint of the Taylor & Francis Group, an informa business

Library of Congress Cataloging-in-Publication Data
Names: Luecht, Richard M., author.
Title: Assessment engineering in test design : methods and applications /
Richard M. Luecht.
Description: New York, NY : Routledge, 2025. | Includes bibliographical
references and index.
Identifiers: LCCN 2024033869 | ISBN 9781032586816 (hardback) | ISBN
9781032586823 (paperback) | ISBN 9781003451051 (ebook)
Subjects: LCSH: Examinations--Design and construction. | Educational tests
and measurements.
Classification: LCC LB3060.65 .L84 2025 | DDC 371.26--dc23/eng/20240906
LC record available at https://lccn.loc.gov/2024033869

ISBN: 9781032586816 (hbk)
ISBN: 9781032586823 (pbk)
ISBN: 9781003451051 (ebk)

DOI: 10.4324/9781003451051

Typeset in Times New Roman
by KnowledgeWorks Global Ltd

Contents

About the Author viii
Preface ix

1 An Overview of Assessment Engineering 1

1.1 Some Definitions of AE 2
1.2 Limitations of Traditional Test Design 2
1.2.1 A Test Assembly Example 3
1.2.2 An AE Perspective on Test Design and Specifications 6
1.3 AE for Comprehensive Test Design Aligned to Proficiency Claims and Score Interpretations 8
1.4 Chapter Summary 11

2 Construct Mapping and Evidence Modeling 13

2.1 What Are Constructs? *14*
2.2 Limitations of Traditional Score Scale Construction and Their Interpretations 15
2.2.1 Traditional Development of a Score Scale 16
2.2.2 Content Blueprints and Standards-Based Alignment 19
2.2.3 Achievement Level Descriptors and Standard Setting 21
2.2.4 Item Mapping 23
2.2.5 Limitations of Traditional Blueprints, Standard Setting, and Item Mapping 24
2.3 Evidence-Centered Design 25
2.4 Construct Mapping: An Ordered Progression of Proficiency Claims and Evidence 27
2.4.1 Choosing a Construct Trajectory 27
2.4.2 Evidence Models and Proficiency Claims as Building Blocks 28
2.5 Creating a Construct Map 30
2.6 Chapter Summary 32

3 Task Models and Task Model Families 34

3.1 What Is a Task Model? *34*
3.2 Task Modeling and Cognitive Complexity 38
3.2.1 Task Model Grammars and the Structure of Task Models 42
3.2.2 Graphical Representations of Task Model Complexity 46
3.3 Item Scale Location (Difficulty) and Task Complexity 47
3.4 Complexity Design Layers 48
3.5 Chapter Summary 49

4 Task and Item Difficulty Modeling 51

4.1 The Need for IDM Research 51
4.2 Isomorphism and Composability in IDM Research 52
4.3 Characterizing Statistical Item Difficulty for IDM Research 53
4.4 Foundations of IDM Research 54
4.4.1 The Roles of Item Features and Complexity Design Layers 58
4.4.2 Some Methods for Statistically Modeling Item Difficulty 61
4.5 Phases in Implementing IDM 64
4.6 Chapter Summary 65

5 Task Model Mapping 67

5.1 Some Limitations of Traditional Test Blueprints and Test Assembly Methods 67
5.1.1 Conditional Measurement Precision in Test Design and Assembly 67
5.1.2 The Consequences for Test Assembly of Using Fallible of Content- and Cognitive-Coded Constraints 71
5.2 Building Task Model Maps (TMMs) 72
5.3 The Alignment of Complexity and Measurement Precision with a TMM 73
5.4 Chapter Summary 74

6 Item Model Families and Automatic Item Generation 75

6.1 Components and Types of Automatic Item Generation 77
6.1.1 AI and GPT Applications for AIG 78
6.1.2 Some Limitations of AIG 78
6.2 AE-Based Item Models 79
6.2.1 Item Model Structures and Content 80
6.2.2 Item Model Quality Control 81
6.3 Chapter Summary 82

7 AE Analytics and Quality Control 83

7.1 Object Analytics 83
7.1.1 Text Analytics 85
7.1.2 Image Analytics 87

7.1.3 Analytics for Audio/Visual Segments 88
7.1.4 Analytics for Tables and Tabular Data 89
7.1.5 Analytics for Mathematical Expressions and Equations 90
7.1.6 Analytics for Numbers/Numerical Sets 90
7.1.7 Analytics for Item Structures 91
7.2 Complexity Scoring Protocols 92
7.3 Psychometric QC Using Conditional Residual Analyses 95
7.4 An Object Analytic Architecture 97
7.5 Chapter Summary 98

8 AE Implementation and Future Directions 100

8.1 What Problems Does AE Actually Solve? 100
8.2 Implementing AE: A System of Integrated Systems 101
8.2.1 Versioning and Robust Integration 101
8.2.2 Quality Improvement Metrics 102
8.2.3 High-Level Procedures and Systems 102
8.3 Future Directions 103

References 105
Index 111

About the Author

Richard M. Luecht is a Professor Emeritus of Educational Research Methodology at the UNC-Greensboro where he taught graduate courses in applied statistics and advanced measurement. His research includes technology integration in assessment, advanced psychometric modeling and estimation, and the application of engineering design principles for formative assessment (i.e., Assessment Engineering or AE). He has designed numerous algorithms and software programs for automated test assembly and devised a computerized adaptive multistage testing framework used by several large-scale testing programs. Dr. Luecht is also a technical consultant and advisor for many state department of education testing agencies and large-scale testing organizations.

Preface

Assessment Engineering (AE) is a principled test design framework that I have developed and modified over past several decades. Much like the iterative design processes advocated in this book, AE has evolved over multiple versions. The current version of AE incorporates aspects of my past work in manufacturing production control and inventory management, cognitive scientific research, test design and item writing, operational psychometrics and statistical analysis, automated test assembly and mathematical optimization, standard setting, graphic design and data visualization, computer programming and database system design, and a more recent interest in generative artificial intelligence. This is admittedly an eclectic mix but this is what testing is—an eclectic mix of technologies, systems, and technical disciplines that need to work together.

The evolution of AE does not solely reflect my own experiences. I have had wonderful mentors and colleagues, perhaps most notably, the late (and great) Ron Hambleton, Wim van der Linden, and Bob Brennan. Thank you for teaching me so many technical things and correcting my misconceptions and mistakes along the way. The motivational writer, William Arthur Ward, wrote that "... *the great teacher inspires.*" I have been inspired not only by my mentors but also by my many graduate students at the University of North Carolina at Greensboro over the past 25 years.

I sincerely believe that we can make tests not only more efficient but also far less expensive while maintaining the best possible quality, regardless of whether they are used to guide instruction in classrooms on a daily basis, for end-of-grade or end-of-course summative purposes, or for high-stakes professional licensing purposes. Despite the many advances in psychometrics as well as computer and information technologies, we continue to design items and tests in much the same way that we did more than 50 years ago. Why? The testing industry has been using automated test assembly for the past three decades to quickly build multiple test forms using a computer algorithm to reconcile competing content and statistical demands applied to a limited supply of items. The industry is also starting to adopt new technologies like automatic item generation as a means of lowering item production costs. However, these technologies provide, at best, indirect connections to our score scales or their interpretive uses. One reason is that these types of technologies—despite their mathematical or statistical sophistication—are only partial solutions. Better alignment is needed between our score scales and their interpretive purposes and the way we go about designing and developing tests to provide the evidence needed to justify those interpretations.

The goal of AE is rather straightforward: to bring an engineering-inspired, multi-disciplinary approach to the field of applied measurement.[1] AE can bridge the chasms between the craft of item writing and test design, the statistical sophistication of psychometric methods for scale development and maintenance, and score interpretations as validity arguments. Psychometrics has continued to progress as a discipline—at least insofar as offering a considerable body of research and ongoing development of increasingly more sophisticated psychometric models and statistical estimation techniques. But psychometric modeling and calibration techniques using advanced statistical estimation procedures, alone, are not comprehensive solutions for test design and development. Psychometrics get us to an ordered series of numbers—a score scale. But effective statistical procedures can only be applied given sufficient data to estimate or calibrate the parameters of a given mathematical model. Furthermore, even when we are given a scale with optimized numerical score properties, we still need to add meaning to the numbers, a challenge often relegated to standard setting and *ad hoc* alignment studies conducted after test forms have been created and statistically calibrated to a score scale.

Consider the following figure showing three important facets of large-scale assessment: (1) test design and development, (2) psychometric scaling and maintenance, and (3) score interpretation. Although our eyes may be drawn to the ellipses, the *gaps* along the three connectors between these facets are equally important. They imply *disconnects*—incomplete linkages or faulty alignments.

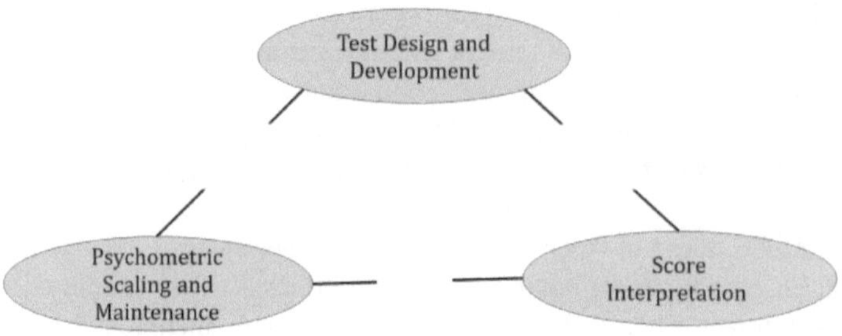

Figure 0.1 Test Triangle: Facets of Measurement

Test developers, editors, and item writers tend to work independently on item and test form design issues that lead to the production of items in an item bank. Psychometricians analyze and calibrate the data that result from operational administrations of the test forms in order to establish and maintain a metric or scale and to support scoring. Score interpretation studies are usually applied only after one or more operational test forms have been administered and scored (e.g., via standard setting). The apparent gaps between the three facets in the above figure are all too real in practice. Arguably, those gaps are due to the lack of a comprehensive design plan for most assessments—a design plan that clearly connects the intended score interpretations with up-front test design and development specifications and practices as well as with psychometric operations.

AE is about principled test design where human judgment and creative license during test blueprinting and item writing are replaced with carefully developed cognitive task models that can generate highly consistent test forms that support intended statistical score scale properties and interpretations over time. AE integrates key technologies and design principles from industrial engineering, cognitive science, information technology, machine learning and artificial intelligence, data science, statistical quality control, and advanced psychometrics to the practice of test design and development. The end goals of AE are: (a) improved and more consistent overall assessment quality; (b) implementation of highly structured designs and scalable automation to reduce item production costs; (c) reduction of item pretesting costs and exposure; (d) improved calibration and scale maintenance over time; and (e) more consistent generation and deployment of very high-quality, low-cost test items to meet both low- and high-volume production demands over time.

AE shares many features and some terminology with other approaches to principled assessment design, including Evidence-Centered Design (ECD; Mislevy, 1994, 2006; Mislevy, Steinberg, and Almond, 2003) and automated item generation (AIG) (Bejar & Yocom, 1991; Bejar et al., 2003; Drasgow, Luecht & Bennett, 2006; Embretson & Kingston, 2018; Gierl & Haladyna, 2012). For example, AE refers to evidence models and claims like ECD, and uses item templates in a manner that is consistent with AIG implementations of item models, families, or shells.

This book integrates four important areas of research and operational practice within the measurement and assessment field that have historically been treated as separate functions in large-scale, operational testing: (1) item generation; (2) test assembly; (3) psychometric scale development and maintenance; and (4) score interpretation and reporting. A key AE premise is that industrial design principles can help us better connect these functions by focusing on creating detailed designs for every item and test form in order to build strong evidence models for score scale design and the interpretation of proficiency along that scale. Everything in AE is *by design*!

This book offers some suggested methods and strategies. It is also intended to serve as a type of functional requirements specification for the systems and technologies needed to realize our visions for our score scales. Beyond that, I hope that it is interesting, useful, and inspiring enough to motivate a change that I see is essential in our testing industry.

Note

1 The seminal work of Deiter Rams on principles for good design is an inspirational way to look at what industrial engineering can offer (see https://en.wikipedia.org/wiki/Dieter_Rams). Given my long-time love of carpentry and along a slightly different tangent, I would also recommend Carroll's book, *Measuring, Marking & Layout* (see references) for insights on how carpenters and home builders approach measurement.

1 An Overview of Assessment Engineering

This book is about Assessment Engineering (AE). But what does it mean to *engineer* a test? A brief answer to this question is that anytime we apply principled, systematic (and possibly automated) procedures for test design, item generation, and test assembly, we are *engineering* the test. For example, modern *automated test assembly* (ATA) procedures employ sophisticated mathematical optimization algorithms and software to build multiple, parallel test forms that can simultaneously meet both content and other qualitatively coded specifications as well as statistical targets like an average item difficulty or Item Response Theory (IRT) test information function. ATA is an engineering process for test construction. If we develop a computer algorithm called an *item generator* to mass-produce items using automatic item generation (AIG), we are effectively engineering the item production process. If we apply multilevel IRT calibration models to empirically investigate residual patterns for item families and then use that quality control (QC) information to tighten the design specifications of item-family templates, we are engineering some facets of item design.

Some testing organizations are already applying various aspects of AE whenever and wherever they use ATA, AIG, or otherwise employing strong psychometric QC mechanisms to help guide and modify their item designs and item creation practices. However, this book is not about *ad hoc* solutions or partial AE implementations. It instead recommends adopting a comprehensive, integrated systems approach that applies well-established industrial engineering principles to the design and implementation of an entire testing *enterprise*—from initial test design and development through score scale design and psychometric QC. That is not to say that readers cannot extract and modify only the required parts of AE for their own purposes; it is certainly feasible. Rather, having a comprehensive and integrated view suggests what is possible in terms of the overall testing enterprise. That is the intent of this book—to describe, discuss, and demonstrate what is *possible*!

However, if organizations are already using various aspects of principled assessment design and engineering to develop new items using AIG or to efficiently assemble multiple test forms using ATA, is there really a need for an integrative framework like AE? There is! It seems to be an all-too-common, implicit assumption in the assessment industry that subject-matter experts such as teachers and test development editors should handle everything having to do with the item and test content, and psychometricians should be the ones to worry about the statistical quality of the items and psychometric properties of a score scale. An integrated efficiency- and quality-oriented view of test design and development and score-scale development and maintenance seems lacking in practice. Furthermore, building an integrated assessment system implies that overall design principles such as scalability, QC, and inter-operability are considered across the breadth and depth of operational activities within the enterprise.

DOI: 10.4324/9781003451051-1

1.1 Some Definitions of AE

AE is an integrated test design and development framework that applies industrial engineering principles to all aspects of item and test design and development while also incorporating strong statistical QC mechanisms to ensure that every test form provides consistent measurement score scale properties and score interpretations over time (Luecht, 2006, 2007, 2008, 2012a, 2013, 2016a, 2019; Luecht & Burke, 2020). In addition to borrowing from the field of industrial engineering, AE draws on research and design innovations from psychometrics and measurement science, cognitive science, information technology and science, and data sciences including machine learning and artificial intelligence. There are five AE design goals: (1) implementation of highly structured designs and scalable automation to reduce item- and test-form production costs while actually improving quality; (2) simplification of the test assembly process and improvement of quality and consistency of test forms; (3) reduction of item pretesting costs and exposure; (4) improved calibration and scale maintenance over time; and (5) detailed evidence-based interpretations across a score scale where every item on every test form is aligned to specific proficiency claims.

1.2 Limitations of Traditional Test Design

Test development is typically a *human-intensive process* calling on the judgments and expertise of subject-matter content specialists, test editors, psychometricians, and other assessment professionals to design and write the test items, pilot test new items, assemble and check the qualitative properties of test forms, etc. In many ways, modern test development remains largely a *craft*—albeit, an all-too-often very expensive, time-consuming, and resource-intensive craft.

Consider a rather simplistic craft example. Suppose that we needed to make 300 circular name tags for a business event. We might be able to handle the printing of the names on sheets of cardstock paper using a computer, a printer, and database software. But we would still need to cut out the 300 name tags. Suppose that our name tag design specification is each individual's name centered within an elliptical shape 4 inches wide (approximately 10 cm) and 2.5 inches (just over 6 cm) tall as shown in Figure 1.1.

We might enlist the aid of five "volunteers" to each cut out approximately 60 name tags. Training might involve showing them how to mark and then use scissors to cut out each name tag—perhaps using a stencil or traceable template. Assuming an average time of two minutes per name tag, each volunteer would need to commit about two hours to the project. Despite our training, there would likely be considerable variability in quality of the 300 name tags due to the cutting skill of our volunteers, the quality of their scissors, etc. So, how might we engineer a more efficient and higher quality process? Perhaps we could locate and rent a machine called a digital die cutter, program in our specifications, and use the die cutter to generate 300 almost perfectly cut elliptical name tags. Of course, we would need to factor in the equipment rental costs and set-up time. But from a production efficiency perspective, this *engineering* solution would certainly be worth considering as a viable method for creating a large number of professional-looking name tags.

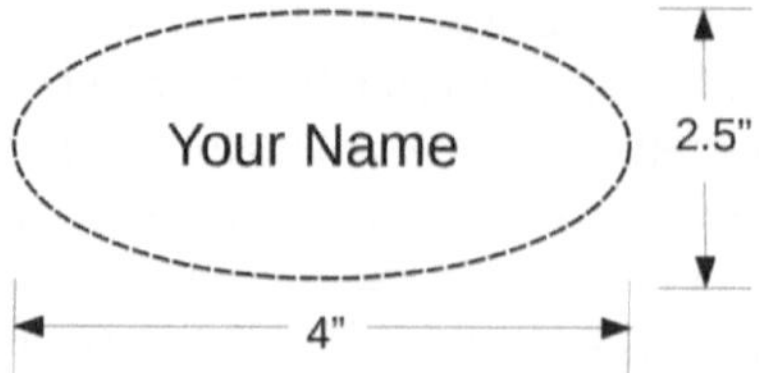

Figure 1.1 Specification for Generating Elliptical Name Tags

1.2.1 A Test Assembly Example

Operational test design, item development, and test form assembly procedures are certainly more complex than generating name tags. Nonetheless, there are many opportunities for quality and efficiency improvements if we stop viewing these practices and procedures as elaborate craft projects where item writers and test developers are given substantial creative license relative to the design and production of unique items and test forms. Imagine the variability we would have if we let our volunteers decide the size and shape of their batch of name tags. This is not meant as a critique of the dedication and hard work that most item writers and test developers put into every item and test form. Rather, it is meant to emphasize that with creative license comes *variability*—variability in design, form, function, and quality. Engineering design seeks to reduce unnecessary variability and costs while maintaining or even improving quality. A relatively simple set of examples can illustrate some of the challenges under a traditional test development paradigm.

Traditional test assembly practices build test forms that comprise some number of items selected from an item bank. Each test form is expected to meet various content requirements and one or more statistical targets such as the average difficulty or IRT functions like a *test characteristic function* (TCF) denoting the expected test scores as a function of the underlying proficiency scale, θ ("theta"), or a psychometric score-precision curve called the *test information function* (TIF; Hambleton & Swaminathan, 1985; Lord, 1980; Luecht, 2016b; van der Linden, 2005). Consider that provided with an item bank consisting of 150 items, there is a very large number of possible combinations—4.6215E+42 combinations to be exact—of 60-item test forms we could build, with a subset of those forms potentially meeting all of our test assembly requirements (i.e., *constraints*).

Figure 1.2 shows an example of test specifications for building 60-item test forms. The rows in the two tables at the left represent the item counts relative to five of the *Common Core State Standards (CCSS) for Mathematics* content areas (National Governors Association Center for Best Practices & Council of Chief State School Officers, 2010). The columns in the upper left table represent three cognitive categories (conceptual, applied, and strategic knowledge). The plot at the right simultaneously shows two possible IRT statistical targets for constructing the 60-item test forms: (1) the TCF denoting the expected test scores and (2) the corresponding TIF indicating the targeted score precision across the proficiency scale. In this case, the majority of the measurement precision is targeted near the center of the scale, slightly to the right of the zero-point on the scale.

In practice, we could employ ATA optimization software to select one or more 60-item test forms that simultaneously meet the content specifications and either the TCF or TIF targets

	Cognitive Skills			
Subdomain	*Conceptual (C)*	*Applied (A)*	*Strategic (S)*	**Totals**
NBT	2	5	2	9
NF	4	8	3	15
OA	3	8	2	13
MD	4	7	3	14
GEO	2	5	2	9
Totals	15	33	12	60

Legend	
NBT	Numbers Base 10
NF	Number and Operations-Fractions
OA	Operations and Algebraic Thinking
MD	Measurement and Data
GEO	Geometry

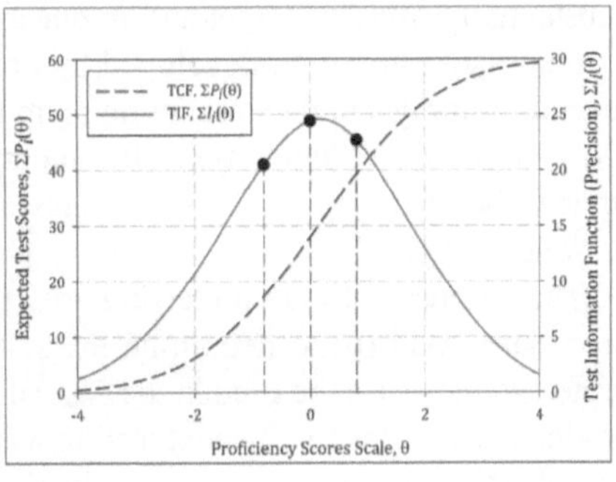

Figure 1.2 A 60-Item Test Form Meeting Statistical and Content Targets

shown in Figure 1.2. The available inventory of items in the eligible item bank would determine the number and quality of the ensuing test forms. For example, an ATA optimization model[1] with exact marginal counts for the content and cognitive item attributes would take on a somewhat intimidating appearance like:

Minimize y

Subject to $$\sum_{i=1}^{I} I_i(\theta) \geq T(\theta) - y \text{ ,} T(\theta) = \{20.5, 24.4, 22.7\}$$

$$\sum_{i=1}^{I} I_i(\theta) \geq T(\theta) + y$$

[List of other equations representing the above marginal content and cognitive constraints specifying exact item-count quantities, minimum or maximums]

$$\sum_{i=1}^{I} x_i = 60 \quad \left[\textit{Test length constraint}\right]$$

$$x_i \in \{0,1\} \quad \left[\textit{Binary item} - \textit{selection}\left(\textit{decision}\right)\textit{variable}\right]$$

$$y \geq 0. \quad \left[\textit{Optimization tolerance variable constraint}\right]$$

The TIF target values at three proficiency scores modeling the requisite amount of score precision implied by the TIF curve in Figure 1.1 are: $T(\theta_1 = -.8) = 20.5$, $T(\theta_2 = 0) = 24.4$, and $T(\theta_3 = .8) = 22.7$. Those points are shown in the plot as dots with drop lines. This type of ATA modeling was developed by applying mathematical programming optimization methods from operations research (van der Linden, 2005). It can find the best (optimal) test form from among our 4.6215E+42 possible combinations. These types of ATA optimization models can be applied to virtually any type of test using Classical Test Theory statistics or IRT.

However, like any manufacturing or production challenge, a major challenge of traditional test development is the creation, sustainability, and maintenance of the item bank. Without sufficient quantities of items (the supply) meeting all of the required content, cognitive, and statistical attributes (the demands), any manual or ATA procedures will be challenged at best and, at worst, can result in substandard or inconsistent test forms (e.g., relaxed or inconsistent *content balancing* constraints or non-parallel statistical properties such as the form-level TIFs that differ substantially from the target and/or one another).

Item banks are often developed by providing subject-matter expert item writers with some level of training and then assigning them to write items meeting particular segments of the *content blueprint*. The items typically undergo additional editorial, appropriateness, and fairness reviews before being assigned to pretest slots on an operational test administration (Schmeiser & Welch, 2006).

The purposes of item pretesting are (a) to verify the item answer keys, rubrics, and scoring procedures, and (b) to determine the statistical operating characteristics of each item. Stable pretest statistics can be used in the type of ATA model shown above for building one or more operational test forms for the next testing window. Nevertheless, pretesting also introduces a subtle complication for our test form production. Items are not "complete" for operational use until they have undergone the pretesting process—a process that adds costs and time to generating the needed supply of items for building test forms. Furthermore, there is inevitably some item loss due to unresolvable quality problems uncovered during pretesting. Because of the potential item loss during pretesting, testing organizations may adopt sustainability policies that require generating, for example, 20–25 percent more new items than needed for populating the test forms to be used during the next test-administration window. However, there may still be item bank deficits stemming from the statistical properties of the available items in the bank within particular content and cognitive categories.

So, let's consider two test assembly scenarios to demonstrate the role of the item bank on the quality of the ensuing test forms. Under each scenario, suppose that we want to generate two parallel test forms each meeting the 60-item test specifications indicated by Figure 1.2 using the above ATA model (see the prior equations). For the first scenario, suppose that we have a fairly healthy item bank consisting of 350 items well representing the form-level content, cognitive, and statistical demands. In contrast, under the second scenario, we are forced to use a more limited item bank consisting of only 150 items—a surplus item inventory of only 25 percent relative to the test assembly demands.

Table 1.1 presents the results of using our ATA model to simultaneously build two test forms from our two distinct item banks using the same system of ATA constraints shown earlier. As we can see, all four forms meet the targeted marginal item counts (i.e., the row and column sums) in terms of the coded CCSS mathematics subdomain item content and cognitive levels implied by the constraints in our ATA model. But consider the "cells" within each block. Forms A and B, assembled from the healthier item bank, each have four cells that differ by one item from the cells in the blueprint shown in Figure 1.2. Forms C and D, generated from the 150-item bank, have far more item count discrepancies in the cells than our *desired* blueprint. Are these four forms really "content balanced" when they only satisfy the marginal content constraints and not the combination of content and cognitive demands implied by our blueprint?

Now let's move to the psychometric quality of our four assembled test forms. Figure 1.3 displays the TIFs relative to the target for Forms A and B (left-hand plot) and Forms C and D (right-hand plot). We would ideally like the TIFs for each form to be coincident with the target TIF. Forms A and B, assembled from the healthier item bank, provide measurement precision across the proficiency score scale that is reasonably consistent with our target. In contrast, the right-hand plot indicates rather sizeable deviations from the target TIF for Forms C and D.

This is neither a contrived example nor is it all that unusual in practice if we actually bother to comprehensively check the quality of operational test forms at a very detailed level. In this case, the test assembly problems for Forms C and D can be largely attributed to the size and quality of the item bank. However, it is not just about increasing the numbers of items in our item banks. Arguably, the underlying problem is the entire way that we go about creating our test specifications and then designing and generating items to populate our item banks.

Table 1.1 Test Assembly Item Counts by Form

	Forms A				*Forms B*				*Form C*				*Form D*			
Subdomain	*C*	*A*	*S*	*Tot*	*C*	*A*	*S*	*Tot*	*C*	*A*	*S*	*Tot*	*C*	*A*	*S*	*Tot*
NBT	**1**	5	**3**	9	2	5	2	9	**3**	**4**	2	9	2	**6**	**1**	9
NF	4	8	3	15	**3**	8	**4**	15	**1**	**10**	**4**	15	**2**	**9**	**4**	15
OA	**4**	8	**1**	13	**4**	8	**1**	13	**2**	**10**	**1**	13	**4**	**7**	2	13
MD	4	7	3	14	4	7	3	14	**6**	**5**	3	14	4	**9**	**1**	14
GEO	2	5	2	9	2	5	2	9	**3**	**4**	2	9	**3**	**2**	**4**	9
Totals	**15**	**33**	**12**	**60**	**15**	**33**	**12**	**60**	**15**	**33**	**12**	**60**	**15**	**33**	**12**	**60**

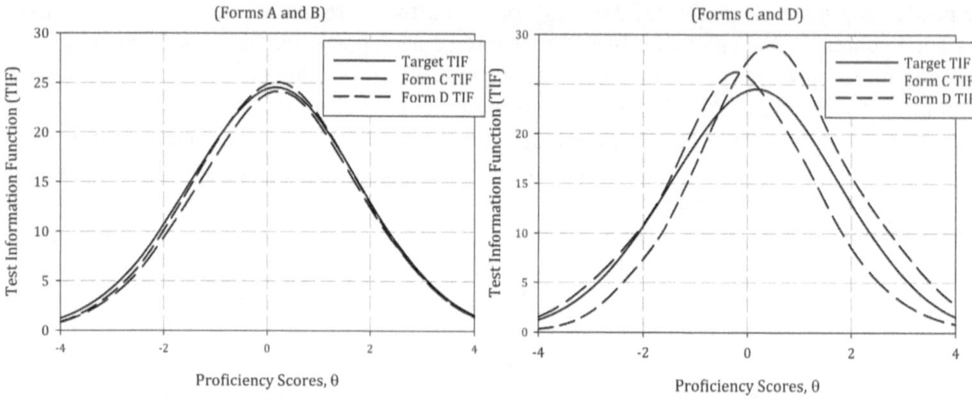

Figure 1.3 ATA Test Information Functions for Two 60-Item Forms Created from Healthy and Restricted Item Banks

As suggested above, testing organizations often use *multiple* schemes or taxonomies for coding the domain-specific item content, references to academic learning standards, cognitive levels of the items, item types, and a myriad of other item features such as word counts, use of images or pictorial materials, and text complexity classifications. These coding schemes are often based on fallible human judgments and worse are often treated as independent item features insofar as generating the test blueprints and guiding item writing. Adding to the problem is our necessary dependence on item pretesting to "complete" each item in terms of empirically estimating its psychometric properties (e.g., statistical item difficulty).

As illustrated in our examples above, we may use an ATA model and associated sophisticated software to attempt to resolve the inherent *competition* between our blueprint and statistical specifications (demands) and the available item bank (supply). In fact, the quality of the assembled test forms is often inversely related to the extent of competition among the available supply of items and then inherent interactions between the demands. The exacting content, cognitive, and statistical item supply demands are seldom *jointly* considered prior to test assembly—that is, during the design and creation of each and every item.

The chapters that follow advocate for changing this process. AE is about designing a single, integrated system of item and test specifications that simultaneously deals with relevant and interacting task content, cognitive task complexity, and the psychometric properties of the items while also reducing or eliminating the need for extensive pretesting.

1.2.2 An AE Perspective on Test Design and Specifications

AE moves beyond ATA by introducing a different type of test form specification. We start with a hierarchical test structure that focuses on *task model families* (TMFs)—rather than individual items—as the primary units of interest (Luecht, 2006, 2012a, 2012b; Luecht & Burke, 2020). A distribution of 60 TMFs is shown in Figure 1.4 as gray-shaded dots. Each TMF (dot) has a *location* on the proficiency score scale corresponding to the difficulty of an entire family of items.

The task models differ in terms of the incremental complexity of the *challenges* presented to examinees where greater task complexity is indicated by darker gray shading of the dots and by larger "ellipses." The extent and complexity of skills or protocols typically needed to successfully complete tasks within that region of the scale are displayed as arrows within the

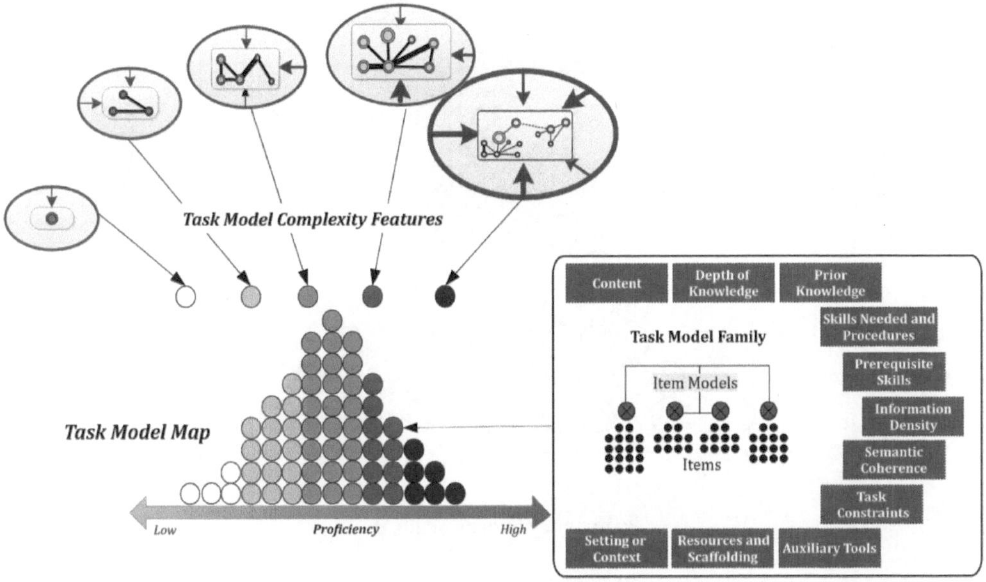

Figure 1.4 A Task Model Map with Task Model Families Comprising Item Models and Items

ellipse. More arrows and thicker lines are associated with tasks that call on more skills and/or higher-level skills, actions, decision-making, or applied procedural protocols. Declarative knowledge features such as the amount and depth of content needed, amount and depth of prerequisite knowledge, text/image complexity, and the density of information associated with the TMFs are depicted as "networks" of differing complexity (e.g., a single dot versus a network of networks such integrated text resources, tables, and graphics associated with a rather complex TMF).

In turn, each TMF consists of one or more item models. Each item model is associated with multiple items as shown in the (rounded) rectangle at the right. This hierarchical structure helps ensure that all of items connected to each task model require the same constellation of knowledge and skills and behave in a highly similar way, statistically speaking—that is, as *isomorphic* items (Bejar, 2002; Luecht & Burke, 2020). The item models specify the item type, presentational or stylistic elements, scoring protocols or rubrics, and shared data structures and constraints for the TMFs. Having multiple item models for each TMF avoids just producing "clones" of a single parent item for that TMF. Instead, there could be multiple parent items or item models associated with a single task model, but all items from those parents are engineered to be completely exchangeable (isomorphic) in terms of both their substantive use of evidence and psychometric properties.

As shown in Figure 1.5, let's compare the task model map (TMM) with our target TIF from Figure 1.2. We can see how the distribution of task models within the TMM closely coincides with our measurement-precision priorities across the score scale and relative to the target TIF. An AE TMM is a complete test form specification because it incorporates into a singular design pattern *both* the statistical specifications like measurement precision across the score scale as well as all relevant domain content related and cognitive requirements. Furthermore, each TMF (dot) is a complete content and cognitive specification for a family of interchangeable (isomorphic) test items that have a designated location within the TMM.

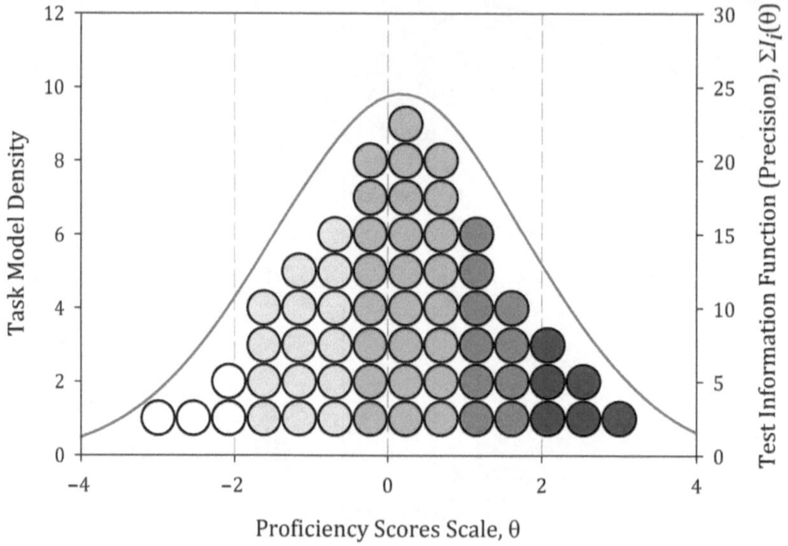

Figure 1.5 Correspondence Between a Target TIF and a 60-TMF Task Model Map

1.3 AE for Comprehensive Test Design Aligned to Proficiency Claims and Score Interpretations

TMM is a complete statistical, content/cognitive complexity, and item-type specification for a test form specification.[2] Each TMF is *located* along the scale. The engineering design goal is to simultaneously maintain that statistical location as well as the designated content and cognitive complexity for the one or more item families created from each TMF.

Meeting that type of engineering design goal is far more than wishful thinking. Figure 1.6 shows the overall alignment between other components of AE. At the top of the figure is *construct mapping* which lays out a detailed assessment progression of intended proficiency claims and score interpretations. The idea of a construct map was "borrowed" from Wilson (2005). Conceptually, a construct map is more or less like range performance-level descriptors suggested by Egan, Schneider, and Ferrara (2012) in the context of standard setting.[3] The assessment progressions forming the construct map are justified by *evidence models*, which are detailed narratives, concrete examples, and artifacts that jointly indicate the requisite assessment-relevant evidence supporting each ordered proficiency claim. The idea of evidence modeling was incorporated using concepts extrapolated from Evidence-Centered Design (Mislevy, 2006; Mislevy, Steinberg, & Almond, 2003). Chapter 2 provides a detailed introduction to construct mapping and evidence modeling.

The evidence modeling justifies each TMF on the TMM. The complexity of the TMFs is engineered by manipulating complexity design layers (CDLs). The CDLs are empirically verified factors or dimensions that jointly control the difficulty of each TMF. This creates a clear alignment (vertically in Figure 1.6) between the proficiency claims, the evidence for each claim, and the TMFs included in each TMM. Importantly, initial versions of this type of engineering design specification can—and probably should—precede the creation of the test items. That is, the item families are generated from each TMF design pattern and are therefore automatically aligned to the intended proficiency claims via the evidence modeling and CDLs. This book delves into each of those aspects of AE in Chapters 3 and 4.

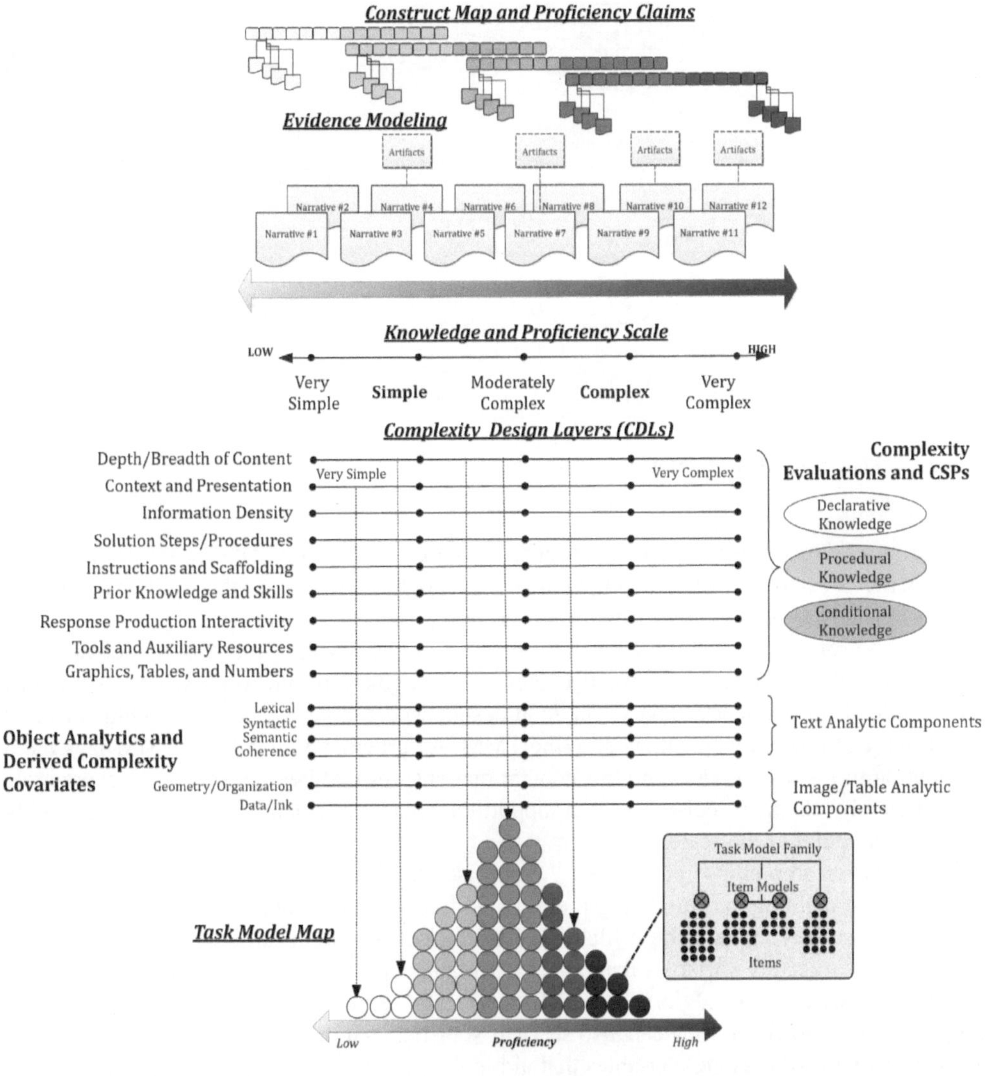

Figure 1.6 Alignment between Proficiency Claims, Evidence, Complexity Design Layers, and a Task Model Map

AE comprises four core technologies that provide the building blocks for principled assessment research, design, and implementation: (i) task modeling and mapping; (ii) item difficulty modeling (IDM) research; (iii) operational item production and test development infrastructure; and (iv) task model and item family calibration and statistical QC. These are depicted in Figure 1.7.

Task modeling and mapping technologies include mechanisms that align to three important aspects of test design related to score reliability and validity. The first is ordered proficiency claims/expectations and evidence requirements across the intended score scale (i.e., supporting construct mapping and evidence modeling). These reflect the tangible priorities for the knowledge, skills, and competencies that can be measured given the practical limitations of most testing situations. This aspect of test design prescribes the intended interpretations of the test scores

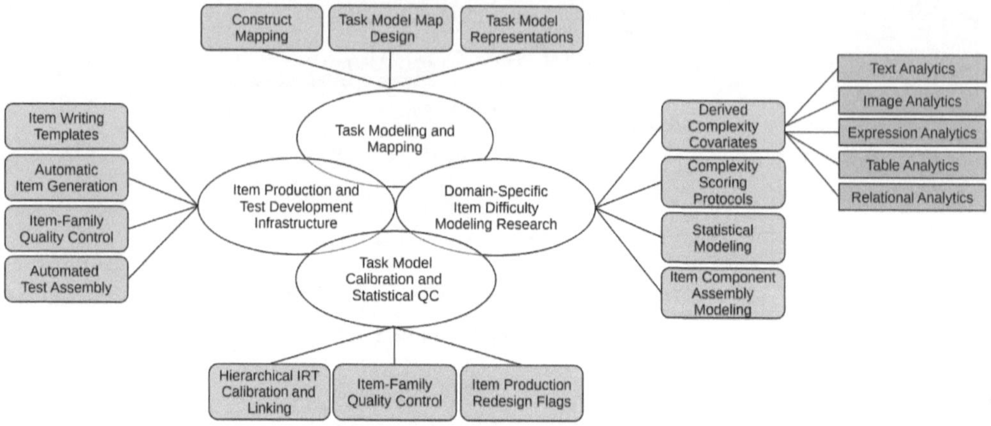

Figure 1.7 Four Core AE Technologies

and therefore addresses some important aspects of score scale validity. The second design aspect involves the development of in-depth, content- and cognitively based task model descriptions that document the composition of item families that provide the intended evidence to support the ordered proficiency claims along the score scale—the TMFs. This task model evidence helps bolster the connections between content- and cognitively anchored score descriptions and the intended proficiency claims. The final design aspect largely relies on building a formal test design and assembly specification—the TMM. As previously noted, the TMM lays out a distribution of the task models and test content that ensures that key regions of the score scale are sufficiently reliable (precise) and that support the breadth and depth of the intended validity claims at that point of the scale.

The IDM research ellipse in Figure 1.7 comprises empirical research and operational practices aimed at defining and modeling measurement conditions indicators and numerical metrics that statistically explain the difficulty of the task-model item families that comprise the TMM. The item feature variables that control, explain, and/or predict item difficulty are called *complexity design layers* (CDLs). These CDLs typically represent manipulated task- and item-design features. However, they can also serve as statistical augmentation covariates to enhance IRT calibration and/or as QC variables that aid in the production of high-quality item families that meet evidence requirements in support of proficiency claims along a score scale. For example, the CDLs can comprise categorical indicators or real-valued variables obtained from machine learning and object analytics, including text analytics and psycholinguistics, image analytics, table analytics, and mathematical/logic expression analytics (e.g., a type-token ratio as a lexical complexity indicator would be a metric indicator). Ideally, the CDL indices can be computed directly from source materials (e.g., text analytics applied to text segments or arrays). The CDLs can also include complexity scoring protocols (CSPs)—that is, rubrics that are used by human raters to denote the more subtle complexity elements underlying items, stimuli, and other test materials (Luecht, 2019; Luecht & Burke, 2020).

The CDL conditions, categories, and numerical indices serve three purposes. The first relates to enhanced development and statistical/psychometric maintenance of a test score scale over time. The second purpose emphasizes improved item calibration capabilities with reduced item pretesting required—a potentially huge cost savings for test developers that also reduces item-exposure security risks. The third purpose involves the capability to develop powerful statistical QC mechanisms to improve the overall quality and quantity of test content available in an item bank by producing isomorphic item families that function exactly as intended. Combined, the IDM components can move item design, and item writing practices production from craft to an efficient assessment production enterprise that incorporates solid manufacturing-engineering practices.

The item production and test development infrastructure ellipse in Figure 1.7 represents all of the operational systems and activities associated with generating test items as well as assembling the final test forms. On the one end of the automation spectrum, these procedures may follow more traditional test development operations (i.e., item-writing and editing employing large numbers of subject-matter [content] experts who craft each and every test item to meet various content requirements and format restrictions—see Schmeiser & Welch, 2006). On the other end of the spectrum would be AIG (Gierl & Haladyna, 2012). AIG uses a three-step process to mass-produce test items, namely, (i) test design specialists create a template or item shell called an "item model"; (ii) subject-matter experts provide lists of content to populate the variable content fields within the item model; and (iii) a software program using a computer algorithm called an "item generator" is developed to create families of test items per each item model. AE accommodates the entire spectrum of item production mechanisms, from manual or computer-assisted item generation to AIG.

The staff at a testing organization often work with item writers and further manage the assembly of the test forms and assign all new, untried items to pilot test slots on the operational test forms (Schmeiser & Welch, 2006). Although some organizations may still engage in manually assembling every test form, many testing organizations now use ATA models and algorithms to optimally build large numbers of operational test forms that meet any variety of psychometric and content-related test assembly specifications called "constraints" (see the prior example and van der Linden, 2005). AE greatly simplifies both item production and test form assembly in many ways. For example, the detailed item production specifications and associated statistical QC mechanisms used under AE ensure a large item inventory that directly reflects the item demands embodied by the TMM. In addition, given that item inventory, we can easily build each test form as needed to exactly match the TMM and, in doing so, simultaneously satisfy all content/cognitive complexity requirements as well as all statistical scale properties like conditional test information (Luecht, 2016b, 2017b).

The task model calibration and statistical QC ellipse in Figure 1.7 include all statistical and psychometric procedures, software tools, and empirical-focused analysis mechanisms for ensuring that (a) all items within a TMF are behaving in an isomorphic way (i.e., item-level variation in the psychometric performance is minimized to acceptable tolerances); (b) design modifications or item-production constraints can be implemented to deal with excessive variation within item families; and (c) scale-calibrated operational item parameter estimates can be updated to ensure that stable and appropriate scoring or classification decisions are reached. Some of the QC procedures may derive from the IDM research (e.g., natural language processing or NLP text analytics to check the complexity of derivative items generated from an AIG item model).

1.4 Chapter Summary

AE is a comprehensive way to design a singular test specification called a task model map (TMM). The TMM includes detailed content and cognitively specified TMFs comprising item families that behave in a statistically and substantively isomorphic way to provide the needed evidence to justify specific proficiency claims along a score scale (i.e., supporting the evidence models for each proficiency claim). An engineering focus helps to iteratively create concrete specifications and design patterns that locate the TMFs along the scale and ensure the needed isomorphism to an acceptable tolerance. The CDLs and related IDM research are essential parts of that engineering effort. Finally, psychometric QC procedures are employed to quantify variation with each TMF as well as unintentional drift in the TMFs over time.

Ultimately, AE is about designing and implementing principled and concrete ways of the intentional alignment between proficiency claims making up a construct map and the items families eventually comprising a TMM. It is not an easy venture. Many of the procedures developed for large-scale test development (e.g., item writing and editing, item pretesting and quality reviews, and test form assembly) need to be reconceptualized and possibly replaced altogether. The potential benefits of AE are eight-fold:

1 Improved validity by direct alignment between items and intended proficiency claims
2 A better understanding of the task design factors underlying item difficulty with direct application to developing new item and TMFs
3 A singular, integrated test form specification called the TMM
4 Simplified test-form assembly (sampling items within TMFs)
5 Empirical QC mechanisms
6 Reduced pretesting within TMFs
7 Full capability with IRT calibration and linking methods
8 Score scale interpretation by design

AE is not about partial implementations or half measures. The simple fact is that modern test design and development practices are not all that modern, nor are they carefully integrated with psychometric scale development practices or even our intended score interpretations. We continue to rely on manual procedures and human judgment to code item content and cognitive complexity using vague taxonomies. We employ data-hungry psychometric calibration and linking methods that require pretesting every test item to estimate sometimes unstable item parameters and associated scale-linking constants. We apply a great deal of human effort to generate and review operational test forms. And, once we have a numerical score scale, we engage in more human judgment via alignment studies and standard setting to map plausible performance interpretations to the scale. There may be better ways to build and maintain a testing enterprise. The remaining chapters offer some suggestions.

Notes

1 This optimization model assumes a mixed integer programming (MIP) solution. In practice, the mathematical model is converted to a set on matrices representing the data and constraints. A mathematical MIP solver (software) would minimize the objective function (tolerance, y) subject to simultaneously satisfying all of the content and statistical constraints listed.
2 Multiple TMMs can be employed for multistage testing (MST) designs and item-level computerized adaptive testing (CAT) with no loss in generality.
3 Egan, Schneider, and Ferrara (2012) proposed a more in-depth, four-tiered framework for proficiency-level descriptors (PLDs), with each tier aimed at different audiences and purposes. *Policy* PLDs are at the highest and most general tier; they describe the expected domain-level performance of examinees in rather broad terms that might be appropriate for administrators and other policy makers. *Range* PLDs are directed toward test developers and item writers. They denote the knowledge and skills expected or demonstrated by examinees within a performance level. *Threshold* PLDs indicate the expected or demonstrated performance exactly at a cut score—assuming some type of standard setting to establish those performance thresholds. Finally, *reporting* PLDs refer to demonstrated performance at the lower-bound (cut score), in the middle, and at the top of each performance category.

2 Construct Mapping and Evidence Modeling

Construct mapping is an iterative visioning process to prioritize, clarify, and document what a score scale is supposed to tell us—ideally long before we begin writing or pilot testing the items. Construct mapping certainly precedes the development of a content blueprint. It incorporates evidence modeling and the subsequent design choices that guide the development of our task models, items, and test forms as discussed in subsequent chapters.

From an engineering perspective, good design begins with clear, well-documented vision of the end product. Designing a score scale without visualizing its properties and intended uses is like addressing a love letter, "*To whom it may concern.*[1]" Failing to reasonably visualize our score scale leaves that endeavor to creative subject-matter specialists and item designers who may invent detailed item specifications and prototype items without even understanding the use or information demands from those items. Items should be designed to provide tangible evidence about proficiency claims. Proficiency claims differ along a score scale with less rigorous claims typically associated with lower scores and more elaborate claims associated with higher scores. Without a clear alignment between proficiency claims and required performance evidence (eventually instantiated as items), the meaning of our scores will be as specific and thoughtful as our generic love letter.[2]

This chapter emphasizes the importance of developing upfront, ordered proficiency claims as part of evidence *modeling*. The term *construct mapping*—adapted from Mark Wilson's 2005 book, *Constructing Measures*—includes the steps from initial visualization of a score scale as a design goal to adding proficiency claims and intended score interpretations, and then layering on detailed evidence requirements for the proficiency claims. This chapter also borrows from some fairly recent work on the development and refinement of performance- or achievement-level descriptors for standard setting.

A discussion of academic standards and alignment is included, but the emphasis is on: (a) working carefully and proactively to lay out the intended, ordered progression of interpretations; (b) adopting versioning strategies and iterative design principles to accommodate modifications of the construct map(s); and (c) verifying that the claims do not generalize too far from the inherent limitations of our assessments (i.e., restrictions on score interpretation implicit in our choices of item types, types of response data, conditions of measurement, etc.). Ultimately, construct mapping is about devising an honest and transparent set of proficiency claims as part of tangible evidence models.

The important objectives covered in this chapter include:

- Understanding the limitations of interpreting scales when the scale was not developed with those interpretations in mind from the onset
- Re-conceptualizing and visualizing constructs as scale scales with well-articulated, ordered assessment progressions jointly representing knowledge, skills, and experiences (KSEs)

DOI: 10.4324/9781003451051-2

- Understanding the components of a *construct map*
- Understanding *evidence models*
- Determining the priorities and density of evidence models along a construct map

Construct mapping can be challenging for existing tests because the score scale(s) already exist(s). In fact, well-established national or state examination programs will undoubtedly have many published and online resources that deal with score interpretations (e.g., normative reports). However, existing testing programs can also benefit from construct mapping as a way to better align the intended inferences and proficiency claims with item and task designs that provide concrete evidence about them. New tests can more directly build draft construct maps before any content blueprinting or item development even takes place.

2.1 What Are *Constructs*?

Constructs are human-generated, theoretical conceptualizations of measurable, continuous traits or latent classes. For example, a test may be developed to measure a construct denoted as *fifth-grade mathematics* or *eighth-grade English language arts*. Similarly, constructs like *anxiety* or *depression* may be measured by psychological instruments. A credentialing examination in the medical field may measure a trait such as *clinical decision-making*. The *Standards for Educational and Psychological Testing* (AERA, APA, NCME, 2014) define a construct as the *intended* concept or characteristic measured by a test and interpretable via the test scores or classifications.

Unfortunately, many construct definitions are vague—sometimes limited to a label or seemingly useful test title. The construct label may imply that other tests measuring the same or similar constructs ought to be correlated with test scores on the intended construct and have predictable interrelationships with dissimilar constructs—what Cronbach and Meehl (1955) called the *nomological net*. For example, we might expect test scores of a fifth-grade mathematics test in one state to correlate rather highly with test scores of fifth-grade mathematics tests in other states if students were administered both tests. We might further hypothesize that scores of a mathematics test ought not be highly correlated with scores of English language test or history test. We can also form hypotheses about the internal structure of a test based on the covariances or correlations between the item responses. For example, a unidimensional test assumes that a single trait adequately explains response patterns with residual covariances or correlations of zero (in expectation). In contrast, a multidimensional test battery may measure two or more possibly related traits.

A score scale operationalizes a construct. For example, Figure 2.1 shows a generic latent construct labeled "θ" (the Greek letter "theta"). The line denotes the construct-based scale. From a statistical perspective, θ is assumed to measure whatever the test items measure. Higher scores reflect greater proficiency or more generally higher levels of the underlying construct or trait.

The scale units are essentially arbitrary demarcations determined by numerical constraints implemented during the estimation of the scale's properties (e.g., constraining the scale unit length of a standard deviation unit to 1.0 or some other numerical constant). The path diagram below the scale (i.e., the ellipse with boxes connected by arrows) provides a graphical representation of the relationship between the scored item response variables (x_1 to x_{60}) and θ. The underlying trait, θ, is assumed to cause or fully explain the examinees' response scores on the 60 items. That is, examinees with higher levels of θ are more likely to receive higher scores on the items, subject to item difficulty. The single-headed arrows are regression weights (λ) indicating the causal sensitivity of each item to θ; they can also act as scoring weights when estimating

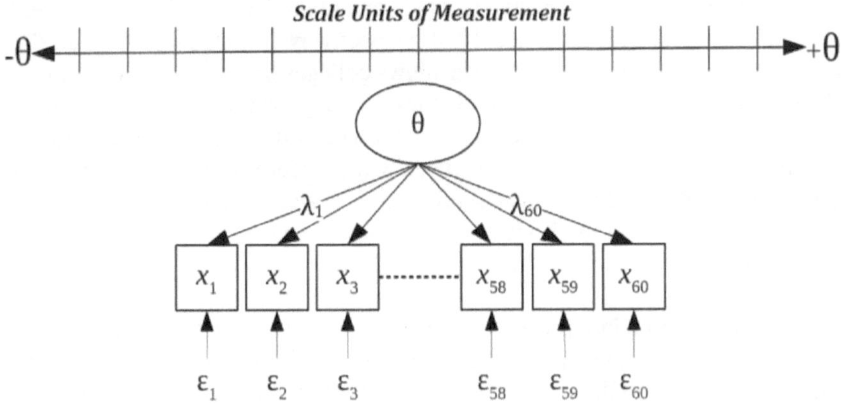

Figure 2.1 Statistical Representations of a Construct-Based Scale

the latent proficiency scores. The variables below each box (ε) are measurement or estimation errors. The observed item response scores are related to the underlying construct scale by the simple statistical measurement model, $x_i = \lambda_i\theta + \varepsilon_i$.

From a statistical perspective, Figure 2.1 seems to be a plausible representation of our construct. We have a number line with scale units. Items are aligned to that line by their estimated statistical characteristics such as item difficulty.

However, consider two very basic questions:

1 What is the construct?
2 What does one unit of change on the scale represent?

Answering these two questions is where construct mapping becomes useful. A construct must be more than a label. We may claim or attempt to make interpretive inferences or assertions about the nature of a construct from a numerical score scale, but most of our interpretations become normative in nature (e.g., relative to the distribution of scores for some reference group of test takers) or rely on *ad hoc* methods such as standard setting to essentially layer criterion- or content-based interpretations onto an existing scale. In order to understand the benefits of formally engaging in construct mapping, it seems useful to first discuss some of the inherent limitations of layering interpretations onto an existing score scale after the scale has been developed.

2.2 Limitations of Traditional Score Scale Construction and Their Interpretations

Test score *interpretation* is an amorphous topic in measurement. There are three broad classes of score interpretations: (a) normative descriptions; (b) domain-based statements about what the examinees can or should do at different score points; or (c) predictions about future outcomes (e.g., progress toward growth targets, college readiness, or success in a job).

Normative interpretations compare an individual's score with a score distribution estimated from some designated group of examinees (e.g., reporting student percentiles). For example, the Scholastic Assessment Test (SAT) used primarily for college admissions has three score scales: (1) Evidence-Based Reading and Writing (EWR); (2) Math; and (3) the SAT Total score composite (EWR + Math). The EWR and Math scales range from 200 to 800 with college readiness benchmarks set at 480 and 530, respectively. High school graduates in 2022 have mean EWR, Math, and Total scores of 529, 521, and 1050, respectively (The College Board, 2023). The normative nature of SAT score interpretations allows colleges or universities to choose students whose SAT scores place them in the top percentiles of a large, national sample of college-bound high school seniors. However, SAT scale scores and percentiles do not indicate the nature of the additional math content that, say, a test taker with a score of 540 on the SAT Math test has compared to an individual who has a score of 510. Instead, we are left with relative score interpretations (e.g., ranks, comparisons to national sample mean, or to benchmark scores that predict reasonable confidence in the likely success of those students in credit-bearing college or university courses).

In contrast, domain-based interpretations assume that the test score represents some intended trait or construct such as mathematics or reading comprehension. Individual scores are essentially predictions of how well the examinee would perform in the domain of generalization (i.e., his or her *universe* score[3]). Higher scores are interpreted as higher/better achievement—that is, more knowledge and/or skill—in the domain. Nonetheless, detailed, well-articulated, and actionable descriptions of the progressive complexity of content explicitly aligned to our domain-referenced score scales seems lacking. Over the past four decades, there have been some attempts to create elaborate and complicated, *ad hoc* content-based, interpretive arguments for our score scales (e.g., Kane, 2006). But there are few demonstrated cases where our score scales can be *empirically* shown to measure an intended, incremental progression of mastered content complexity in a clear and consistent way that transcends performance on an individual test form.

There are at least three reasons for the interpretive shortcomings of most existing practices. First, there seems to be an implicit assumption in the assessment industry that subject-matter experts (SMEs), such as teachers and test development staff, should handle almost everything having to do with content and psychometricians should be the ones to worry about the statistical properties of a score scale. An integrative view of test design/development and score scale development seems lacking in practice.[4] Second, it is extremely difficult to add detailed, content-based interpretations to a numerical scale *after* it has been developed (e.g., carrying out a standard setting exercise to map theoretical achievement level descriptors to designated regions of the score scale). The intended interpretation needs to be anchored into the meaning of every unit or point along the scale. Furthermore, every item needs to be justified in terms of the quality of evidence it provides in support of those point-by-point proficiency claims or assertions. Third, most prevailing domain-sampling paradigms treat items as *incidental* to the score scale and fail to demonstrate concrete connections between item difficulty and the manipulable content complexity and presentational feature of those items.

This chapter summarizes some of the more popular methods for incorporating meaning about and interpretations of a score scale. Some concrete suggestions are provided for designing better scales with interpretation and meaning inherently included in the score scale design and development process. The concepts of *construct mapping* and *assessment progressions* are also introduced in this chapter as ways to develop up-front, comprehensive specifications for the ordered proficiency claims toward which all the other components of Assessment Engineering (AE) are directed.

2.2.1 Traditional Development of a Score Scale

Most educational assessments are assembled to measure knowledge and procedural skills in a subject area—that is, a *domain*. Content domain framework documents may be developed to the intended scope of content knowledge and measured skills within the domain (e.g., see some excellent examples such as the *Reading Framework for the 2026 National Assessment of Educational Progress*, NAGB, 2024).

Given the frameworks and associated content blueprints, the test items are written by SMEs (e.g., teachers who are familiar with both the intended test content and the students who will take the tests). The SMEs often go through extensive item-writing training and the generated test items may further undergo extensive qualitative reviews and experimental tryouts in the examinee population (i.e., pretesting) to qualify their eventual use on a test form (e.g., Schmeiser & Welch, 2006).

Similarly, in professional certification and licensure, the domains are often described in terms of often used and/or critical KSEs applied by entry-level professionals (e.g., medicine and health care or accounting). A practice or job analysis survey is typically employed to determine the KSE priorities. Given the purpose of these types of tests, the interpretive focus of the score scale is often isolated to minimum competency (Raymond & Luecht, 2012).

In contrast to our content-based conceptualizations of constructs, most score scales are statistical constructs developed and maintained over time by somewhat sophisticated psychometric modeling analyses implemented using data collection sampling designs. For example, a score scale may be derived from factor analyses and use number-correct scoring or their transformations (e.g., Anastasi, 1988; Kolen & Brennan, 2014). More commonly, nowadays, score scales are developed using Item Response Theory (IRT). One or more IRT models and fairly advanced statistical procedures, such as maximum likelihood or marginal maximum likelihood estimation, are employed to *calibrate* a collection of test items to an underlying metric using a large matrix of binary- or polytomously scored item-responses to the underlying proficiency scale (Bock & Aitkin, 1981; Hambleton & Swaminathan, 1985; Lord, 1980; van der Linden, 2016). Estimated IRT proficiency scores can then be computed using the calibrated statistical item characteristics analogous to conducting measurement using calibrated laboratory equipment. Through statistical linking, an entire bank of items can be calibrated to the same proficiency scale making it possible to generate and score multiple test forms on a common scale. For example, an IRT-calibrated item bank is essential for implementing computerized adaptive testing (CAT) where the average item difficulty of individually tailored test forms is tailored to each examinee's apparent level of proficiency.

However, even the most technologically complex IRT models, calibration and scoring methods merely get us to a number line[5]—the score scale. This is a very important point to understand! Most traditional test score scales are represented by an ordered series of numbers. It is easy to lose sight of that interpretive restriction given the sophistication of our measurement models and advanced estimation techniques. Although we may claim that we can make probabilistic inferences about examinee performance—that is, about their knowledge, skills, or competency in a specified domain from the numbers—the validity and quality of those stochastic assertions are often left empirically unverified and only justified by somewhat circular reasoning based on vague, theoretical domain-sampling arguments (Haertel, 1985).

The scale points or units are, more often than not, arbitrary, subject only to restrictions on the types of mathematical scale transformations allowed.[6] For example, most IRT proficiency scales are referred to using the Greek letter θ ("theta") and span a range of $-4 \leq \theta \leq +4$ where zero is the center-most location of the scale.[7] Reported scores are typically (rounded) linear transformations of estimated θ scores. For example, consider the transformation formula, $y = round\left(A + B \cdot \theta\right)$. We may set the intercept (A) of the transformed scale relative to a cut score or to the intended population mean and determine the unit size (B) of the scale using two conveniently chosen data points or the standard deviation of some designated *reference group* of examinees (e.g., eligible first-time test takers completing the examination within a specified time frame).

Once we have the score scale—the numbers—it is relatively easy to develop *normative* interpretations. For example, achievement tests like the *Iowa Test of Basic Skills* (Riverside Publishing) are *normed* using a nationally representative sample of students in particular grades. An individual's test performance in the test is compared to the performance of other examinees. For example, the test scores can be converted to percentile ranks or grade-equivalents that sequence the scores on a test relative to the distribution of scores for a chosen reference group. However, norm-referenced interpretations have little or no content-based interpretation (Glaser, 1963). We do not know the extent of differences in mathematical knowledge and/or levels of skills for of students scoring at the 60th versus 70th percentiles.

Several decades ago, there was significant interest in developing *criterion-referenced tests* (CRTs)[8] as an alternative to norm-referenced testing (Glaser, 1963; Hambleton, Swaminathan, Algina, & Coulson, 1978; Popham & Husek, 1969). As Glaser succinctly stated, "*Along such a continuum of attainment, a student's score on a criterion-referenced measure provides explicit information as to what the individual can or cannot do. Criterion-referenced measures indicate the content of the behavioral repertory, and the correspondence between what an individual does and the underlying continuum of achievement*." (p. 519).

The assessment design, creation, and implementation challenges for CRTs were not trivial then, nor have they necessarily been resolved today despite the passage of time and incremental improvements in test design and development practices. With CRT, test developers first [concretely] determine the "*well-defined behavioral domain*" by articulating the behavioral claims and criterion (evidence) needed to support the intended claims (Popham, 1975). Next, they design items that justify making plausible inferences about satisfying the requisite evidence in a consistent (reliable) and interpretable way. Finally, test developers may field test the item, calibrate the obtained response data, and then rely on unsubstantiated sampling assumptions to justify performance interpretations. As Haertel (1985) stated regarding the validity of CRTs, "*... we are left with the theory of statistical sampling to justify our generalizations from a test score to an item domain, but with no theory at all to justify generalizations beyond that domain*." (p. 25).

It is interesting to note that those same test design, development, and implementation challenges are still prevalent across the assessment landscape. While easy to make, most domain-sampling arguments are largely unsubstantiated by practice or empirical studies. Tests are considered valid if the items are created by SMEs familiar with the domain and further align to some taxonomy of content and/or cognitive categories. However, from an inferential sampling perspective, those same arguments may fail as validity arguments unless we can concretely specify the sampling frame—the collection of procedural and content-based knowledge and skills from which we are supposedly [randomly] sampling items—and demonstrate how the sampled content relates to the reported proficiency scores.

Although we talk emphatically in assessment circles about supporting evidence-based inferences, our test design and development efforts remain largely divorced—at best siloed or insulated—from the design and development of our score scales. It seems far easier for testing organizations to create a well-intentioned behavioral and/or content-focused taxonomy of standards or objectives, and then they rely on that taxonomy to develop and classify the item content that determines how test forms are constructed. Next, we build our score scales from empirical item response data—i.e., determine the numbers and the scale properties. It is only afterward that we attempt to layer on one of more content-based interpretations of the knowledge and skills using standard setting and related methods. We make the case here that those practices need to change in some fundamental ways to improve the connections between score scales and their interpretations.

Most educational (and, for that matter, most professional credentialing) examinations employ up to three types of *descriptors* to reflect the content of a test and to supposedly provide substantive meaning of the scores. The first type of descriptor is called a content *blueprint* or content outline. The blueprint typically specifies the allocation of items or score points to key content, academic standards, and/or related score-reporting categories. (Note that some content blueprints can be both comprehensive and highly detailed.) The second class of descriptors are called *achievement-level descriptors*[9] (ALDs). ALDs are written explanations of proficiency-based expectations or claims about of the scope of knowledge and skills required within different regions of a score scale. ALDs are usually linked to the score scale via standard setting that determines the thresholds or cut scores separating the ordered categories. The final type of descriptor is called *item mapping*. In this, actual test items are mapped or *located* along the score scale based on their statistical item difficulty. The choice of items helps to provide exemplar content explanations at a specified level of mastery (e.g., statements like, "Students at this score point have a likelihood of answering 80% of the items like this one.")

2.2.2 Content Blueprints and Standards-Based Alignment

A content *blueprint* (or outline) indicates the types of content to be covered in a test. The blueprint specifies the allocation of items or score points to key content categories. For example, Chapter 1 introduced a sample test assembly model that was based on the *Common Core State Standards* (CCSS; NGACBP & CCSSO, 2010) for Grade 5 Mathematics. The fifth-grade standards concentrate on three areas of mathematical practice: (a) fluency with addition and subtraction of fractions; (b) integration of decimal fractions into the place value system and developing fluency with whole number and decimal operations; and (c) developing an understanding of volume with real-world applications. The sample problem in Chapter 1 included a content blueprint for a 60-item test form. A reasonable question is, "Where did the blueprint come from?"

Most blueprints start with conceptual outline or hierarchical view of a subject area or discipline. For example, Figure 2.2 displays the five CCSS domains for fifth-grade mathematics: (1) numbers and operations—base ten (NBT); (2) numbers and operations—fractions (NF);

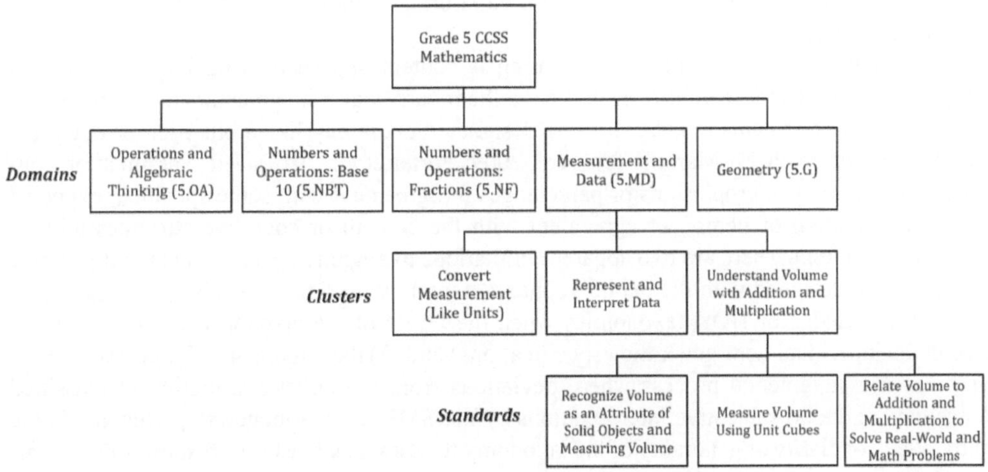

Figure 2.2 CCSS Domains, Clusters, and Standards for Grade 5 Mathematics

(3) operations and algebraic thinking (OA); (4) measurement and data (MD); and (5) geometry (G) with further breakdowns for the MD domains (clusters and standards). The NBT standards involve understanding and interpreting the place value system using base ten (e.g., recognizing the numerical meaning of digits in a multi-digit numbers as multiples of ten) and being able to deal with decimals to thousandths. The NF standards cover adding and subtracting fractions as well as making connections to multiplication and division (e.g., dividing by a whole number, x, is the same as multiplying the number by $1/x$). The OA standards focus on writing and interpreting numerical expressions using numbers, parentheses, and brackets as analyzing ordering patterns and relationships. The MD standards deal with converting measurement units, interpreting simple scales used in plots or geometric images, and understanding and applying the concept of "volume." Finally, the GEO standards focus on graphing and interpreting data points on the coordinate plane to solve problems and classifying two-dimensional figures into feature-based categories.

Committees of mathematical educators familiar with the CCSS might be convened within a state to prioritize the five domains shown in Figure 2.1, yielding the item counts included in the blueprint depicted in Chapter 1 (see Figure 1.2). In practice, more detailed subdomains or score reporting categories, genres or settings, use of images or graphics, availability of auxiliary tools like calculators, and item types can also be included in a content blueprint.

A content blueprint serves three functional purposes: (1) helps establish item writing priorities where higher demand dimensions and categories should prompt more extensive item writing in those areas; (2) constrains the categorical content distributions for assembling each test form (e.g., using the blueprint in Figure 1.2 to set exact item counts or count ranges—minimums and maximums—to which the test assembly process would need to strictly adhere, and subject to also meeting various psychometric targets such as the distribution of item difficulty or score scale reliability or precision target); (3) reports subscores in key subdomains.

In some cases, a content blueprint may be too broad or deep to ever measure with test of typical length—say, 40 to 60 items. Instead, various item-content categories are priority sampled over time under the assumption that plausible performance-based inferences can be made using an extended domain-sampling rationale that incorporates both items and a multi-year sampling frame for examinees. Conversely, some professional credentialing tests—for example, medical licensure examinations—can be quite long and cover content blueprints that include hundreds of content categories organized in an outline with up to four or five levels.

An approach closely related to blueprinting is content *alignment*. Under most alignment approaches, researchers select SMEs and have them carry out a judgmental study where they classify existing test items relative to some designated taxonomy like a blueprint or cognitive schema (e.g., Forte, 2017; Martone & Sireci, 2009; Porter et al., 2013). The classification consistency is reported as proportions or percentages of agreement with some specified, expected content distribution of items—or agreement with the content or cognitive attributes already coded for each item. There are two apparent limitations to alignment studies: (1) the items may not have been designed with the explicit content taxonomy used in the study (e.g., aligning to depth-of-knowledge or DOK taxonomies when the levels of the taxonomy are not explicitly used in the individual item-generation specifications) and (2) the alignment is based exclusively on an *ad hoc* judgmental process where deviations from the target distribution of classified items may be due to subjective interpretations by the SME raters solicited to participate in the study, a lack of clarity or generality of the taxonomy to assessment tasks, or features of the items included in the alignment study.

2.2.3 Achievement Level Descriptors and Standard Setting

The use of ALDs—also interchangeably called *performance level descriptors* or PLDs—has been a hallmark of the *National Assessment of Educational Progress* (NAEP). NAEP, often called the Nation's Report Card, is administered in ten subject areas: arts, civics, economics, geography, mathematics, reading, science, technology and engineering, U.S. history, and writing. The examinations are administered to students sampled from across the country in select grades on a designated multi-year schedule to gauge academic performance in U.S. public schools. There are four NAEP achievement levels for every examination and grade: (1) *below basic* proficiency reflecting a lack of even sufficient partial mastery of knowledge and skills in a domain; (2) *basic* performance denoting partial mastery of knowledge and skills that are fundamental for proficient work at a given grade; (3) *proficient* performance usually articulated as solid mastery of subject-matter knowledge and analytical skills appropriate to that grade as well as competency over challenging subject matter related to real-world applications; and (4) *advanced* performance denoting superior demonstrated levels of proficiency on the most challenging academic knowledge and applied skills measured by each grade-specific NAEP examination.

Figure 2.3 provides a detailed listing of the NAEP Grade 4 Mathematics ALDs for the *proficient* category. These statements reflect the likely mathematics knowledge and applied skills that fourth-grade students in U.S. public schools should be able to demonstrate at a level of solid mastery. Furthermore, an implicit assumption is the expectation that at the proficient level, students should be able to demonstrate ALL of the listed knowledge and skills.

Demonstrate an understanding of the relationships between the four operations (addition, subtraction, multiplication, and division); *add and subtract multi-digit whole numbers, fractions, and decimals in single and multi-step problems*; apply basic properties of operations to solve problems; divide with whole numbers using one-digit divisors and understand remainders; *solve problems with real-world contexts involving fractions with like denominators*; identify and explain factors and multiples; *compare and order whole numbers*; identify, understand, and sort even and odd numbers; *identify and compare decimals, fractions, and whole numbers on a number line*; identify reasonable estimates; *identify appropriate units or tools of measurement within the same system*; convert measurements within the same system; *measure lengths of objects to the nearest whole or ½ unit*; solve or estimate problems involving area; *demonstrate knowledge of 2D shapes by identifying, comparing, contrasting, and analyzing their attributes and describe attributes of 3D shapes with support of visual aids*; select the final image of translations and reflections with no dashed lines and create parallel lines; interpret and analyze data with scales of 2 or greater to solve problems; *identify possible outcomes in probability events*; determine the probability of events using terms of likelihood; *select expressions and equations to represent real-world situations*; solve one-step equations with whole numbers; *determine and/or apply rules to write, identify, or extend values in input/output tables*; and locate and name points on a map/grid system with whole number or letter coordinates.

Students at the NAEP PROFICIENT level are likely to ...

Demonstrate an understanding of the relationships between the four operations (addition, subtraction, multiplication, and division), *add and subtract multi-digit whole numbers, fractions, and decimals in single and multi-step problems*, apply basic properties of operations to solve problems, divide with whole numbers using one-digit divisors and understand remainders, *solve problems with real-world contexts involving fractions with like denominators*, identify and explain factors and multiples, *compare and order whole numbers*, identify, understand, and sort even and odd numbers, *identify and compare decimals, fractions, and whole numbers on a number line*, identify reasonable estimates, *identify appropriate units or tools of measurement within the same system*, convert measurements within the same system, *measure lengths of objects to the nearest whole or ½ unit*, solve or estimate problems involving area, *demonstrate knowledge of 2D shapes by identifying, comparing, contrasting, and analyzing their attributes and describe attributes of 3D shapes with support of visual aids*, select the final image of translations and reflections with no dashed lines and create parallel lines, interpret and analyze data with scales of 2 or greater to solve problems, *identify possible outcomes in probability events*, determine the probability of events using terms of likelihood, *select expressions and equations to represent real-world situations*, solve one-step equations with whole numbers, *determine and/or apply rules to write, identify, or extend values in input/output tables*, and locate and name points on a map/grid system with whole number or letter coordinates.

Figure 2.3 NAEP Proficient Category ALDs for Grade 4 Mathematics

Examinations like NAEP as well as most state sponsored end-of-grade and end-of-course tests usually engage in standard setting to connect the ALDs to the score scale. There are numerous standard-setting methods, each with benefits and issues. In general, standard setting involves having a panel of SMEs, such as teachers and other qualified individuals, evaluate the content of one or more test forms and the ALDs. The panel usually engages in a deliberative rating process to then determine cut scores that delimit each of the performance categories. It is important to note, however, that standard setting does not inherently add meaning to a score scale. Indeed, some standard-setting activities can be almost entirely based on normative policy decisions (e.g., market-based decisions that might lead to a policy to restrict the proportion of eligible professionals who are issued a credential or license).

Egan, Schneider, and Ferrara (2012) proposed a more in-depth, four-tiered framework for ALD development. Each tier is aligned to different audiences and purposes. *Policy ALDs* are at the highest and are most general tier. They describe the expected domain-level performance of examinees in rather broad terms that might be appropriate for policy makers (e.g., see Figure 2.1). *Range ALDs* detail the knowledge and skills expected or demonstrated by examinees *within* an achievement level. Egan et al. envision range ALDs as directed toward test developers and item writers. *Threshold ALDs* describe performance exactly at a cut score—assuming some type of standard setting to establish those performance thresholds. Finally, the reporting ALD tier refers to demonstrated performance at the lower bound (cut score) of a category, in the middle, and at the top of the performance category. Their four-tiered framework argues for better and certainly more granular definitions of expected performance traditional approaches to specifying ALDs. Yet, there remains the tendency to primarily focus on what the examinees can or should bring to the testing situation, rather than the complexity and challenges offered by the items.

ALDs are typically connected to a score scale—the numbers—by an *ad hoc* judgmental process called *standard setting*. The final outcome from standard setting is to determine cut scores on a score scale that delineate the conceptual, ordered performance categories associated with the ALDs. Most standard-setting activities involve recruiting qualified panelists highly familiar with the test content and the target examinee population (e.g., classroom fourth-grade teachers). The panelists are trained to apply a designated standard-setting method and then use that method to evaluate items, a distribution of examinee scores, or the examinees' performance or response patterns on a designated set of items. The standard-setting activities may further include in-depth discussions by the panelists concerning the meaning of the ALDs, as well as iterative training in the prescribed rating or classification method. Most standard-setting studies also include various types of statistical feedback mechanisms that allow the panelists to modify their ratings or classifications across two or more rounds (Cizek, 2001, 2012).

Some of the more popular standard-setting methods include variations of the modified Angoff procedure (Angoff, 1971), the Bookmark procedure (Mitzel et al., 2001), and various methods that require the panelists to evaluate and classify examinee performance relative to the performance categories implied by the ALDs (e.g., contrasting groups, body-of-work, analytical, and integrated judgment methods). The modified Angoff method(s) have the panelists consider a group of "borderline" candidates at the conceptual cut score delineating each ordered pair of performance categories. Using an intact test form or some other collection of items, they rate the proportion of borderline candidates likely to correctly answer each item. Those ratings are aggregated across items and panelists to determine the final cut score(s). The Bookmark method employs an "ordered item booklet" (again, an intact test form or a collection of item items specifically chosen for the standard setting). The panelists place their bookmarks between the pair of items that, in their opinion, best delineates the examinees correctly answering the items at a designated probability of success like $p_i(\theta) = 0.8$. The bookmarks are aggregated across the panelists.

Most of the more examinee-centered methods require the panelists to classify examinees into the proposed, conceptual performance categories inferred by ALDs. Those classifications and the examinees' actual scores on the test can be used to statistically determine the cut scores. More thorough discussions of standard setting are provided by Cizek (2001, 2012) and Cizek and Bunch (2007).

2.2.4 *Item Mapping*

Item mapping—sometimes synonymously called scale anchoring—has its origins in criterion-referenced testing (CRT). It is also conceptually related to the bookmark standard-setting method (Mitzel, et al 2001) and the item descriptor process (Ferrara, Perie, & Johnson, 2002). The idea is to define a response probability as a prescribed level of mastery (e.g., $p = 0.8$). Then, using a set of IRT-calibrated items, we can locate the items on the underlying scale corresponding to that probability value. Each item therefore serves as a concrete example of the type of actual test content that the examinees would be very likely to correctly answer at its corresponding scale location point.

For example, suppose that we have 50 items calibrated using an IRT model of choice. If we define "mastery" as an 80 percent likelihood of correctly answering each of the 50 items, the item locations become $prob(x_i = 1|\theta) \equiv P_i(\theta) = 0.8$. Figure 2.4 presents the IRT item characteristic curves[10] (ICCs) for each of the 50 items. As we progress from the lower regions of the scale (e.g., $\theta \leq -1$) to the upper regions of the scale (e.g., $\theta \geq +1$), the probability of a correct response increases from near zero to one. Depending on the IRT model used, the item difficulties fall approximately or exactly where $prob(x_i = 1|\theta) \equiv P_i(\theta) = 0.5$. Easier items are *located* to the left and harder items are located to the right. The item locations on the horizontal axis where the target response probability is set at 0.8 are shown by the dots with vertical drop lines.

The mapped items are meant to provide concrete examples of the types of items that examinees at particular scale-score points are likely to get correct with a specified probability.[11] While item mapping has a fair amount of pragmatic appeal, there is a subtle complication. Using actual items can lead to item-specific interpretations of performance, and those types of interpretations run counter to usual theoretical intention to have a given proficiency scale,

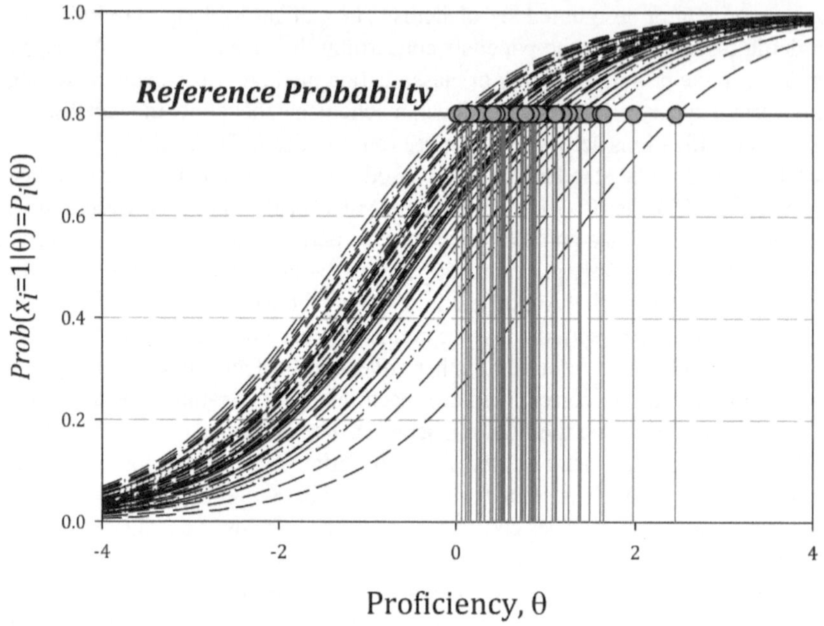

Figure 2.4 Item Mapping for 50 Items

provided domain-level inferences that go beyond the detailed content represented by the items are included on a particular test form (Haertel, 1985).

2.2.5 Limitations of Traditional Blueprints, Standard Setting, and Item Mapping

Large-scale testing organizations apparently feel comfortable with their numerical scales and *ad hoc* interpretations of the score points. Figure 2.5 shows a scale with three normative distributions (curves), cut scores corresponding to four achievement levels, and an item map. The underlying score scale is assumed to be based on IRT where the proficiency scale range shown is $-4 \le \theta \le +4$. We can assume here that the test assembly process ensures that the test forms meet some specified content blueprint. Viewed from this perspective, we can understand an organization's comfort with their score scale and interpretive framework. They have a numerical scale and a combination of ALDs and item content to provide a sense of what the numbers mean. Depending on the distributional characteristics of the examinee population, we can further include normative reference values such as means, medians, or percentiles.

Still, there are nontrivial limitations of relying on content blueprinting, standard setting, and item mapping for the purpose of adding interpretive meaning to a scale. For example, most content blueprints, no matter how detailed or well conceptualized by content experts, are neither ordered in any way nor aligned to the scores or properties of a scale. The same can be said for academic standards. Very easy and very difficult items can be coded as belonging to the same content category or standard. The reason is simple. Content codes and standards are nominal categories. In contrast, an assessment scale is an ordered series of numbers. There is an inherent mismatch between the categorical and statistical features of items that cannot be easily or convincingly resolved by *ad hoc* alignment studies.

Of course, we can augment our content blueprints with standard setting studies. The ordered PLDs do give us some expectation-based inferences about progress along the score scale.

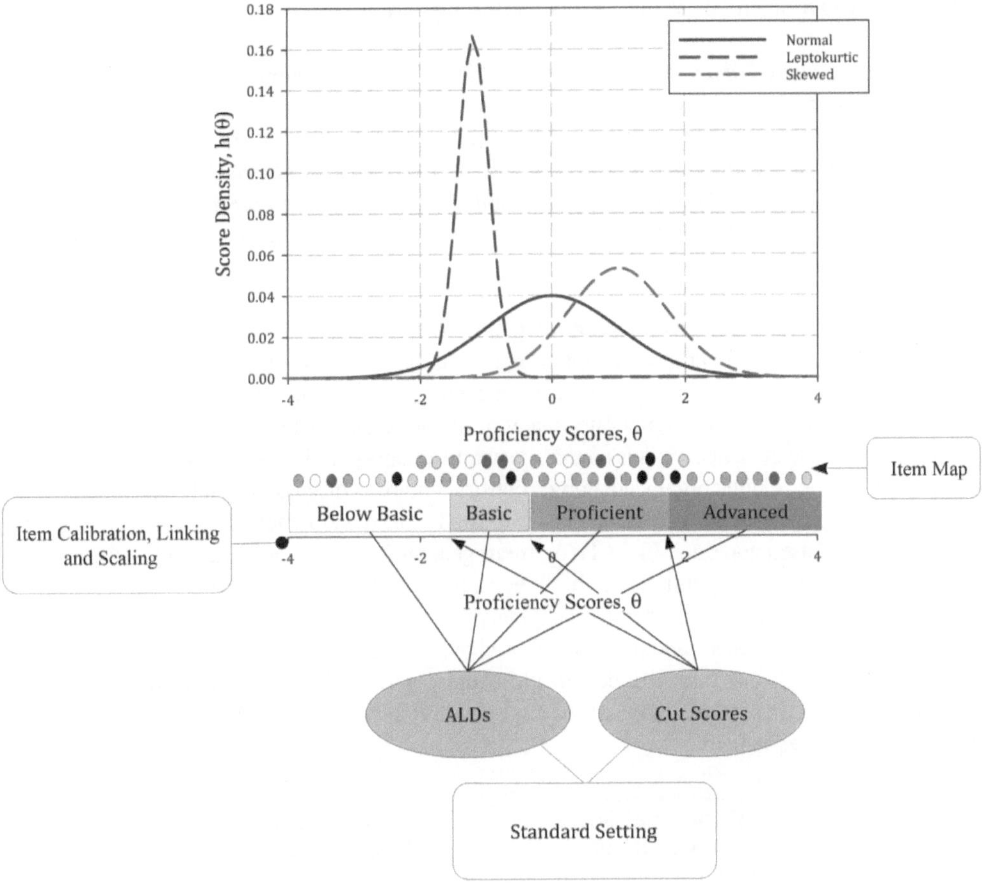

Figure 2.5 Items and Achievement Levels Mapped to an IRT Score Scale

However, those descriptions usually not detailed enough to describe the specific nature of the changes in the content mastered. Nor do PLDs tell us about the actual changes that occur in the progression of knowledge and skills from one score point to another.

Finally, our third content-based approach to adding interpretations to a scale score—scale anchoring—offers a rather detailed set of descriptions about the types of items examinees are likely to answer correctly at different points along a scale. Nonetheless, the ensuing interpretations of performance depend on the content of the selected items and their calibrated item locations. By somewhat circular reasoning, we derive our interpretations of the scale values through item anchoring while having no way to justify that the scale itself aligns to our intended inferences about proficiency.

2.3 Evidence-Centered Design

Mislevy and his colleagues at the Educational Testing Services (ETS) generated a seismic shift in assessment design with the introduction of what they termed *Evidence-Centered Design* (ECD; Mislevy & Riconscente, 2006; Mislevy, Steinberg, & Almond, 2003;). ECD has its conceptual roots in the legal profession, that is, developing and documenting evidentiary arguments to support inferences, propositions, warrants, or claims.

ECD evolved from an assessment design philosophy originally advocated by Messick (1994):

> *A construct-centered approach would begin by asking what complex of knowledge, skills, or other attributes should be assessed, presumably because they are tied to explicit or implicit objectives of instruction or are otherwise valued by society. Next, what behaviors or performances should reveal those constructs, and what tasks or situations should elicit those behaviors? Thus, the nature of the construct guides the selection or construction of relevant tasks as well as the rational development of construct-based scoring criteria and rubrics.*
> (p. 16)

This philosophy has served as a beacon for good assessment design by focusing on what we wish to say or infer about the examinees and then reasoning backward to the evidence to justify those inferences or claims. The task designs, in turn, concentrate on providing the required evidence from scored student responses. AE incorporates many of the principles of ECD into what are called *evidence models*. These evidence models dictate the nature, quantity, and quality of the evidence needed to justify proficiency claims organized along a construct map, as discussed in subsequent text.

Figure 2.6 compares more traditional test design and scale development practices with a systematic, evidentiary-based approach like AE (or, more generally, ECD). AE starts with a vision of the scale that can be iteratively refined and modified as needed. All test development and scale design activities are subsequently directed toward engineering the intended scale—including supporting its upfront proficiency inferences and interpretations about what examinees know and are able to do.

AE is fully consistent with the design philosophy and intent of ECD. In fact, AE can be viewed as a set of concrete mechanisms to engineer and implement ECD. Construct mapping is one of those AE mechanisms.

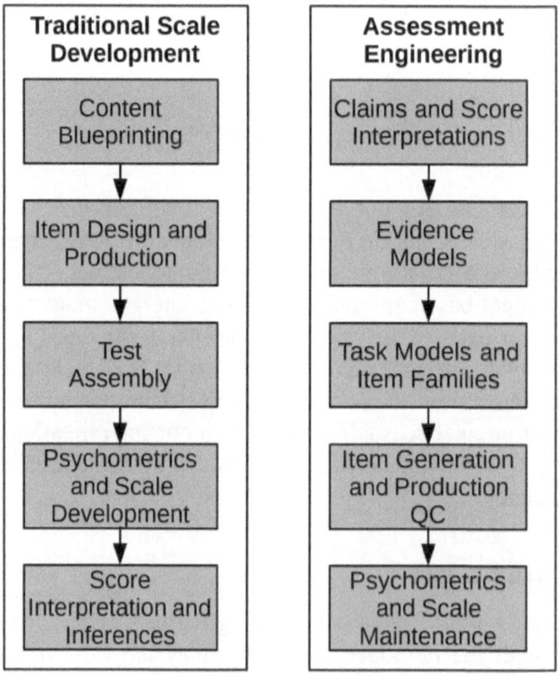

Figure 2.6 Comparison of Traditional Scale Design and AE-based Scale Design

2.4 Construct Mapping: An Ordered Progression of Proficiency Claims and Evidence

There are four aspects to construct mapping, namely, (1) choosing a construct trajectory; (2) developing detailed proficiency claims and inferences as building blocks for the map; (3) creating the construct map as an assessment progression that determines the scope, sequencing, and allocation of the building blocks; and (4) iteratively refining the construct map to reflect pragmatic priorities, assumptions, and constraints.

2.4.1 Choosing a Construct Trajectory

A *construct map* is an assessment progression (i.e., a conceptual "scale") that documents the measurable knowledge- and/or skill-based proficiency claims or assertions that we wish to make as we move from the low to high ends of the "scale." A construct map emphasizes that the examinees must demonstrate increasing levels of specific skill or that they must deal with incrementally more complex data, scenarios, or problems, or both as well-articulated progressions along the construct. Figure 2.7 shows three trajectories in what we might call the "*cognitive construct space.*"

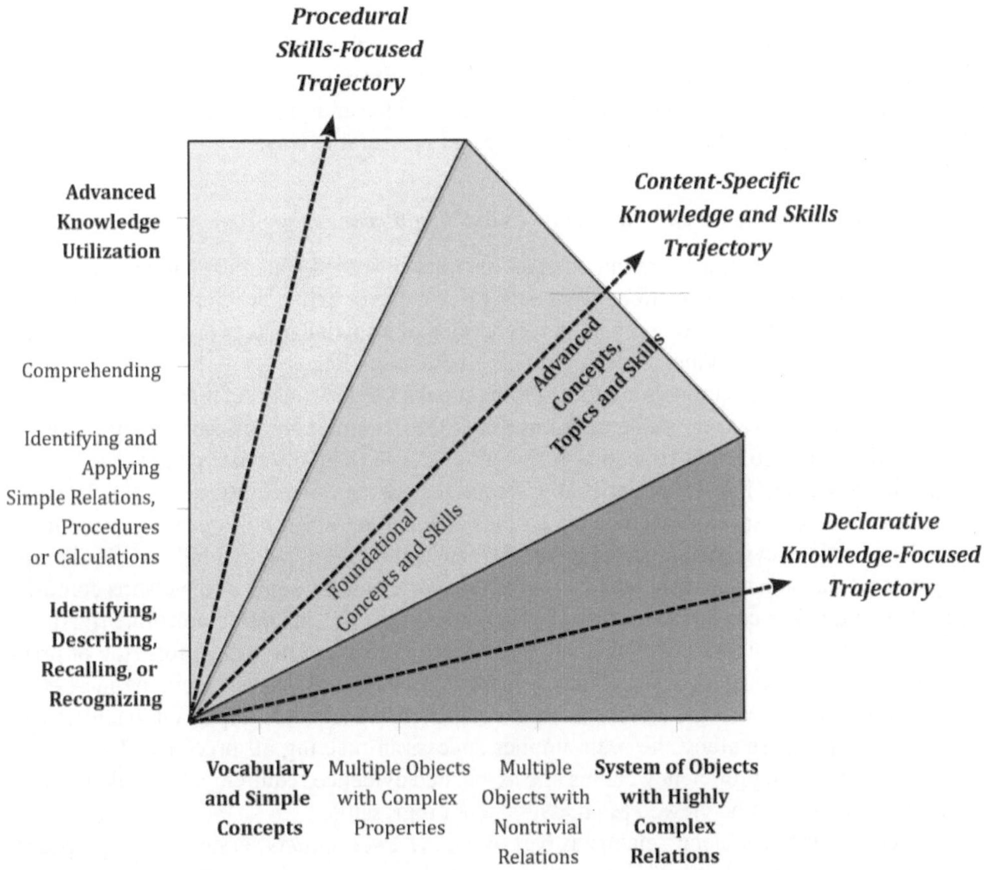

Figure 2.7 Three Construct Map Trajectories in a Cognitive Construct Space

If we assume a skills-focused trajectory, our proficiency claims should concentrate on the incremental changes in demonstrable actions or products of actions that require increasing or decreasing levels of cognitive skill or the application of more and more advanced procedures, schema, or protocols. Alternatively, a declarative knowledge trajectory calls for dealing with increasingly more complex content (e.g., incrementally more complex text, from isolated words or text segments to reading passages). The content knowledge trajectory focuses on the depth and breadth of domain-specific knowledge that we expect examinees to know—for example, from the identification or recall of basic or foundational knowledge of concepts, facts, and terminology to analysis, synthesis, or strategic use of a more complex and highly integrated subsystem of domain-specific knowledge.

A construct dealing with reading comprehensions or language development might follow the *declarative* trajectory where examinees are expected to encode, process, interpret, and otherwise work with incrementally more complex text (or, more generally, information in a particular media). The *procedural* trajectory focuses on the incrementally higher complexity of inferred skills or procedural steps that examinees must apply to information or data. For example, a mathematics construct map might focus on simple procedures or operations within the lower regions of the construct map and incrementally compound those procedures at the higher end. The content-specific trajectory is a blend of the procedural and declarative trajectories where content knowledge, the amount of information and its presentation, and applied skills all increment in lock-step complexity.

The idea of keeping a more-or-less straight-line trajectory in mind avoids the tendency to view each construct as the compensatory amalgamation or mixture of differing content categories and levels of declarative content and concept knowledge and procedural skills. Everything along the trajectory must increase in a systematic and measurable way.

2.4.2 Evidence Models and Proficiency Claims as Building Blocks

Proficiency claims or warrants are knowledge- and/or skill-based statements about the examinees.[12] Claims can reflect foundational concepts, knowledge or skills, or refer to the application of advanced cognitive skills to complex constellations of knowledge, text or other data. When connected with concrete evidence requirements, these proficiency claims become part of an evidence model. Evidence models are the building blocks for our construct map. They prioritize and connect what we want the scale to tell us about the examinees—our proficiency claims—with how we need to go about collecting sufficient evidence to justify those claims.

A proficiency claim in assessment is an inferential statement about the examinees. It specifies our performance expectations on a class of tasks under certain conditions of measurement. These claims and the evidence required to justify them can be short, behaviorally oriented proficiency-related statements or more lengthy narratives. For example, some of the claims comprising an initial draft of a construct map could be an ordered list of "can do/demonstrate [this] …" statements derived from task statements rated as very frequent and/or critical for a job or practice analysis survey. Since a construct map is a conceptual type of "ruler" depicting increasing levels of skills and/or dealing with increasingly complex materials, it is important to understand that successful progress along the scale implies success in meeting all preceding lower-level claims. Ultimately, the proficiency claims and associated evidence requirements (models) along the construct might also be viewed as an assessment progression.

Incorporating the proficiency claims as part of the *evidence models* serves several purposes. First, it demands that every proficiency claim we make within a domain has clearly defined specification for the assessment-related evidence. That is, our inferences must be anchored in and justified by the evidence. Second, we must prioritize the quantitative and qualitative nature of the proficiency claims and evidence requirements included within each model. It is important to understand that virtually all tests contain a finite number of items. We likewise need to conceptualize our proficiency claims and evidence models as finite in number. This can become a challenging endeavor when policy makers and others devise elaborate hierarchies of learning standards or extended content and cognitive outlines containing collections of hundreds or thousands of entries and no clear mapping of those standards or content outline entries to the score scale.[13]

Figure 2.8 shows the refinement process leading to a single evidence model. The source of the proficiency claims can be learning standards or other documentation that describes key proficiency-anchored outcomes or expectations. The assessment purpose and priorities govern the target rigor of the claims. For example, a placement or mastery test would likely prioritize foundational claims involving the content knowledge and skills expected by minimally competent individuals. An end-of-grade or end-of-course achievement test would be more likely to involve a wider range of proficiency claims: from foundational to advanced. The contexts and settings provide guidelines for the complexity of applied settings, texts, images, etc. to help contextualize the proficiency claims. Teaching and learning resources are self-explanatory.

An evidence model has a singular proficiency claim and six types of (ideally detailed) documentation: (1) performance expectations that state what the examinee must do to demonstrate the prescribed proficiency claim; (2) concrete activities or procedural sequences of solution steps that successful examinees must reveal; (3) documents, data, or information that examinees must work with; (4) facilitative or required tools or resources available to the examinees (e.g., software tools or auxiliary informational resources); (5) critical decisions to be made; and (6) level and depth of content knowledge—including prior knowledge—presumed by the claim. As noted above, keeping the evidence requirements connected to each proficiency claim is essential.

We also need to realize from the onset that our construct map will be comprising a finite number of evidence models distributed by their apparent complexity relative to one another. That "finite number" requirement does, however, imply the need for serious prioritization—likely over multiple iterations involved relevant groups of content experts. When moving from the generalities of the ellipses in Figure 2.8 to the specifics of an evidence model, there are obviously going to be competing assessment priorities that reflect the criticality emphases and

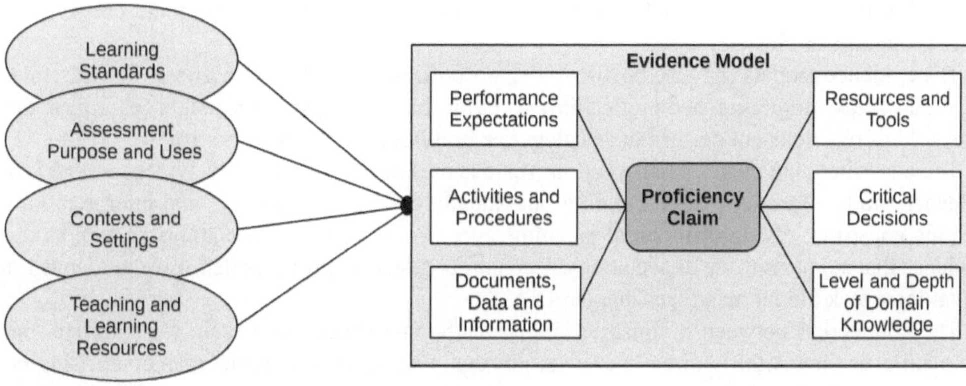

Figure 2.8 Iterative Refinement of a Proficiency Claim

preferences that different SMEs in a domain may make with respect to various learning standards, contexts, etc. This type of competition of priorities is real. It is also a matter of policy, not something that AE can resolve. The simple fact is that not all learning standards in a given domain can be represented by a finite collection of evidence models. In fact, not all learning standards can be assessed in a reliable and valid way. However, the most common and critical standards need to be identified as starting points for construct mapping.

There is no required format for an evidence model. It is a well-organized and understandably communicated collection of documentation. It is important to pay careful attention to the language used to articulate the six types of documentation used. The proficiency claims and evidence documentation should be detailed yet understandable to more than just scholars or educational experts in a domain. The language used should certainly avoid obtuse inferences or evidence requirements that go far beyond what we can actually assess. In addition to being well organized and understandable, the documentation should be clear enough to distinguish each evidence model from other evidence models in terms of their scope and complexity. Finally, it is essential to keep in mind that evidence models can be modified and refined (within reason) over time.

2.5 Creating a Construct Map

As mentioned earlier, a construct map is a plausible distribution of evidence models. Since each evidence model contains a singular proficiency claim and its associated evidence requirements, we can begin to develop our construct map by sorting the evidence models according to the implied complexity of the proficiency claims relative to other proficiency claims. (Note: a useful assumption is that more complex proficiency claims will have more complex evidence requirements such as higher performance expectations or dealing with more complex data).

Figure 2.9 presents a construct map comprising 60 evidence models, which is our finite limit. We presuppose here that one or more groups have engaged in a carefully deliberated and systematic consensus-leaning endeavor to decide on the top 60 proficiency claims to be assessed. There are four content subdomains represented by the corresponding levels of shading. (Note that the shading neither represents increasing/decreasing complexity nor the levels of proficiency. Also, the fact that there are exactly 15 evidence models is merely a convenience for this illustration.) Considering the apparent complexity of the proficiency claims and evidence requirements associated with each evidence model, 3 groupings of 20 evidence models each are mapped to our construct—essentially low, moderate/medium, and high groupings. Less complex, lower-level proficiency claims are located to the left and more complex claims (i.e., evidence models) are grouped to the right. Through additional clarifications and refinements, we could create even more groupings or clusters.

The evidence models can also be distributed proportionally to the test purpose. For example, we might stack more evidence models in the region of critical decision points (e.g., near the threshold of two adjacent performance categories or a pass-fail decision point).

The construct map makes clear what our scale is measuring—essentially evidence model by evidence model. That is, we are building our (ideally concrete) inferences and interpretations into the construct, giving differential meaning to our performance expectations as well as the evidence that supports those expectations. A construct map also provides definitive guidance for designing a task model map (see Chapter 4).

The connection between a construct map and the statistical score scale we calibrate and maintain over time is fairly direct. For example, again consider a construct map comprising 60 evidence models. For illustrative purposes, let's further assume that four content subdomains are more or less ordered in complexity as shown in Figure 2.10 (top-left, where lighter shades denote less complex proficiency claims and evidence requirements). The bottom plot in Figure 2.10

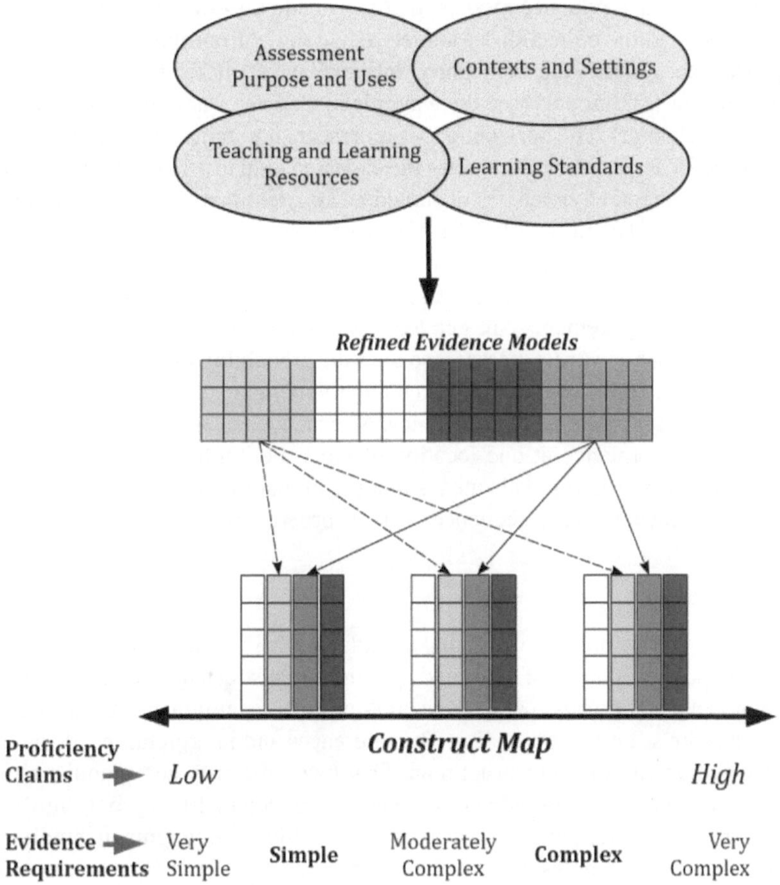

Figure 2.9 Building a Construct Map as a Distribution of Evidence Models

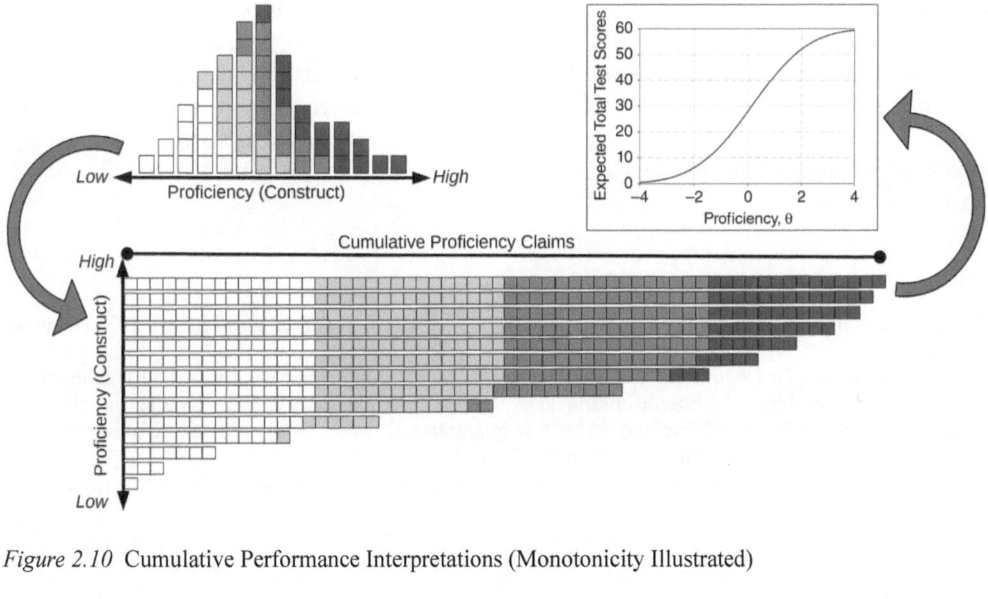

Figure 2.10 Cumulative Performance Interpretations (Monotonicity Illustrated)

is a cumulative plot of the evidence models, that is, we add all lower-level evidence models—our building blocks—to the collection of models as we move from the lower to higher regions of the construct map. Finally, the top-right graph displays an IRT test characteristic function (TCF) for 60 items or task models (see the example in Chapter 1 and the discussion of a latent scale earlier in this chapter). The horizontal axis represents the statistical proficiency scale—our measured construct. The vertical axis denotes the expected total test scores (e.g., number-correct scores). With a bit of mental gymnastics, it should be apparent that the cumulative distributions of the 60 evidence models and the TCF are highly consistent with each other. The cumulative construct map, however, provides point-by-point meaning for the construct.

Figure 2.10 also illustrates an important statistical property conveniently assumed to exist for most educational measurement scales called *monotonicity*. It implies that as the underlying proficiency scores on our construct increase, so does the probability of attaining higher observed item scores (e.g., Lord, 1980). It also implies cumulatively higher performance in terms of total test scores as a function of increasing proficiency. A consequence of satisfying the monotonicity assumption is that performance at one location of the scale implies an equal or higher probability of success on easier items. This means that the probability of successful performance is cumulative and incremental over a sequence of items ordered by their difficulties.[14]

2.6 Chapter Summary

Construct mapping is a visioning process that articulates what we want from our score scale before moving into the creation of test items and applying sophisticated psychometric models. Using evidence models, this process can lead to an interpretative argument that strongly supports the validity of a score scale point by point. The inferences and interpretations demanded of the score scale are embodied in the construct map. That level of clarity and granularity is difficult to achieve by layering *ad hoc* normative or domain-referenced interpretations onto a numerical scale via standard setting, item mapping, or content/cognitive item alignment studies.

These construct map examples presented here obviously gloss over the extensive work that must go into the development of the proficiency claims and evidence models. Nonetheless, they demonstrate three important things. First, we can conceptualize and map out—quite convincingly—what we want to say about the examinees by keeping the relative complexity of our proficiency claims in mind. The (intentional and prioritized) differential complexity ordering of the evidence models provides the basis for the construct map, itself. Second, a construct map provides a systematic and incremental distribution proficiency claim (i.e., content-based expectations and interpretations of proficiency) that is fully consistent with the properties of most statistical score scales. Third, the distribution of evidence models making up the construct map provide direct guidance for the development of task models and task model maps (Chapters 3 and 4, respectively).

Notes

1 Adapted from a quote about presentation designs by Ken Haemer, Presentation Research Manager at AT&T.

2 Carrying out standard setting after a score scale is in place is an *ad hoc* way of adding meaning to a score scales. Similarly, aligning or linking an evidence-based taxonomy or vague academic standards to items after the fact is fallible and offers few guarantees that the stated evidence requirements are actually supported by the items on a given test form.

3 Note that the domain-referenced predictions or inferences are usually never empirically verified from a validity perspective.

4 A simple way to test this assertion is to ask, "What does a one-point change mean [on this scale] in terms changes in the depth and breadth of subject-matter content knowledge that the examinees can handle or level and nature of skills they can bring to bear on a problem?"

5 Okay, in fairness, there are multidimensional IRT methods that can also simultaneously calibrate items to multiple continuous or discrete scales (e.g., van der Linden,2016).

6 Stevens (1961) introduced four classes of scales: nominal, ordinal, interval, and ratio. He characterized each by the types of allowable mathematical transformations possible to still maintain the properties of the original scale.

7 The central location of a scale may represent a specified population mean such as $\mu(\theta) = 0.0$, a mean item-bank difficulty, $\mu(b) = 0.0$, or almost any other convenient mathematical constraint(s) imposed on the otherwise unknown distribution of numbers making up the scale.

8 Criterion-referenced tests are sometimes called domain-referenced tests and objectives-referenced tests. In a criterion-referenced test, the items are a representative set of items from a clearly defined domain of behaviors measuring an objective, whereas with an objectives-referenced test no domain of behaviors is specified and items are not considered to be representative of any behavior domain. As Hambleton et al. (1978) point out, this distinction may have important implications and consequences for the kinds of generalizations that can be made from criterion-referenced test scores—at least compared with objectives-referenced test scores.

9 These descriptors are sometimes synonymously called *performance or proficiency-level descriptors*.

10 This example assumes that the items are calibrated using a Rasch one-parameter logistic model. Other IRT models like the two- and three-parameter models would produce non-uniformly shaped ICCs that can somewhat cloud the concept of *locating* an item at a specified probability of mastery or competence like 0.8.

11 The mapped items provide concrete examples of the types of items that are likely to get correct with a specified probability. For example, items may be located on the scale using IRT item-parameter estimates such that examinees at that score point have an 80 percent likelihood of correctly responding to that item. A similar approach uses a difficulty-ordered "reference test"—that is, a complete test form—to concretely describe the score levels needed to correctly respond to the items on the test with a specified probability.

12 Claims can also be made about psychological traits or affects.

13 Content standards or cognitive alignment studies are sometimes used for this purpose but rarely aid in the interpretation of the scores in any concrete way.

14 See, for example, the "item map" shown earlier in Figure 2.5.

3 Task Models and Task Model Families

This chapter is about ways to turn our evidence requirements (models) into families of test items. The focus is on the design-specified *complexity* of collections of generated items comprising *task model families*. The art and science of task modeling is certainly not new (e.g., Bachman & Palmer, 1996; Kirsch & Mosenthal, 1990; Mislevy et al., 2003). However, this chapter introduces some useful and novel ways to think about, develop, and implement task models using complexity ordered conditions and metrics called *complexity design layers*. Various ways to represent task model complexity are also presented.

3.1 What Is a *Task Model?*

A *task model* is a detailed, cognitively oriented description of the challenges, features, and conditions of measurement for a family of items. These models replace individual items as the design units of interest and focus attention on the controllable aspects of item creation, not on the characteristics of individual items. As noted above, each collection of items is called a *task model family* (TMF).

Task models are actionable specifications for item design and development, not just vague references to learning standards, proficiency claims, or cognitive processes. They are conceptually similar to recipes used in cooking. A recipe typically includes a list of ingredients and instructions for combining, cooking, and preparing the final food product. Even if a recipe is followed exactly, there will likely be slight (acceptable) variations in flavor, texture, coloring, etc. Different chefs may further intentionally or unintentionally vary the ingredients or other parts of the recipe—for example, to substitute healthier or more flavorful ingredients. Nonetheless, if the recipe is followed faithfully, highly similar outcomes can be expected in terms of appearance and taste.

Consider the example of a multiple-choice question (MCQ) that asks kindergarten students to sum the counts for two sets of objects.[1] Figure 3.1 presents the MCQ. Which features of this item impact the cognitive complexity of the task for typical kindergarten students? The number of books in each set (i.e., constraints on the set counts)? The complexity and extent of instruction provided in the MCQ stem? The familiarity of the objects? The sameness of the objects to one another? The inclusion of the images? The choice of distractor options?

There are numerous choices we can make when designing items in a domain. We can put constraints on the number and types of objects, the inclusion of images and their properties (e.g., color, size, spacing or orientation, relationships to one another and to the problem), the explicitness and extent of instructions provided, etc. For example, suppose that we augment the second part of the MCQ stem with the explicit problem-solving instructions, "(*Hint: count the number of books in each stack and add those two numbers together*)." Of course, that type of hint might make the item significantly easier and would not necessarily by useful to students who apply a perhaps simpler strategy of counting all of the books.

DOI: 10.4324/9781003451051-3

Molly and Keith each have a stack of books as shown here.

How many total books do Molly and Keith have if they combine their stacks?

A. 6
B. 7
C. 8
D. 9

Figure 3.1 A Four-Option MCQ for Kindergarten Mathematics

The cognitive complexity ingredients in our task model recipe should be intentional choices and specified in as much detail as possible. For example, we might create a narrative description of the task model as follows:

Each four-option MCQ item in this family should present two sets of same-type objects familiar to most kindergarteners (e.g., books, foods, common household items, or toys). Each set should have 3 to 7 of the objects accompanied with a total count smaller than 10. The objects should be described in the stem and accompanied by a relevant image clearly showing both sets of objects grouped by count (e.g., a two stacks of books). The text should be at an appropriate level of complexity for kindergarteners. The two-part task of counting and summing the objects [should/should not] be explicitly stated. Incorrect MCQ distractor options should be plausible with a clear rationale related to faulty counting, summation or reasoning about the nature of the task.

Table 3.1 presents a more detailed description of the key complexity-oriented features of a potential task model for this type of test item.[2] The leftmost column describes the features followed by a more detailed description in the second column. The third and fourth columns respectively describe key properties and constraints on those properties. The rows detail each of the features.[3] The kindergarten mathematics standard is included, followed by the intended grade level(s), the nature of the data provided, likely solution steps or cognitive actions/procedures, the context, tools (e.g., calculators), the item types or structures to be used, and text and image complexity descriptions and constraints. The text and image complexity and composite difficulty rows in this table represent metric-based designations that are ideally based on empirically verified object analytics and item difficulty modeling (IDM) research (see Chapters 4 and 7).

Although the number of task complexity features documented in Table 3.1 may seem a bit daunting at first glance, it is important to remember that each task model represents a common set of design specifications for an entire *family* of items, not for individual items. Easier or more difficult task models in the domain would appropriately manipulate the complexity of these features, properties, and constraints. This type of task model data specifications sheet merely documents the key complexity features.

Table 3.1 Example of a Task Model Data Specifications Sheet

Task model features	*Values/Descriptions*	*Key properties*	*Constraints*
Standard(s)	K.AT.O.CC.2: Solve addition and subtraction word problems with 10 or fewer numbers using objects or drawings to represent the problem	–	$x_1 + x_2 \leq 10$
Grade level(s)	Kindergarten (K)	–	–
Description of data	Two discrete object sets: $s_1(n_1)$, $s_2\ (n_2)$	Set size, object types	$n_1, n_2 \in (3,\ldots,7)$ familiar objects
Actions/procedures	Recognize objects: add(count(n_1),count(n_2))	–	–
Context	Word problem: counting two object sets	Descriptions of objects and groupings	No direct instruction provided
Tools	None	–	–
Structure	MCQ-4	Stem, image, options (4:1)	Single answer
Text complexity	Kindergarten (K)	–	–
Image complexity	Common objects stacked or grouped together as "sets"	Images of discrete objects and groupings: $s(n)$	Distinct sets of common, same type objects
Composite difficulty	Moderately easy	–	–
Prototype item/example	KM00238	–	–

Back to metaphors, a task model data specifications sheet is a crude recipe that includes a detailed description of the cognitive task ingredients and the way in which the ingredients should be combined to generate items within that TMF. The recipe specifies the nature and complexity of content-specific information provided, available data or resources, the proposed context(s) covered by a TMF, and the skills and likely actions to be undertaken by the examinees. Further on, we present some alternative and more efficient ways to represent the task model ingredients and task challenge preparation instructions.

Another task-modeling analogy is a *schema* detailing the environment, rules, active and passive components, and flow of play for a computer game session.[4] The schema specifies the complexity of the game environment and context of play; navigation options; the timing and intensity when activating each challenge; the speed of play; hints, clues, or scaffolding; resources, weapons, or tools, the complexity of the game content and context, etc. Each game session presents a unique combination of schemas, parameters, and challenges that more or less determine the session's difficulty for an average player.

The underlying complexity features in each task model are carefully documented using one or more schema to describe the environment, content, challenges, features, and relevant conditions of measurement. Each task model has its own schema that can be used to generate item within the associated TMF. Easier TMFs will tend to have simpler schema than complex ones.

Each TMF schema is subsequently implemented by applying the task-model specifications to one or more item models. Item models are highly detailed templates or constraints, and are variabilized content input to an automated item-generator components for producing items that follow the task model design schema[5] (see Chapter 6). Simply put, each task model is instantiated by one or more item models and each item model can generate multiple items. The three-tiered hierarchical structure of task models, item models, and items is depicted in Figure 3.2.

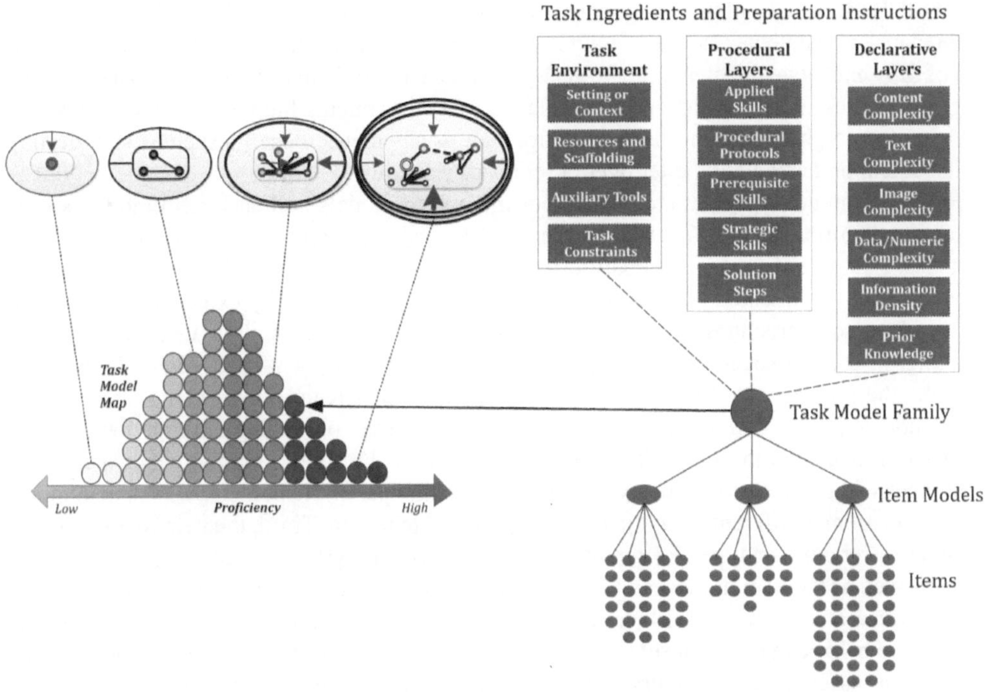

Figure 3.2 A Task Model Map with a Task Models→Item Models→Items Hierarchy

The left-hand distribution of dots in Figure 3.2 is called a *task model map* (TMM). The TMM serves multiple purposes as discussed in Chapter 5. What is important to understand here is that a TMM is composed of an intended *distribution* of task models, each of which has a prescribed location along our proficiency continuum—the construct map and, later, along our emergent score scale.

The four ellipses above the TMM graphically represent the content and cognitive complexity of an easier, moderately easy, moderately difficult, and difficult TMF. The number and line thicknesses of the ellipses represent the overall complexity of the task environment for each TMF (simple or isolated contexts for the task model challenges versus complex problem environments). The arrows within each ellipse denote the scope, intensity, and complexity of required actions, use of tools or resources, and interactivity of items in each TMF (i.e., procedural knowledge requirements). Increased numbers of arrows and thicker arrows denote greater complexity. Finally, the "networks" within each ellipse suggest the complexity of content and other information acted upon by the examinees (i.e., the complexity of the declarative knowledge). More "nodes" and connectors (links) denote increased complexity.

The top-right section of Figure 3.2 describes the task environments, procedural knowledge layers, and declarative knowledge layers corresponding with the graphical ellipses, arrows, and link-node networks. Each task model can vary these layers. More complex layering is applied to increase complexity and generate more difficult item families. Finally, the lower-right section presents the hierarchical relationship among a task model, item models, or templates used to generate items, and the items within each TMF.

Each task model provides a content-oriented, cognitively focused representation of potentially large families of items. The concept of empirically supported *isomorphism* (Bejar, 2002;

Luecht & Burke, 2020) plays a huge role in the development of each TMF and the creation and maintenance of the items associated with it. Isomorphism implies that a potentially large collection of fully exchangeable items can be generated for each TMF; items that incorporate the same types of features at constant levels of complexity as well as having highly similar statistical difficulties. Isomorphic item families offer important psychometric benefits such as significantly reduced item pretesting and better overall score scale stability.

Each task model is instantiated by one or more item models and each item model is used to generate multiple items. This type of hierarchical design structure has several important advantages. First, the shared, complexity-oriented specifications for each TMF can be concretely aligned to our documented progression of assessment evidence and, by extension, to the proficiency claims comprising our construct map(s). That is, task models allow us to describe in a meaningful, content-specific way the cognitive complexity for each TMF. These descriptions can take the form of any combination of methods including feature lists, content task model grammars, graphical TMF depictions, and narratives. Second, producing multiple item models per TMF implies that the full collection of items generated provides similar challenges to the examinees without necessarily being clones of a particular parent item. Instead, each item model may derive from a different parent item or a designated template. Third, the item models are not limited to a certain item type like a multiple-choice or technology-enhanced items. Finally, each TMF, as well as the item models and families of items associated with them have a more or less fixed *location* on our scale. This latter point implies that individual items within each family are expected to behave in an isomorphic way substantively and statistically. Part of the engineering process, discussed in later chapters, involves methods for ensuring isomorphism.

To summarize, the task models simultaneously describe the nature of the content-based challenges presented and what the average examinee in the population needs to do to solve that type of problem. Like a recipe used in cooking, the task model also provides item-generation guidance. For example, how much prior knowledge should be assumed or implied—versus made explicit? What types of tools or resources will be provided? How complex are the instructions and information provided? How much complex are the text, images, graphics, or tables provided? How many solution or protocol steps are likely? What types of cognitive actions will typical examinees follow given their knowledge and skills? How complex are the solution steps or protocols?

3.2 Task Modeling and Cognitive Complexity

Task modeling is the most comprehensive aspect of AE because it directly applies industrial engineering principles to item and test design and production practices. However, task modeling is only possible through empirical research, the development of operationally efficient procedures and protocols, and the use of applied analytic technologies that complete the alignment between proficiency claims and associated evidence requirements derived from construct mapping and the actual test items created to provide the intended evidence.

Cognitive complexity plays an integral role in AE. It concretizes the evidence models by creating detailed design specifications for every TMF of items. From a task modeling perspective, we focus on the context and challenges to be presented to a population of examinees rather than the knowledge and skills that examinees bring to a given task or item. This subtle juxtaposition of focus—from speculations about the examinees' knowledge and skills to task complexity by design—is one of the central tenets of AE. That is, we cannot control what the examinees bring to a given task. However, we can engineer the complexity of the items associated with each TMF.

There are numerous learning, behavioral, psychosocial, and cognitive theories (e.g., behavioral psychology, cognitive developmental, social cognitive and information processing). AE neither advocates nor requires a strong theoretical basis for implementation. The notion of controlling the complexity of item families via intentional design choices may seem to align with certain information processing theories of cognition—for example, controlling the cognitive load and the depth/breadth of knowledge provided or assumed to be accessible by examinees and then controlling the structure/organization and formatting of data, information, or ideas. Still, no attempt is made to exactly reconcile AE with any information-processing theories. The metrics and score interpretations we develop under a principled assessment design framework like AE can certainly be used to test or evaluate hypotheses and various aspects of grander theories of cognition and the human condition assuming that such theories also attend to construct mapping, evidence modeling, and task modeling.

AE is about creating detailed, replicable, and scalable *designs* that lead to the carefully controlled production of high-quality items and test forms that provide the intended evidence to support the ordered proficiency claims comprising a given construct map. Fulfilling this engineering design purpose ideally leads to consistently *controlling* the difficulty and other statistical properties of items within acceptable tolerances for each TMF. If the empirical results fail to achieve that purpose we need to repair (re-engineer) the design and carryout additional research to better understand complexity-oriented factors impacting the task model difficulties or go back to the construct mapping and evidence modeling stages to find gaps or deficits in the documentation and reasoning processes.

Various cognitive complexity schemes or taxonomies have been proposed over the past 60+ years. Perhaps the most well-known are Bloom's *Taxonomy of Educational Objectives* (Bloom et al., 1956) and Webb's *Depth-of-Knowledge* (DOK; Webb, 2005). While providing a general sense of increasing or decreasing complexity these types of schemes nonetheless have serious limitations in terms of their utility for item or task design. First, they tend to focus on underlying cognitive processes of examinee or students rather than tasks as challenges developed under a principled design framework like AE. Second, they conflate different types of knowledge[6] and skills that might be tapped by careful TMF design (e.g., varied levels of declarative knowledge, procedural knowledge, generative knowledge, and/or strategic knowledge). Third, they ignore differences in populations.[7] Finally, their ignore contexts, settings, tools/scaffolding, and resources that can impact task complexity in facilitative or punitive ways.

In contrast, AE focuses on the cognitively oriented features or attributes of the task challenges presented to the examinees. The proficiency claims developed via a construct map document what we wish to say about the examinees along a scale. The task models provide documentable evidence to support those claims. Examinees are only considered in terms of their average or expected performance on each TMF. That is, on average, examinees are expected to perform well on simpler tasks and less well on more complex tasks.

The cognitive science literature has typically distinguished between two types of knowledge (e.g., ten Barge & van Hezewijk, 1999). *Declarative knowledge* refers the complexity of content, data, information and the way in which it organized and presented. *Procedural knowledge* refers to how examinees need to access, manipulate, or otherwise act upon the declarative knowledge. Metaphorically, procedural knowledge is like a computer algorithm and software that does something. Declarative knowledge is conceptually like structured or unstructured data to which the algorithm is applied (i.e., simplistically procedural knowledge acts upon declarative knowledge). The declarative knowledge presented in a test item typically needs to be encoded, possibly manipulated, and then acted upon. The declarative knowledge can be explicit and static (i.e., provided as text, images, or numerical data) or considered as prior or implicit knowledge the examinees need to retrieve or recall. Declarative knowledge can also be generative in nature—that is, the result or outcome of one or more applications of procedural knowledge to declarative information or data (e.g., the result of classifying information or carrying out calculations and then using the result, or of pulling together information and abstracting concepts or patterns). In Figure 3.2 (shown earlier), procedural knowledge is represented by the arrows where more arrows indicate more procedural steps and the thickness of the lines denote more complex skills. Declarative knowledge is represented by the network diagrams. More complex networks more elaborate constellations of knowledge or data with many different types of relationships between the component knowledge objects (nodes) in the network.

Consider an example of an MCQ that asks examinee to identify the author's main theme or purpose in a 300-word fourth grade reading passage. If the purpose is a literally presented in the first sentence of the paragraph, the procedural knowledge requirement is a basic *identification* task (e.g., clearly recognizing the first sentence as a summary statement and matching it to the correct MCQ answer—perhaps slightly paraphrased). If the main-purpose sentence is instead located elsewhere within the text passage, additional steps may be needed to isolate and evaluate that sentence relative to the answer options. Those additional steps could subtly increase the amount of procedural knowledge required.

Now consider having high school students read a 600-word science passage comprising lexically, syntactically, and semantically complex text using somewhat technical jargon that is not necessarily defined within the passage. The directive is similar: to identify the author's main purpose. Compared to our fourth-grade reading passage, this high-school science reading passage requires more strategic problem-solving and procedural steps to process to correctly answer the question about the author's purpose. That is, the text is obviously more complex in nature, possibly stressing the cognitive load-management capabilities of an average high school student. (However, if the author's main purpose was explicitly provided in the first sentence of the passage, even the increased text complexity might be somewhat irrelevant for some students test-wise.)

Further contrast these types of reading comprehension tasks with an MCQ item that requires the examinees to identify two or three less-than-obvious idea units, compare them, and then infer the author's main theme. The procedural knowledge is more than just locating information (i.e., identification). If the idea units were implicit rather than explicit within a fairly dense academic reading passage, our MCQ question about author's purpose may prove to be quite difficult.

Prior knowledge and the organization of the key information presented to the examinees also play key roles in task model complexity. If the data or information we present to the examinees is highly familiar knowledge and is clearly presented in an organized way, we theoretically *reduce* the cognitive load of inputs as well as the magnitude of preprocessing steps needed to solve the problem. Conversely, if the amount of information or data is extensive and contains non-essential distractions such as nuanced vocabulary, complex sentence structures, poorly organized data tables, or complicated figures, we are likely increasing the cognitive load of the task—naively or intentionally. For example, using text-based vignettes or word problems to present the data and context for mathematics problems may seem more *authentic*, but can also increase the cognitive complexity of the task.

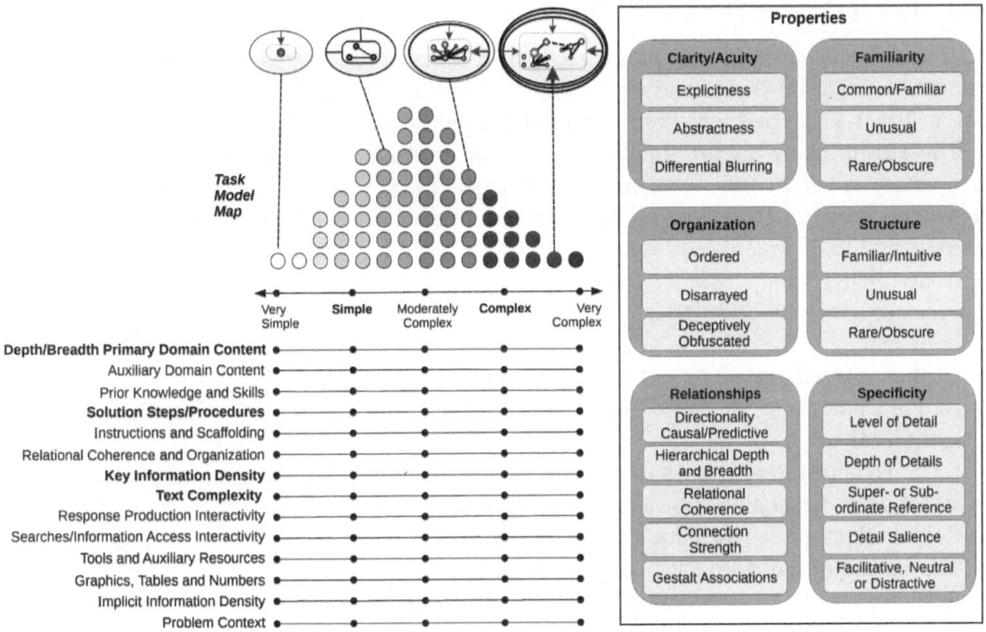

Figure 3.3 Task Cognitive Complexity from as Layers with Properties

Figure 3.3 presents an expanded view of the TMM presented earlier. The layered "scales" below the TMM denote different types and magnitudes of cognitive complexity that could be manipulated to increase or decrease the level of challenge provided by each task model. Although it is certainly possible to classify these layers being more procedural or declarative in nature, that is not a requirement. Rather, these task complexity design layers (CDLs) indicate how different levels and types of knowledge should be represented within a given task model. Furthermore, in practice, the layers are domain-specific. For example, a different constellation of layers would be present for a fifth-grade science scale than for a fifth-grade mathematics scale. And a fifth-grade science scale might incorporate a different set of layers than an eleventh-grade science scale. These task CDLs are completely under the control of test developers, with the proviso that they should be empirically verified as discussed in Chapters 4 and 7.

It is far beyond the scope of this book to provide specific strategies or models for developing a cognitive understanding of the content associated with all possible domains, constructs, and examinee populations. One helpful conceptualization, however, has to do with focusing on the trajectories of the task challenges within a *cognitive construct space* (see Section 2.3 in Chapter 2). The *dimensions* of a cognitive construct space can simultaneously represent the complexity-oriented progression of different types of declarative and procedural knowledge as *trajectories*. As discussed in Chapter 2, these types of trajectories remind us how the *task* complexity changes—a perspective that seems lacking with traditional content blueprints. For example, if we assume to latter content-specific knowledge and skills trajectory, we would not design task models requiring simple or basic skills applied to complex content; nor would we apply advanced skills to relatively simple, foundational content. While not a strict requirement, staying *on-trajectory* can help to avoid later psychometric complications regarding the properties of the eventual statistical scale(s) we devised for calibrating the TMFs and scoring the examinees.

3.2.1 Task Model Grammars and the Structure of Task Models

Task model grammars (TMGs) provide a domain-specific way to simultaneously represent the content-focused knowledge and procedural components for each task model (Luecht, 2006, 2012a, 2013). Other useful representations and schemes are described further on.

The idea of using a representational grammar was adapted from work on semantic text complexity developed by Kintsch and van Dijk (1978; also see Kintsch, 1988). A TMG provides a fairly compact way to represent series of actions applied to potentially complex, inter-related data[8] and also provides a relatively easy way to distinguish the task models in terms their primary content foci and contexts The basic structure of TMG statement represents:

a Explicit instructions, goals and response format(s)
b Actions, processing, analysis, and solution steps, or procedural protocols typically applied to the TMF
c Data, documents, concepts, variables, numerical quantities, and images comprising the constellation of declarative knowledge provided as part of the problem
d Relationships among the data, documents, etc.
e The context or setting in which the task must be solved
f Resources such as reference materials, formula sheets, or look-up tables
g Primary or auxiliary tools such as search engines, calculators, grammar or spell-checkers, software applications

These components can be compactly organized into an equation-like structure:

$$goal\left\{\mathbf{actions}\left[relations\left(\mathbf{data}\right)\mid setting, resources, tools\right]\right\}.$$

This is not a "one-size-fits-all" formulation. Some task models may exclude certain components and other task models will have an expanded set of actions or likely processing steps and multiple types of data. By assigning fixed or designer manipulable properties to the various components, we can also distinguish between levels or magnitudes of complexity.

TMGs are *domain specific*! Unlike other "cognitive complexity" schemes that attempt to generalize the extent of knowledge and examinee's supposed cognitive processes across domains, each TMG should be developed by cognitively astute subject-matter experts using clear and meaningful domain-specific choices of action verbs, procedural steps, data types, content representations, contexts, etc.

Luecht, Devore and Burke (2009) developed a TMG for computerized accounting simulations in a task modeling proof-of-concept study. Fourteen computerized simulation exercises were reverse engineered by having expert accountants generate cognitively oriented descriptions. Training was provided and the experts worked together to come to consensus about the task descriptions. The experts considered three classes of task complexity features: (1) the number and complexity of actions or procedural steps needed; (2) the amount and organization (i.e., density) of the data or information provided in each exercise; and (3) the complexity of the accounting context. Figure 3.4 presents 3 of the 14 "task models" and the corresponding complexity feature values. The gray-shaded (light to dark) vertical scales denote increasing complexity of each feature. (Note that a linear composite of these

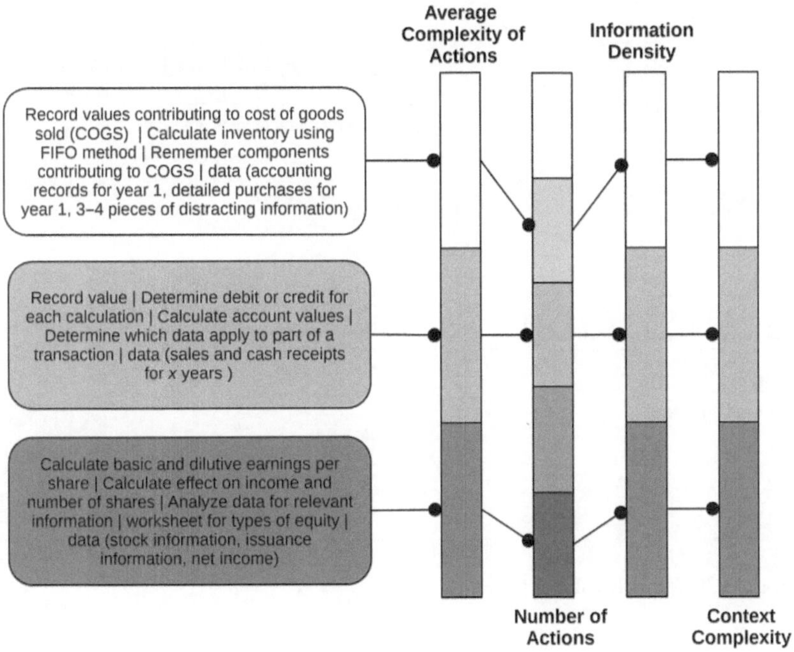

Figure 3.4 Accounting Task Complexity (Adapted from Luecht et al., 2009)

features correlated nearly perfectly with empirically estimated item difficulties for the 14 simulations.)

Changing the complexity of individual test items—or more generally, TMFs—can involve simultaneously manipulating multiple design features (Irvine, 2002). For example, using more complex vocabulary or syntax can increase the overall text complexity of an item and its statistical difficulty within an examinee population. Similarly, item difficulty can be affected by the collection and properties of numbers used in a mathematics problem or the complexity of images or graphics used. Requiring examinees to recall and then apply formulas or procedural steps/protocols, rather than, providing them with a formula or step-by-step instructions, is likely to also inflate item difficulty. Under AE, these are complexity design elements—the ingredients and problem-solving steps and resources—that go into each task model.

Consider the four variants of an MCQ in Figure 3.5. The tasks seem simple enough. Each item asks the examinee to count[9] the number of objects—in this case, squares, rectangles, or blocks. Implicit in the selected-response task type is that the examinee must also match their count to one of the available MCQ options.

Question **(a)** has six identical squares. Question **(b)** instead uses rectangles where the shading, size, and orientation of each rectangle is irrelevant to the counting task. (*Note that those irrelevant properties could actually artificially increase the apparent task complexity for some examinees. The item writer is further assuming that all examinees will understand what a "rectangle" is.*) Question **(c)** increases the total number of squares to a value larger than ten. Finally, Queston **(d)** introduces two set of blocks. It can be solved by simply counting the seven blocks (ignoring the groupings), adding together the two counts of the blocks

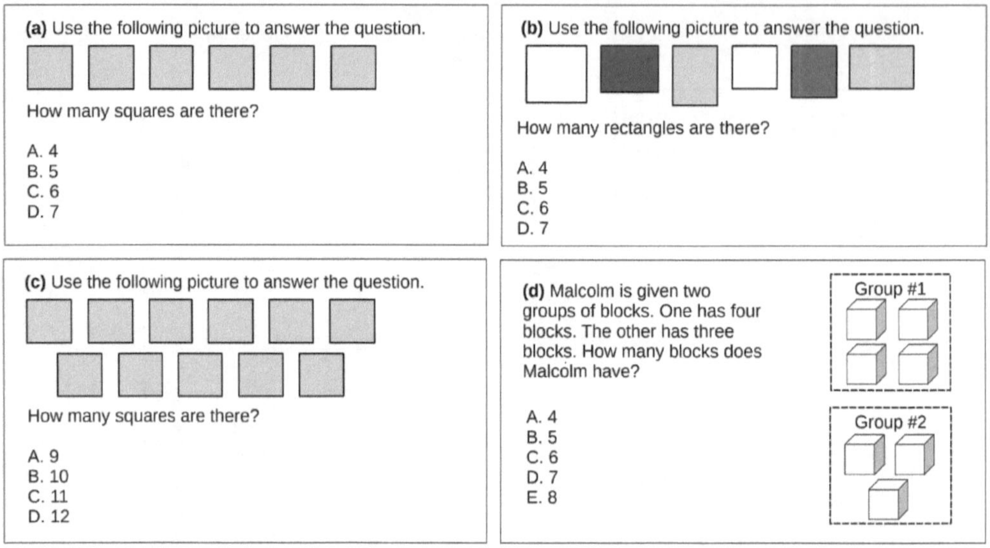

Figure 3.5 Four MCQ Items Involving Counting

within each group, or adding the stated numbers, "*four*" and "*three.*" Question (d) also introduces additional text in the stem to provide a bit of context but might pose issues of the [unexplained] groupings of the blocks.

Table 3.2 presents four task model representations for each of the items. The implied tasks are decomposed down into three classes of complexity features or components (see "Description" rows for each question). The *procedural* components (second column) describe the basic solution steps or procedures. The *declarative* components indicate the nature of the static information or data provided within each problem. Included are the conditions or constraints on the information data (e.g., 5–9 identical, familiar geometric objects). Finally, the *task environment* components specify the relevant complexity of the setting that can directly impact item difficulty and/or moderate various procedural and declarative components. The TMG rows labeled "TMG" provide abbreviated, formulaic cognitive representations of the basic task $count\left\{objects\right\}$. The counting function is applied to the list of objects in brackets where "*n*" refers to the actual number of shapes shown.

The descriptions of the procedures or actions likely to be taken by the examinees and the key data they are given to work with highlight the intricate differences in the potential complexity of these four items. For example, items (a) and (b) differ in terms of the properties of the squares/rectangles shown. Items (a) and (c) differ in the number of squares to be counted. Finally, item (d) adds the grouping featuring and a short vignette description. This leads to two possible TMG representations: one that reflects students ignoring the groupings and merely counting all of the objects and the other embedding the two counting operations within addition. The vignette text is described by a simple "*has*(*P*, *G*)" propositional form where *P* is the name or label for the "agent" and *G* is the description of the object groups.

This type of propositional form of a TMG is not a complete cognitive description of a TMF. It is merely a shorthand way of representing the key task features or attributes related to procedural and declarative knowledge as well as the context of task. Nor is it a required format for

Table 3.2 Task Model Representations for Four Items (see Figure 3.6)

Q	*Format*	*Procedural components*	*Declarative components*	*Task environment components*
(a)	Description	Determine how many by counting	5–9 identical, familiar geometric shapes	Direct instruction with *mcq*(4) format
	TMG	$\boldsymbol{count}\left\{\boldsymbol{objects} = \boldsymbol{squares},\ \boldsymbol{n} < 10\right\}$		
(b)	Description	Determine how many objects there are by counting	5–9 familiar geometric shapes that vary in size (height, width), orientation, and color or shading	Direct instruction with *mcq*(4) format
	TMG	$\boldsymbol{count}\left\{\boldsymbol{objects} = \boldsymbol{rectangles.ignore}\left(\boldsymbol{shape},\ \boldsymbol{shading},\ \boldsymbol{size}\right),\ \boldsymbol{n} < 10\right\}$		
(c)	Description	Determine how many by counting, ignoring irrelevant shape properties	10–20 identical, familiar geometric shapes	Direct instruction with *mcq*(4) format
	TMG	$\boldsymbol{count}\left\{\boldsymbol{objects} = \boldsymbol{squares},\ \boldsymbol{n} \geq 10\right\}$		
(d)	Description	Determine how many objects there are by counting and/or simple addition or summing of two integers or counts	5–9 identical, familiar geometric shapes grouped in two sets or familiar containers (1–5 shapes per group)	Short narrative with limited procedural instruction (simple text or description) with *mcq*(5) format
	TMG	$\#1{:}\ \boldsymbol{count}\left\{\boldsymbol{objects} = \boldsymbol{blocks} \mid \boldsymbol{ignore}\left(\boldsymbol{groups}\right)\right\}$ $\#2{:}\ \boldsymbol{add}\left\{\begin{array}{c\|c} count\left\{\boldsymbol{objects} = \boldsymbol{Group_1}\left(\boldsymbol{blocks}\right),\ \boldsymbol{n_1} < 10\right\}, & text = \\ count\left\{\boldsymbol{objects} = \boldsymbol{Group_2}\left(\boldsymbol{blocks}\right),\ \boldsymbol{n_2} < 10\right\} & has\left(\boldsymbol{P},\boldsymbol{G}\right) \end{array}\right\}$ ***text elements:*** ***P*** = *person,* ***G*** = *groups of objects*		

representing our engineered task models. Rather, the TMG statements attempt to efficiently document the high-level complexity components related to actions, protocols, or likely solution steps (procedural knowledge) applied to the explicit or implicit data or information provided (declarative) knowledge all within a given context ranging from isolated information to deeply embedded concepts and prior knowledge requirements.

While we are not required to adopt the use of TMGs to engage with AE-based test development, we do need to keep our focus on task model complexity. That is, for assessment design and item writing purposes, test developers and psychometricians must move away from focusing on what the examinees know and can do and should instead concentrate on controlling various design layers related to declarative and/or procedural knowledge associated with each task model. That is, task models are focused evidence in support of particular proficiency claims along the construct map (Chapter 2). Multiple task models are used to both build the body of evidence across the proficiency levels on a construct map as well as ensure sufficient magnitudes of score precision and/or decision accuracy along the scale.

In aggregate, the collection of TMFs make up on a new type of test-form specification called a *task model map* (TMM)—a concept introduced in Chapter 1 and discussed/illustrated in Chapter 5. That is, the TMM serves as an *integrated* test content blueprint and a statistical specification (i.e., if we build a test form using the TMM, we satisfy both all content and statistical test assembly requirements). The familial, hierarchical relationship between task models and items also ensures that the supply of items in a bank can consistently meet the test form production demands over time.

3.2.2 Graphical Representations of Task Model Complexity

Graphical or visual representations of task models can be useful to represent procedural, declarative, and contextual features of the task models relative to each other. In fact, several types of graphical elements have been used thus far to represent: (a) the position of a task model within a larger TMM (i.e., the task model locations); (b) the complexity of the contexts or settings, where one or more ellipses, and where thicker or narrower lines might indicate more or less complexity in the setting; (c) arrows where the number of arrows and their properties (line thickness and size of the arrow heads) represent solution steps or applied procedural skills; and (d) network blocks that show the extent and relationships between key declarative knowledge features.

We can also use graphics elements to depict the properties of information or data. Figure 3.6 shows six examples denoting various complexity-related properties (left to right, top to bottom): (1) resolution or sharpness of an image, concepts, or idea units; (2) density of the setting, problem context, or background noise; (3) pacing, speed, or other time-related features; (4) depth of prior or implicit knowledge required; (5) the number of key properties or constraints on those properties associated with each task model; and (6) the presentation or organization of the key information presented.

As already noted, these types of visualization aids are not intended to provide detailed information about each task model. Rather, they serve as design reminders about the cognitive challenge features that make up of each task model and how those features are symbolized in more

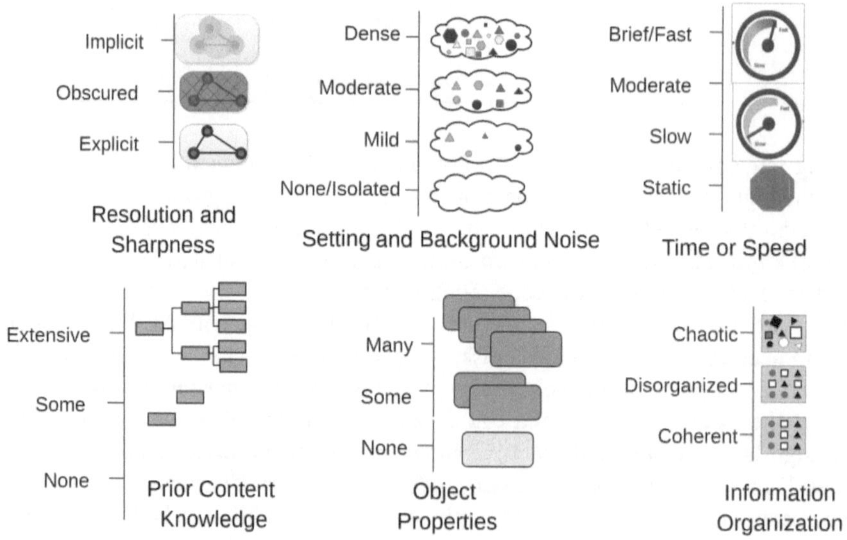

Figure 3.6 Examples of Six Graphical Representations of Complexity-Oriented Task Features

versus less complex TMFs. They can further help to visually compare the ordered complexity of task models in terms in terms of key declarative, procedural, and contextual task model features.

3.3 Item Scale Location (Difficulty) and Task Complexity

Each TMF has a *location* (statistical difficulty) along a scale[10] that is empirically verified for all items within that family (Luecht & Burke, 2020). This location connects the content and cognitive complexity features of the TMF with its statistical operating characteristics within a given population and also serves several quality control functions when items are generated within the family. As such, a given TMF must incorporate a fixed set of cognitively focused conditions, parameters, constraints, and other design specifications meant to establish and maintain that location. For example, Figure 3.7 isolates the four task models highlighted in the TMM shown earlier.

The task models shown in this figure become more difficult/complex as we move from left to right and simultaneously provide evidence about the underlying proficiency claims. *Easier* TMFs (left) might present simplified, foundational content in somewhat isolated contexts, provide task-relevant, easy-to-use tools and scaffolding, and only demand the use of well-practiced basic skills in a domain. In contrast, the more difficult TMFs might demand complex, specialized, or nuanced content knowledge presented in more complex context and the use of more advanced reasoning or strategic skills or multiple applied (integrated) skills.

It is important to emphasize that task models are not themselves proficiency claims nor performance level descriptors (PLDs). Rather, each task model details the nature and complexity

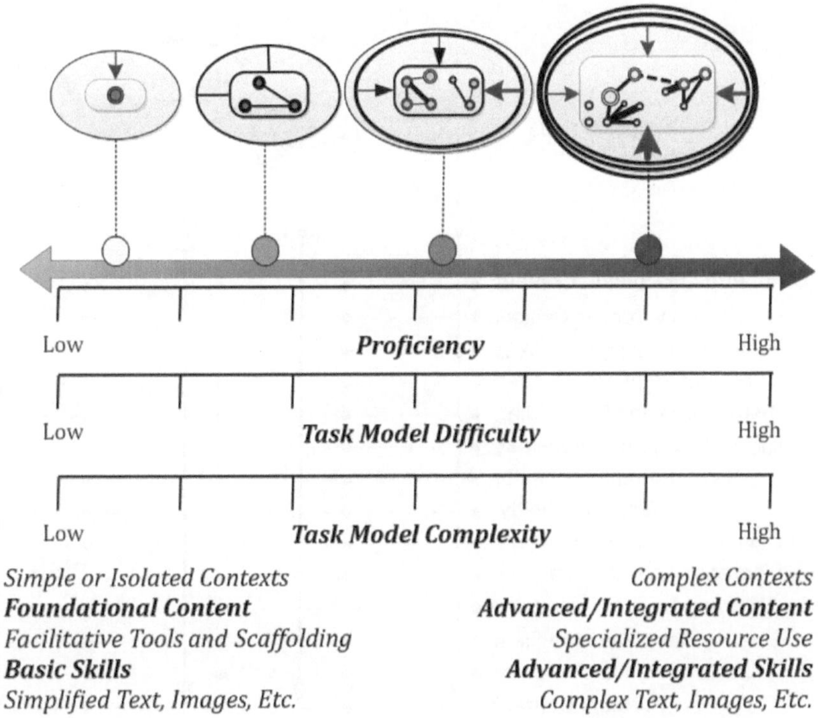

Figure 3.7 Item Difficulty (Scale Locations) and Task Complexity for Four Task Models

of a family of exchangeable test items that present a highly comparable set of challenges to the examinees within a specified context and requiring a designated type and level knowledge within a domain.

3.4 Complexity Design Layers

Complexity design layers (CDLs) decompose a more general conceptualization of declarative and procedural complexity within an assessment domain or subject area into metric-based factors or dimensions. These factors are used when designing the task models and controlling the difficulty of the TMFs. They may reflect discrete categories or continuous complexity-focused metrics.

As discussed in Chapter 4, the CDLs are determined using IDM research. Here, we lay the groundwork for developing a collection of CDLs within a domain. Consider four task models that differ in overall complexity. Figure 3.8 shows the four models with 14 CDLs below them.[11] The dots along each CDL represent both qualitative and quantifiable changes in complexity for that CDL. Compared to the simplified view of a cognitive space depicted earlier in Figure 3.4, this figure essentially represents each task model as a point in a cognitive task space with 14 dimensions.

The vertical drop arrows in this figure idealize how the complexity of each task model changes with respect to each of the underlying factors or conditions represented by the 14 CDLs.[12] Six CDLs are boldfaced in the list: (i) the depth and breadth of primary content, (ii) the number and complexity of solution steps and procedures, (iii) the amount of instruction or scaffolding provided, (iv) the density of key information, (v) text complexity (i.e., the amount and complexity

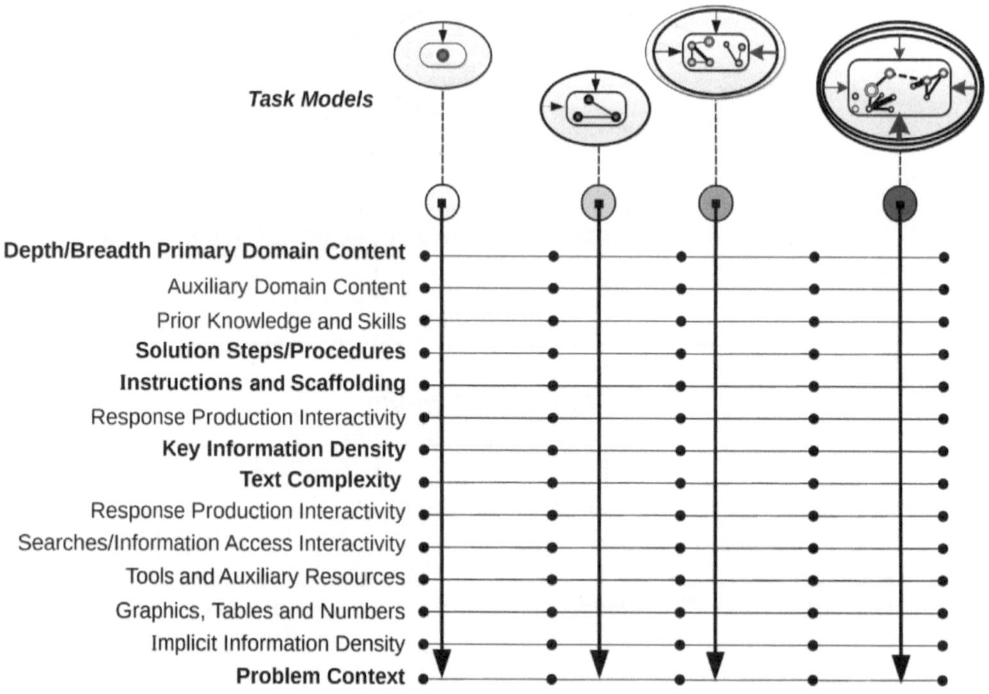

Figure 3.8 Four Task Models Mapped to 14 CDLs

of text used to present the items with each TMF), and (vi) the complexity of the problem context or setting. These may be the six principal complexity drivers for this conceptual domain. However, there are also eight other domains that could come into play.

What is germane to this discussion is how the CDLs decompose the rather vague notion of cognitive complexity into 14 understandable and potentially manipulable factors or task design-focused conditions. But where do we get the CDLs? The answer to that question may be best answered using a story from the fabled Turkish hero Nasreddin Hodja. When asked by the king to discover all manner of knowledge in the world, Nasreddin went out for a year into the world. Upon returning, he reported to the king:

> *Knowledge is like the carrot, few know by looking at the green top that the best part, the orange part, is there. Like the carrot, if you don't work for it, it will wither away and rot. And finally, like the carrot, there are a great many donkeys and jackasses that are associated with it.*
>
> (n.d.)

Our knowledge and understanding of the intentional cognitive assessment space and relevant CDLs is like the carrot. Without a great deal of work and with too much philosophizing about its nature and structure we may never get to useful results—our isomorphic TMFs. In Chapter 4, we discuss some of that necessary empirical work.

3.5 Chapter Summary

This chapter introduced task models as a way to realize the evidence requirements (models) for families of test items. The focus is on the design-specified complexity of collections of statistically and substantively isomorphic items comprising TFMs, that is, exchangeable items within TMFs.

Task modeling accomplishes several important goals. First, it focuses our design efforts for the TMFs not for individual items. Since the TMFs are essentially detailed instantiations of the evidence models discussed in Chapter 2, we begin to build our validity arguments into our task designs. Second, task modeling assumes that content and cognitive task features are not constant across a score scale (or construct map). This assumption allows us to move away from complexity-generic perspectives on content (e.g., a table of content specifications that treats easier and more difficult items as exchangeable content).

Various ways to represent task models were discussed, including TMGs, graphical representations, and more detailed tables or narrative descriptions. The concept of cognitive design layers (CDLs) was also introduced; they are discussed in greater detail in Chapter 4.

Notes

1 The kindergarten mathematics standard might be to "*Solve addition and subtraction word problems with 10 or fewer numbers using objects or drawings to represent the problem.*"

2 In practice, we would develop the task model prior to generating items and refine it as needed to capture all salient complexity features. One or more prototype items merely exemplify each task model family.

3 The list of components or features is population- and domain-specific. For example, the features of task models in kindergarten mathematics would likely be different than for higher grades and would certainly be different than other domains like reading comprehension.

4 A game architecture typically extends the usual structural design of computer software to also include specifications for the graphics engine and interface, sound/audio controls, production and rendering, user inputs and outputs, and interfaces with a browser or operating system.

5 At this juncture, the use of the term "item generator" does not distinguish between items generated by human item writers, generative artificial intelligence, or other implementations of automatic item generation (AIG).

6 Human memory and cognition researchers have historically distinguished between procedural knowledge (how to do things) and declarative knowledge (stored symbolic representations of facts, data, concepts, or information to be retrieved and acted upon using procedural knowledge)—see Squire (1987) and ten Barge and van Hezewijk (1999). The terms *generative knowledge* and *strategic knowledge* are included here as further clarifications of different knowledge types. Generative knowledge denotes dynamically created information, data, or content presented in an assessment task. Strategic knowledge refers to metacognitive protocols or planning strategies for choosing action sequences, selecting declarative repositories in memory or understanding.

7 In fairness, attempts have been made to align DOK levels to different grade levels within subjects like mathematics or reading.

8 AE TMGs can employ a relatively straightforward equation-like format that also mimics the declaration format of functions and procedures used in computer programs. This potentially makes the TMG, itself, useful for subsequently developing software code supporting "calls" to automatic item generation and/or other generative artificial intelligence applications.

9 None of the questions explicitly tell the examinee to "count." Rather, we might assume that the "*How many blocks are there*?" question makes it clear to all examinees that they must engage in a nominal counting exercise.

10 At this point, numerical properties of the scale are not important. The location of each TMF is relative to other task models.

11 There can obviously be more or fewer CDLs, depending on the domain and nature of the measured construct.

12 In practice, not all CDLs may apply to all task models. Furthermore, the arrows may not so neatly track in a straight line across all of the CDLs. Some moderately complex task models, in particular, may show more variation in how the drop arrows would track across the CDLs by design.

4 Task and Item Difficulty Modeling

A key component of Assessment Engineering (AE) is the development of task model families (TMFs) comprising *isomorphic* items. That is, our goal is to engineer the design of the TMFs to ensure the production of statistically exchangeable collections of items that present highly specified content at designated levels of cognitive complexity. Developing isomorphic items is far more than just cloning a parent item by variabilizing and then substituting into designated tokens specified in an item shell or template (see Chapter 6). Rather, we need to sufficiently understand and be able to manipulate, or at least statistically account for, the key features, contexts, and difficulty-related factors that allow us to generate and maintain each TMF.

Task modeling (Chapter 3) can help develop complexity design layers (CDLs) to characterize the essential and intended cognitive-complexity components making up the task models. This chapter describes how empirical research helps operationalize those components using *item difficulty modeling* (IDM; Bejar, 2002; Graf & Fife, 2012; Luecht, 2017b, 2019). That is, IDM allows us to develop quantitative metrics and conditions tied to CDLs that statistically explain and maintain the statistical locations of the TMFs within a task model map (TMM; Chapter 5) and aid in the design of the task model families.

4.1 The Need for IDM Research

IDM research is an investment justified by three challenges. The first challenge involves large-scale item production demands. Testing agencies often require large item banks to meet operational testing needs—especially for on-demand formative assessments (Ackerman & Luecht, in press). The second challenge includes overall item production costs. Organizations need more efficient item design and production mechanisms that reduce per item costs while increasing item quality. The third challenge is item pretesting. There are usually significant costs as well as test assembly and logistic issues associated with pretesting every item as the primary means of determining and evaluating its statistical characteristics.

The latter pretesting challenge, in many ways, may be the most significant one. Many, if not most, testing programs now use Item Response Theory (IRT) models to calibrate their item banks. IRT calibration is a way to statistically pre-equate test forms. That is, once calibrated to an underlying item bank scale, IRT scores can be computed even if examinees take different test forms—including administering computerized adaptive test (CAT) forms (Hambleton & Swaminathan, 1985; Lord, 1980; van der Linden, 2016). However, IRT calibrations tend to require substantial amounts of scored item response data from a finite pool of eligible test takers in the target population.

There are nontrivial costs, logistic complications, and exposure risks associated with pretesting. Successful IDM research can help to significantly reduce and possibly eliminate the need

DOI: 10.4324/9781003451051-4

for item pretesting altogether. In addition, the careful attention to designing items can lead to higher-quality items meeting detailed item inventory requirements over time. The transition from item-writing as an artform or craft, where subject-matter experts (SMEs) largely make most content-related decisions about item design, to a more automated, production-oriented manufacturing engineering view of item and test design and development was succinctly stated by Drasgow, Luecht, and Bennett (2006):

> *The demand for large numbers of items is challenging to satisfy because the traditional approach to test development uses the item as the fundamental unit of currency. That is, each item is individually hand-crafted—written, reviewed, revised, edited, entered into a computer, and calibrated—as if no other like it had ever been created before.*
>
> (p. 473)

4.2 Isomorphism and Composability in IDM Research

Although IDM is applied to individual items, the ultimate goal—at least from AE perspective—is to create a test development *system* capable of generating high-quality items on demand. The AE focus is therefore on TMFs (Luecht & Burke, 2020). One of the core principles for designing and building viable TMFs is *isomorphism* (Bejar, 2002; Bejar & Yocom, 1991; Luecht, 2019; Luecht & Burke, 2020). A second principle involves the engineering concept of *composability*.

Isomorphism is generically defined as "*having similar form or shape.*" In an AE context, isomorphism implies indifference with respect to choosing any particular item from a TMF. More specifically, the isomorphic items within a given TMF must be completely exchangeable in terms of key criteria including the apparent item content, the nature and level of challenge/cognitive task requirements, and the statistical item characteristics. Luecht (2019) and Luecht and Burke (2020) distinguish two types of isomorphism, both of which are ideally informed as part of a successful IDM research study, namely, (1) statistical isomorphism and (2) substantive isomorphism.

Statistical isomorphism implies that a common set of parameter estimates can be used for items belonging for test assembly and scoring purposes. This is a decidedly pragmatic, operational definition. It does not necessarily mean that the statistical item operating characteristics are perfectly coincident. Rather, the implication is that any item-level variation or covariation among the parameter estimates within task families are ignorable for all practical scoring and decision-making purposes—that is, it ought to be a matter of indifference to a test taker which items across TMFs comprise his or her test form.

Substantive isomorphism implies that the items within a family are comparable in terms of the content complexity and cognitive task requirements specified by controls and constraints associated with a given task model. Each task model is a complete design specification for a collection (family) of items. The item models provide mechanisms for generating items that each meet the design specifications of the task model. This implies that every item in each TMF must (i) involve highly similar content, (ii) be at the same depth of knowledge, (iii) comprise the same constellation of problem skills and/or procedural steps, (iv) require the same prior knowledge, (v) encompass the same level of semantic coherence (i.e., integration of the task components), (vi) reflect similar magnitudes of information density of the problems (data density, text and/or graphical complexity), (vii) include the same task constraints or conditions, (viii) demonstrate comparable instantiations of the settings or contexts, and (ix) involve the same available problem-solving resources and scaffolding, and auxiliary tools.

Composability implies that different components or elements can be combined and/or connected in various ways to create larger, more complex components, systems, or structures. It is an important principle in software and industrial engineering that promotes reusability and design efficiency under the umbrella of a robust design architecture.

Traditional item writing often considers each item as a creative, monolithic design process that is fully controlled by the item writers. That is, each item is written as unique challenge based largely on the item writer's preferences. Items are not composed in a principled manner involving component parts.[1]

Composable task design instead implies that the complexity of the content, its presentation, and the scoring of TMFs can be robustly modularized. This principle allows for efficiently combining the components to create isomorphic items within each TMF at targeted levels of complexity, and also understanding how we can decompose the difficulty or complexity of an item family into its constituent parts—the CDLs and TMF specifications and tolerances.

4.3 Characterizing Statistical Item Difficulty for IDM Research

The research quest to identify the causal precursors of item difficulty starts with selecting an appropriate dependent variable—*item difficulty*. The dependent variable can be a simple item mean or *p* value, or a function of multiple, estimated item parameters that statistically characterize each item in the population—such as IRT difficulty, discrimination, and pseudo-guessing parameters that artificially shape a statistically fitted response function to empirical response patterns (Hambleton & Swaminathan, 1985; Lord, 1980).

Luecht (2019) recommended using an expected response function (ERF) as the dependent variable for most IRT models, rather than the item parameter estimates, themselves (also see Ackerman & Luecht,in press; Luecht & Burke, 2020). IRT item parameters are merely shaping parameters rather than meaningful outcome features. For example, the one-parameter (1PL or Rasch) logistic model is:

$$prob\left(u_i = 1|\theta; b_i\right) \equiv P_i = \left[1 + exp\left(b_i - \theta\right)\right]^{-1} \tag{4.1}$$

where P_i is the probability of success on a binary-scored item response (u_i=1 if correct or u_i=0 otherwise), θ is the underlying score scale, b_i is an item difficulty parameter. Equation 4.1 is also the conditional ERF: $ERF\left(u_i|\theta\right) = \left(0\right)Q_i + \left(1\right)P_i = P_i$ where $Q_i = 1 - P_i$ as the probability of incorrect response to item *i*.

In contrast, the more complicated three-parameter logistic (3PL) IRT model characterizes the item response probability by:

$$prob\left(u_i = 1|\theta; a_i, b_i, c\right) = P_i = c_i + \left(1 - c_i\right)\left\{1 + exp\left[-a_i\left(\theta - b_i\right)\right]\right\}^{-1} \tag{4.2}$$

with θ again representing the underlying proficiency score scale and b_i denoting the item difficulty. In addition, the model includes a "discrimination" parameter, a_i, that functions as both a type of scoring weight as well as an indicator of the sensitivity of the item to the changes in the underlying proficiency scores, and a "lower asymptote" parameter, c_i, that adjusts for noise in the response function at the lower end of the proficiency scale—sometimes called the "pseudo-guessing" parameter (Hambleton & Swaminathan, 1985; Lord, 1980).

Luecht's rationale was borrowed from Horst (1933) who offered a definition of item difficulty that remains useful today. Horst defined item difficulty as the expected proportion of correct responses within a prescribed examinee population.[2] This definition lets us reconcile the differences between a classical p value and various IRT-modeled response functions. For example, under either the 1PL or 3PL IRT models shown above, an expected (dichotomous) item response score can be expressed as the following integral (summation) over an examinee population with a distributional proficiency score density, $g(\theta)$:

$$E(u_i) = p_i = \int P_i(\theta)g(\theta)\, d\theta. \tag{4.3}$$

This ERF also readily extends to polytomously scored items having more than two (binary) categories, i.e., $E(u_i) = \int \sum_{j=1}^{J_i} X_{ij} P_{ij}(\theta)g(\theta)\, d\theta$. If desired, we can also normalize the latter expectation relative to $max(X_i)$ to put it onto a proportional scale.

Therefore, when we talk about task model difficulty or *locating* task models on a scale, we will be dealing with a metric that ranges from zero to one, were higher values imply easier challenges and lower values denote more difficult challenges. This scale choice does not preclude using more sophisticated item response modeling strategies. It merely provides a highly intuitive metric for describing the difficulty of the TMFs relative to one another—an essential component of building the TMMs.

There are four advantages of characterizing task model difficulty on an ERF (proportional) scale. First, item mean scores and p-values are usually readily understood by non-psychometricians such as SMEs and test development staff. Second, an ERF avoids conditional treatment of the task model difficulties within restricted regions of the proficiency scale. For example, if we accept some of the lessons from designing games, we see that the game challenges are not directed at examinees within a narrow skill range. Rather, those challenges are evaluated relative to the expected performance (or average perceived difficulty) within the population of players. Third, using the proportional ERF scale easily reconciles the various parameterization differences between IRT models (see Equation 4.3). Finally, following Luecht's (2019) rationale, the ERF can be further transformed to other convenient metrics for statistical analysis purposes—for example, to a logit, a probit, or a arcsine metric that avoids some of the inherent heterogeneous variance issues at the extremes of a distribution associated with proportions and percentages.

4.4 Foundations of IDM Research

IDM research has evolved along two different, but not incompatible, pathways. The *strong theory pathway* prefers the starting with strong cognitive and learning theories about the knowledge, skills and experiences (KSEs) in an examinee population to justify the item design choices that are subsequently made (e.g., Embretson, 1998, 1999; Gorin & Embretson 2006, 2012; Nichols, 1994; National Research Council, 2001). The other *statistical-control* pathway is somewhat more relaxed with respect to the theoretical underpinnings of IDM.

This latter pathway does not preclude the development of strong cognitive explanations of examinee performance; it encourages that where feasible. However, this pathway argues that from a task and item/test design perspective, we simply cannot control or otherwise discover what the examinees bring to a test in terms of their unique KSEs; nor can we deal with all of the potential multilevel interactions between item and task design characteristics or features and examinee characteristics (Attali, et al., 2022; Drum, Calfee, & Cook, 1981; Luecht, 2013, 2019; Luecht, Burke and Devore, 2009; Meisner, Reckase & Luecht, 1993; Settles, Laflair & Hagiwara, 2020).

Some of the computational psychometrics research that employs machine learning and artificial intelligence text analytics are examples of *statistical controls* (e.g., Enright, et al.,

2002; Gorin & Embretson, 2006, 2012; Settles, LaFlair, & Hagiwara, 2020). This line of research at *Duolingo™* leverages readily available psycholinguistic features like word length (character count), word popularity relative to a large lexical corpus, sentence length, etc., with task complexity aligned to the *Common European Framework of Reference* (CEFR), an international standard for describing the proficiency of foreign-language learners.

As discussed further on, text analysis software packages like Duolingo's proprietary IDM modeling system as well as publicly available online packages like *CohMetrix* (Graesser & McNamara, 2011; McNamara et al., 2014), Google's *Bidirectional Encoder Representations from Transformers* (BERT) for natural language pre-processing, and numerous open-source packages/libraries available for the *R* and *Python* programming environments can generate numerous psycholinguistic variables from input text segments. If some of those variables prove useful to explain and control item difficulty in a particular testing domain, it does not really matter if they likewise fit into an accepted, well-articulated theory of the cognition of language.[3] Therefore, while strong cognitive theories that help guide task designs can be useful to help guide the design of constructs and evidentiary requirements to support performance claims, they are of secondary importance from this IDM statistical-control perspective which seeks to identify and manipulate key design variables that empirically explain statistical item difficulty.

Fischer (1973) attempted to integrate hypothesized (theoretical) causes of cognitive task complexity with a formal IDM strategy. By applying linear constraints to the Rasch model, Fischer (1973) proposed the *Linear Logistic Test Model* (LLTM), which he stated was "*appropriate for the analysis of subject areas in instructional research if the subject area comprises tasks or items*" which are solved using a combination of "*cognitive operations or rules.*" His work empirically tested specific hypotheses about the impact of manipulating cognitive features on item difficulty using operational test items.

Embretson (1998, 1999) extended Fischer's LLTM by adding a discrimination parameter and then empirically demonstrating how to connect strong cognitive theories to item design by manipulating features hypothesized to impact the cognitive complexity of the tasks. For example, in her article in *Psychological Methods,* Embretson (1998) describes the careful application of Carpenter, Just and Shell's (1990) processing theory based on the *Raven's Progressive Matrices Test* to the development of a small item bank that manipulated the number of rules and presence or absence of abstract relations for purposes of measuring an abstract reasoning trait. She was able to account for about 80 percent of the variation in the item difficulties as a function of the manipulated item design features.

Bejar and Yocom (1991) termed these strong-theory methods as "*generative approaches*" because the items are specifically generated using design features hypothesized to impact item difficulty (also see Bejar, 2002). For example, Bejar and Yocom studied the manipulation of glyphs hidden in a larger image as a means of directly impacting cognitive load (i.e., glyph shape, manipulating the extent of edge detection needed, amount of distractive information). They were able to demonstrate modest effectiveness, statistically explaining about 50 percent of the variance in the empirical item difficulties.

Bejar et al. (2003) expanded this type of research to a more traditional academic test—the computer-adaptive *Graduate Record Examination* (GRE®) developed and administered by Educational Testing Service. They used 147 GRE items from the general test to develop item models (i.e., as parent items) and then designed several variant items per parent. Their study demonstrated reasonable control over the variant items associated with each of the 147 items. Although they only demonstrated a moderate amount of explained variance between the empirical difficulties and the predicted values (i.e., they reported R^2 values of 0.67–0.76), they were able to demonstrate the feasibility of actually using the predicted values in scoring with results on par with GRE test-retest correlations.

Meisner, Reckase, and Luecht (1993) demonstrated the feasibility of controlling item difficulty for mathematics items appropriate for the ACT Assessment Mathematics test using an algorithmic approach to generate items. Eight item families developed per each of 16 generating algorithms that were hypothesized to systematically differ in complexity. For the most part, the eight items per were shown to be statistically exchangeable when pretested on operational ACT test forms—that is, *isomorphic* (Bejar, 2002).

Daniel and Embretson (2010) also investigated the impact of systematically manipulating select cognitive variables in computer-generated mathematics items. They used Embretson's (1998, 1999) generalized LLTM to show that a "solution planning" stage is easier for examinees when equations are provided in the item; conversely, when a key equation is not provided in the item, the solution planning stage becomes more cognitively complex and requires additional cognitive processing steps.

The research literature on IDM for reading comprehension and related areas of receptive language assessment is perhaps the most extensive for three reasons. First, there are several well-developed frameworks of language acquisition and development such as the aforementioned CEFR, the *Interagency Language Roundtable* (ILR) on foreign language, and the *ACTFL Performance Descriptors for Language Learners* (ACTFL.org). These frameworks include detailed guidance about the expected (ordered) performance and functional capabilities of language learners at different levels of proficiency, including ordered descriptions of contexts, content, and text types. Second, the lexical, syntactic, and semantic features of static reading passages can be readily linked to cognitive processing language concepts like encoding, fluency, and cognitive loads on short-term memory. Third, with the proliferation of open-source software platforms like *Python* and *R*, numerous text analytic software packages are now readily available to independent researchers, including cloud-based AI-analytical engines such as Google's *Bidirectional Encoder Representations from Transformers* (BERT) that including natural language preprocessing for applications like question answering and sentiment analysis.

Drum, Calfee, and Cook (1981) conducted one of the first large-scale IDM studies looking at reading comprehension assessments. They hypothesized six skills are used in a reading comprehension test: (i) accurate and fluent word recognition (lexical); (ii) knowledge of specific word meanings (lexical); (iii) knowledge of syntactic/semantic clause and sentence relationships (syntactic); (iv) recognition of the superordinate/subordinate idea structure of passages (semantic); (v) identification of the specific information requested in questions (semantic); and (vi) a dynamic evaluation of the alternate choices (multiple-choice distracts) to select the one that best fits both the syntactic/semantic requirements of the question and the idea structure of the reading passage. Drum et al. looked at seven national reading tests for younger children and computed 16 predictors from the item content they felt should predict item difficulty. The 16 predictors fell into one of four classes: (a) passage components; (b) item stem components; (c) correct answer choice components; and (d) incorrect response choice components. The regression analysis results across the seven tests impressively produced R^2 values (proportion of variance explained) of 0.58–0.95. Reducing the number of predictors to ten did not significantly result in degenerate regression solutions. However, when these researchers looked at the strength of the predictors the familiarity of words (word recognition and/or word meaning) emerged as the primary sources of item difficulty on these studied reading comprehension test.[4]

One of the more comprehensive and successful IDM studies was carried out by Sheehan and Mislevy (1990). Sheehan and Mislevy analyzed three classes of variables obtained by Kirsch and Mosenthal's (1990—also see Mosenthal and Kirsch, 1991) in-depth cognitive analysis of items written for the *Document Literacy scale on the Young Adult Survey* included as part of the *National Assessment of Educational Progress* (NAEP): (1) materials variables that characterized the length and organizational complexity of the document referred each the item; (2) directive variables that related to the length and organizational complexity of the task directive (item instructions); and (3) process variables that considered the difficulty of the task solution process. What was unique in these studies is that some of the predictive/explanatory variables were based on cognitively anchored ratings, rather than just surface item features. The quantified cognitive item features accounted for a sizable amount of variance in the estimated item difficulties with reported the R^2 values ranging from 0.59 to 0.81. The apparent success of Sheehan and Mislevy (1990) relative to some of the more recent IDM research seems to have been due to the additional work by Kirsch and Mosenthal (1990) to incorporate an in-depth cognitive analysis of the document literacy items, including the development of a formal grammar for representing the item content. Unfortunately, their procedures may have been too time-consuming and/or complex to operationally implement.

More recently, Ferrara, Steedle, and Frantz (2022) conducted a meta-analysis and found 31 IDM studies[5] related to reading comprehension alone. Of those, only 12 demonstrated predictive R^2 values of 0.5 or higher. They went on to identify 6 classes of passage-related feature variables that appears most strongly related to item difficulty across the 12 studies: (i) text structure and rhetorical features; concreteness of passage information; (ii) passage content demands; (iii) reference to information outside the passage; (iv) passage and sentence length (effort demands); (v) passage linguistic demand related to passage grammar and syntax variables; and (vi) passage linguistic demand involving passage vocabulary variables. They also identified seven classes of predictive item-level feature variables: (a) text rhetorical and language features such as imagery, metaphor and persuasive language; (b) lexical and semantic match between the passage and item; (c) concreteness of information requested in an item; (d) cognitive load of matching information in the item and passage; (e) location in the passage of information needed to correctly identify and respond to the item (e.g., located in the first and/or second sentence versus embedded); (f) familiarity of information needed; and (g) competing information in the item and passage.

Applied IDM studies have likewise taken place in content domains like K-12 mathematics, high school biology, science reasoning, pictorial reasoning (e.g., rotation of shapes or figures), clinical decision-making in nursing, biostatistics and evidence-based medicine, and even professional accounting. For example, Luecht, Burke, and Devore (2009) conducted a small-scale study using computerized accounting simulations from a national accountancy examination. They used an accounting-based, cognitive-feature-ordered *task model grammar* (TMG) to classify 14 accounting simulations according by 3 cognitive complexity metrics: (1) the number of apparent cognitive actions needed by an entry-level accountant to arrive at a solution; (2) the average level of complexity of the required actions; and (3) the complexity of the setting or problem context (extent of supporting information per simulation, density of the information provided, distractive information, etc.). Luecht et al. were able to almost perfectly reproduce empirically estimated item difficulties and associated statistical properties[6] for the 14 simulations and furthermore resulted in correlations between IRT scores estimated from the IDM-computed difficulties and the empirically estimated difficulties of over 0.99.

In another study, Luecht (2019) used regression-based analytics to explore the difficulty of biostatistics and evidence-based medicine items from a national medical licensing examination. Luecht included a combination of statistical component metrics derived using linguistic features of the items and human-rated cognitive features of the items to predict the items' difficulties (e.g., the density of information provided—including text, graphics tables or numerical information, the extent of procedural skills or protocol knowledge needed, the depth, breadth and specific of auxiliary content, the extent of prior knowledge or prerequisite skills needed). This combination of text-derived and rated features resulted in R^2 values of nearly 0.9—a very promising IDM finding for any test.

Luecht, Burke, and Devore's (2009) study and Luecht's (2019) study help highlight an important point also apparent in the Mislevy and Sheehan (1990) study and at least alluded to by Ferrara et al. (2022) in their meta-analysis involving reading comprehension tests. Extracting surface features alone is not sufficient to adequately explain item difficulty! Rather, it seems that using human raters to effectively score items relative to some of the fuzzier aspects of cognitive complexity like requisite prior knowledge. The abstractness of the relationship between the item stem and directions and specific distractors in a multiple-choice item is essential to augment the item-difficulty predictions. That insight is the motivation for reconceptualizing IDM predictors as CDLs. Some CDLs computationally derived by analytical processing of source materials using software and others by using human raters to efficiently and effectively score the items (or task models) relative to features that are not amenable to computer-automated analytics.

No further attempt is made in this chapter to comprehensively review the expanding repositories of past IDM-related literature. Rather, the remainder of this chapter focuses on what is needed to carry out a research program aimed at moving IDM research into operational item and test design and production under the AE framework.

4.4.1 The Roles of Item Features and Complexity Design Layers

The predictors or explanatory variables used in IDM can either be available surface features associated with individual items or stimuli, computed variables such as psycholinguistic or natural language processing (NLP) indices applied to text segments, or more subtle, manipulated task-design features of the response instructions, items, stimuli or even scoring evaluators and rubrics. The goal is to [ideally] explain as much of the variation in the dependent variable(s)—item difficulty—as possible. These predictors are generically referred to as *item feature* variables[7] in this chapter. Guttman and Schlesinger (1966) may have been the first researchers to undertake the identification of what they termed "facets" that could be systematically varied as part of the item writing process. They investigated limited number of facets that related to both content features as well as the format and presentation of the items. Although their results were, at best, inconclusive, they helped to illustrate the apparent importance of linking intentional item design to item complexity, and by extension, to item difficulty.

While the selection of an appropriate dependent variable—an item difficulty indicator—is relatively straightforward, the selection of the item feature variables can be far more nuanced and will likely vary across different content domains and item types (Luecht, 2012a, 2013, 2019). For example, Ferrara, Steedle, and Frantz (2022) proposed a framework of item response demands for predicting item difficulty that included (1) the complexity of the stimulus (e.g., reading passage, map, diagram), (2) the selected- or constructed-response mechanism(s) used, (3) the depth and breadth of content or domain-specific terminology and concepts used; (4) the apparent cognitive level of the items, and (5) the linguistic response demands such as grammar, syntax, and vocabulary in an item stem and/or passage. As noted earlier, Ferrara, Steedle, and Frantz (2022) applied their framework to look at 31 IDM studies related to reading/paragraph comprehension. As shown in Table 4.1, they identified two broad classes of response-demand features: (i) features related to the selected or generated reading passage and (ii) features related to items and distractors.

Table 4.1 IDM Features of Reading Passages and Items

Passage-Item Demands
Text rhetorical and language features (e.g., imagery, metaphor, characterization, foreshadowing, persuasive language, literary terms, theme) or text language (e.g., concrete/abstract concepts, vocabulary, syntax, colloquial language, dialect)
Lexical and semantic match degree of overlapping words, phrases, and concepts between the item and passage
Concreteness of information requested from concrete (e.g., person, thing, place, action, or event) to abstract (e.g., purpose, pattern, difference, condition, reason, or evidence)
Cognitive load of matching information in the item and passage
Location of information needed (e.g., main idea in first and/or second sentence of first short paragraph, main idea in first sentence of second paragraph)
Familiarity of information needed
Competing information in the passage or item
Item-Stem/Distractor Demands
Stem content demands (amount/categories of information in the stem)
Stem response vocabulary demands
Stem response cognitive processing demands (abstractness and item type/comprehension processes)
Correct response vocabulary demands (new content words)
Correct response position demands
Distractor plausibility (vocabulary, match and language)

Source: Adapted from Ferrara et al. (2022).

Yet, it becomes an empirical question as to whether or all of some these features apply equally to reading comprehension tests for different purposes (e.g., academic achievement or growth in reading, for college admission testing, as part of certification or licensure test that employs extended reading sections). Nor is it clear to what extent these same response demands even apply on academic achievement across grades or grade bands. That is not a criticism of Ferrara et al.'s (2022) study. Rather, if helps emphasize the serious challenge in attempting to over-generalize specific classes of cognitively oriented task or item design features across different populations, test types, subject areas or contexts.

Luecht (2019) and Luecht and Burke (2020) instead introduced two broad classes of predictors/explanatory variables that they termed *complexity design layers* (CDLs): (i) derived complexity covariates (DCCs) that can be computed from feature vectors of a wide range of metadata variables computed or coded for intact items and (ii) complexity scoring protocols (CSPs) and other human-rated indicators that supplement the DCC indicators. The CDLs are *domain-specific*! There is no expectation that a collection of CDLs that work in one domain or assessment context will work in another domain. Rather, the CDLs should represent all salient item features that best predict item difficulty—regardless of the number of indicators needed, type of IDM metrics involved, or whether particular CDLs can be theoretically justified by some preferred or prevailing cognitive theory. It should be noted that the concept of CDLs can also be more generally incorporated into nominal, categorical contextual conditions that moderate the item-difficulty predictions (e.g., design states such as testing modes or classes of item types).

Figure 4.1 shows a flexible variable-focused, analytical architecture to support IDM research and, eventually, operational implementation where the IDM input data are efficiently collected for automated or semi-automated. The outputs from the analyses (e.g., regression weights,

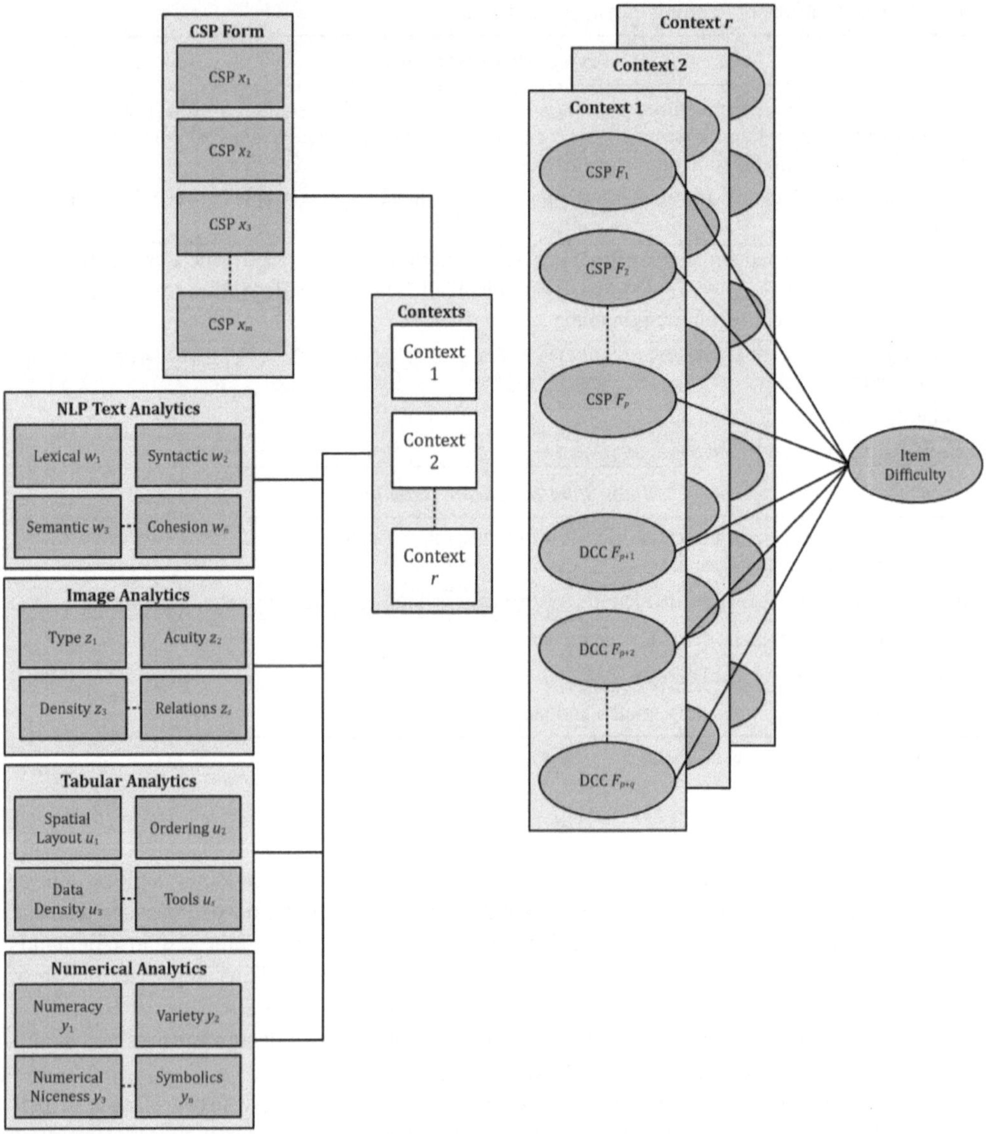

Figure 4.1 An Analytical Architecture for IDM Research and Operational Implementation

predicted item-difficulty values and residual statistics to be monitored) would ideally be automatically uploaded to a repository for use in assembling items.

There are two notable distinctions in this AE representation of IDM research. First, the CDLs focus on assessment task (item) complexity features, not on the characteristics of particular examinees in the population. The rationale is straightforward. Test developers can control the design and production of the assessment tasks they generate but have little to no control over the knowledge, skills, and abilities the examinees bring to each task. Rather the CDLs control the nature and complexity of each TMF and ideally provide tangible performance-based evidence about proficiency claims along the score scale (Luecht, 2012a, 2013, 2019, 2020; Luecht & Burke, 2020). Second, the CDLs may or may not fit into some generalized cognitive schema like Bloom famous taxonomy (Bloom et al., 1956) or Webb's (2005) depth of knowledge (DOK) levels. Rather, every test may have its own set of *content-anchored, domain-specific CDLs*!

Implementing IDM is not sufficient to ensure successful AE research. It serves as an important part of the overall AE framework linking the conceptual task models and CDLs to quantitative metrics and qualitative data. However, operationalizing IDM also requires software and data system to efficiently capture, store, and use the item feature variables and CDLs in operational item production and test assembly. For example, the development of effective CDLs in a domain can augment that data with numerous other computed and rating-based indicators, possibly numbering in the hundreds or even thousands of numerical and categorical variables. Those variables can furthermore be associated with individual items or item families derived from common TMFs. In short, the requirements and design specifications for the item and test data is an order of magnitude more complex than most testing organizations currently support in their item banking and test form assembly and processing software systems.

4.4.2 Some Methods for Statistically Modeling Item Difficulty

Given the dependent variable and a set of independent variables from an item corpus, we could use the mainstay linear regression model to predict/explain the item difficulty variable, Y, as a linear combination of q item features, X, as:

$$\hat{Y} = \beta_0 + \sum_{j=1}^{q} \beta_j X_j \tag{4.4}$$

by estimating the coefficients, β_0 (intercept or bias offset term) and β_j for j = 1, …, q that minimize the sum of squared residuals,

$$arg.min\left[\sum_{i=1}^{N}\left(y_i - x_i^T\beta\right)^2\right]. \tag{4.5}$$

That is, using matrix notation for N observations and q+1 coefficients with, the least squares solution for the vector of coefficients is

$$\hat{\beta} = \left(X^T X\right)^{-1} X^T y \tag{4.6}$$

where the "T" superscript denotes the transpose matrix function.

More elaborate regression models can also be used including quantile regression models, multilevel models, nonlinear models, and even latent structural models comprised of both observed and latent variables. Ultimately, the estimated item difficulty parameters can be directly used as surrogate item difficulty estimates for purposes of test assembly and scoring. Optionally, they can serve as transitional difficulties for test assembly until a more formal set of operational item parameters can be estimated using large samples of response data and an IRT model of choice. The predicted difficulties can likewise be used as strong "priors" in most types of IRT Bayes estimation to calibrate the items.

It is important to realize that test-development researchers must still select, compute, or otherwise create the item features variables to be used. When incorporated as item features, the researchers may employ specific *a priori* hypotheses about which features of an item will affect its difficulty and then empirically verify or nullify those hypotheses. The *a priori* approach forms the basis by which other forms of principled assessment design have been used to create groups of items with similar properties from a single item model, or template (Daniel & Embretson, 2010; Embretson & Kingston, 2018; Luecht, 2013; Mislevy et al., 2003). Although this research has shown promise as a basis to produce effective item models (Enright, Morley, & Sheehan, 2002; Gorin & Embretson, 2006, 2012) the potential need manually code the item features for an entire item bank can be difficult to employ on a large scale. One of the arguments in this chapter is that focusing on the most efficient methods for identifying potentially salient item features, augmenting those decisions with strong engineering-based quality control (QC) mechanisms as part of an item manufacturing-production system, and finally automating as much of the process as possible can help overcome the apparent limitations of incorporating human-determined item features (Luecht & Burke, 2020).

An alternative to merely predicting item difficulties involves directly modeling an item response function using the item-feature variables. As noted earlier, Fischer (1973) introduced the linear logistic test model (LLTM) to predict statistical item characteristic as linear combinations of design-focused covariates (item features), q_{ik}, for $k = 1, \ldots, K$ complexity-based design attributes going into the design of each task model. The probability of a correct response to a dichotomous item can be expressed under the LLTM as:

$$prob\left(u_{i:f}=1|\theta;\eta_i\right)=P_i(\theta)=\left[1+exp\left[\left(\sum_{k=1}^{K}\eta_k q_{ik}-\eta_0-\theta\right)\right]\right]^{-1} \tag{4.7}$$

where $\boldsymbol{\eta}_i$ is a vector of coefficients (weights) associated with the item features variables, $\boldsymbol{q}_i$.

Embretson (1999) extended the LLTM by adding an item-discrimination parameter. Generalizing from individual items to TMFs, this constrained two-parameter model can be expressed as:

$$prob\left(u_{i:f}=1|\theta;a_f,b_f\right)=P_f(\theta)=\left[1+exp\left[-a_f\left(\theta-b_f\right)\right]\right]^{-1} \tag{4.8}$$

where $u_{i:f}$ is an observed binary item score for an item in TMF f, a_f is a TMF discrimination parameter,

$$a_f=\tau_1 q_{f1}+\tau_2 q_{f2}+\cdots+\tau_K q_{fK}=\sum_{k=1}^{K}\tau_k q_{fk}, \tag{4.9}$$

with characteristic weights, τ_k. The family-level item difficulty can be similarly expressed as

$$b_f=\eta_1 q_{f1}+\eta_2 q_{f2}+\cdots+\eta_K q_{fK}=\sum_{k=1}^{K}\eta_k q_{fk} \tag{4.10}$$

with a different set of coefficient weights, η_k, that determine the item difficulty, b_f, as a linear combination of other item or TMF design features. This modeling approach can provide relatively stable item parameter estimates since all of the item responses per family are used (e.g., see empirical results reported by Shu, Burke, & Luecht, 2010; also see Sinharay & Johnson, 2012). The downside is that it ignores variability within the TMFs[8] (Glas et al., 2010).

The weights, τ_k and η_k can be empirically estimated from the response data, denoting predetermined predicted TMF item discrimination and difficulty (i.e., estimated effects of the design-based covariates making up each task model, q_{kf}), or could in principle be directly specified by the task designers if items can be reliably generated from the same design features. A slight simplification of the generalized LLTM for TMFs would set the discrimination parameter inversely proportional to the estimated residuals of items within each family (Luecht, 2019; Luecht & Burke, 2020). That is,

$$a_f \propto \left\{ \sum_{i=1}^{I:f} \left[p_{i:f} - \int P_f(\theta)\phi(\theta)d\theta \right]^2 \right\}^{-1} \tag{4.11}$$

where $p_{i:f}$ denotes an empirical item mean (p-value for dichotomously scored items) and $\phi(\theta)$ is the probability density function for θ within the target population. The logic of using a family-level weight to be the reciprocal of the residual variance is to "reward" TMFs that are working well and "penalize" those that are not—at least insofar as the effect of the item parameters on scoring/decision making (also see Luecht & Burke, 2020).

More complex hierarchical IRT models have been proposed (e.g., Glas et al, 2010; Geerlings et al., 2011; Sinharay & Johnson, 2012). In most cases, these models introduce a family-level covariance matrix to account for potential dependencies among the parameters of models like the 3PL (Equation 4.2) and several partial-credit IRT models for polytomous data. Empirical investigations have demonstrated that the added complexity of these models, while improving (family-wise) item fit, does not substantially improve scoring accuracy (Glas et al., 2010; Sinharay & Johnson, 2012).

Shu, Burke, and Luecht (2010) offered a more pragmatic view of the IRT calibration process and recommended a calibration design that allowed for items within a TMF to be treated as single items for calibration purposes. Any IRT model for dichotomous and polytomous data can be used for calibration and linking under this type of design. The stability of the IRT item parameter estimates will tend to improve substantially because of the combined, scored response data from all items connected to each TMF. Sinharay and Johnson (2012) called this an "identical siblings design" (i.e., exchangeable items within families). Under this approach, we identify the item feature variables and use them as a combination of item-production constraints and QC indicators applied to entire families of items. However, we still calibrate the entire TMF and use those IRT parameter estimates for test assembly and scoring purposes while simultaneously monitoring the variation of individual items within each family.[9]

Figure 4.2 demonstrates how item response can be systematically collapsed within a TMF for calibration purposes. The top figure shows 48 non-isomorphic items that are (ideally) below to four TMFs. Each shaded block represents a sample of examinees exposed to that item. Because the items are not functioning isomorphically, we have to treat them as unique items and deal with smaller calibration samples. The middle figure shows 12 item models (three per each of the four TMFs) with sufficiently isomorphic items within each item model. We can therefore collapse the response data and increase the sample sizes per calibrated item model. Finally, the bottom image shows four TMFs with all items isomorphic within family. The data is again collapsed across the item models and we have maximum sample sizes (given the available data), which should ensure more stable and better quality TMF parameter estimates.

Note that IDM serves two purposes under this approach to calibrating item parameters. First, as noted, the predicted difficulties can serve as strong QC indicators to ensure that newly generated items are within item-engineering tolerances for inclusion on operational test forms. Second, the predicted difficulties can be used to augment available response data as prior information under a Bayesian calibration framework.

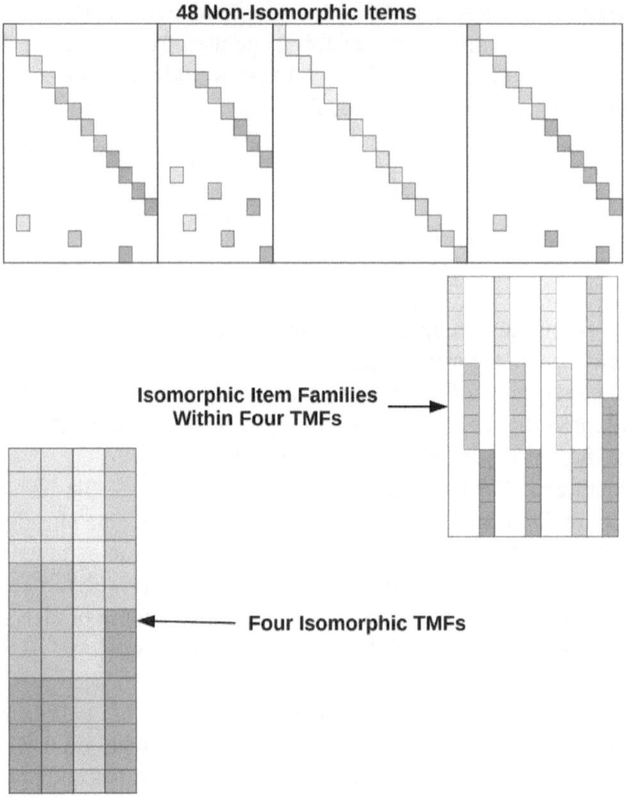

Figure 4.2 Collapsing Response Data Based on the Quality of Isomorphism with a TMF

A thorough comparative discussion of the merits of various statistical modeling approaches is beyond the scope of this chapter. In general, a parsimonious solution like the identical-siblings model may be a good place to start for several reasons. First, the identical sibling model allows all available data from each TMF to be included in the calibration. This ensures that stable item parameter estimates can be obtained using commercial off-the-shelf IRT calibration software. The only minor complication involves the data management needed to reliably collapse the response data across items within task-model or item-model families. Second, the identical siblings model and similar direct-calibration methods avoid the complications of explaining the nuances of complicated calibration and scoring procedures to end users or policy makers. Finally, an item calibration approach using hierarchically associated response data simplifies QC, allowing variation and data-model fit statistics (computed within the item families) to be used to evaluate the quality of the task-model design features and item writing/generation within each TMF.

4.5 Phases in Implementing IDM

When carried out by academic researchers, IDM studies may just be isolated research in service of supporting or refuting particular theory of learning or cognition. However, for operational implementation as part of a larger principled assessment initiative, IDM implementation will usually involve three phases.

In Phase 1, researchers attempt to demonstrate the feasibility of IDM using existing item banks—that is, items creatively designed and written by trained human item writers. These studies are often seen as *proof-of-concept* investigations to demonstrate that available or easily derivable item features can statistically explain a sufficient amount of variation in item difficulties (e.g., using linear regression modeling to predict empirical item difficulties from various text-based surface features of the items and coded item metadata). Some of the AE CDLs, described further on, can include these types of explanatory item-feature variables.

The obvious limitation of this type of Phase 1 IDM research is that the studied items are probably not designed with much attention to the very complex features that are subsequently "discovered" by statistical analysis to likely impact item difficulty. Rather, human item writers may have been trained according to an organization's item writing guidelines and then assigned to create a set of items from a designated content blueprint category. The item feature variables may not be same ones that could be used under a principled assessment design process that affords item writers far less creative license than before. In any case, despite sometimes very promising statistical results in terms of "item difficulty variance explained" few testing organizations seem willing to move beyond this first phase of IDM. Perhaps their reluctance is due to the serious upfront costs and resources needed to essentially re-engineer entire item design/production and test assembly systems and procedures. Or decision makers may accede to internal resistance by editorial test development staff and content experts who see any form of "automation" as a threat to their role(s) within a testing organization.[10]

Phase 2 of IDM implementation involves formally incorporating the explanatory CDLs and item-feature variables into the item design and production process. This might include developing template-controlled item writing using human item writers or even formally adopting computer-based automatic item generation (AIG) software with strong IDM-based QCs. The primary goal of Phase 2 is demonstrating the feasibility of an item design and production system capable of effectively and efficiently creating items and test forms to meet demands—whatever those may be—with significantly reduced human involvement in the production phase and limited empirical item pretesting. The concept of using CDLs to control the *location* of AE TMFs (see Section 2.6, further on) assumes this second phase of IDM implementation to ensure the statistical and substantive isomorphism of items within each TMF.

The third phase of IDM involves item design and generation. This phase may or may not incorporate generative AIG, if the latter can be integrated with IDM to carefully control the production of every item or assessment task (cf. Bejar & Yocom, 1991; also see Bejar, 2002). Under a generative approach, statistical and substantive isomorphism of TMFs, for example, is almost guaranteed in the same way that industrial manufacturing-engineering plants can create an inventory of "widgets" to exact specifications. Phase 3 no longer requires any item pretesting, and either limited or no direct human involvement is required in the production of the items and test forms. Items are likely to be composed by AIG on-the-fly to meet any and all assessment demands. To repeat, every item is created to meet exacting IDM specifications by design, including the automated production of scoring rubrics/evaluators. Note that IDM is still relevant in Phase 3 but is primarily applied during the specification phase for the construction of items and as a QC mechanism for TMFs prior to releasing the items for operational purposes.

4.6 Chapter Summary

This chapter characterizes three purposes for incorporating an IDM research agenda in AE. The first is to provide a relative *location* for each TMF as an estimable linear function of the CDLs (i.e., the analytically derived complexity components or DCCs and indices computed using human-rated CSPs). The statistical distribution of the TMF locations becomes the task model map (TMM). The second purpose is to provide QC metrics and indices that can be used to monitor the production of items within each TMF. Items generated by subject-SMEs or by AIG can be monitored and flagged if their predicted locations fall outside of established tolerances—all without pretesting the items. Finally, the predicted locations can be used as "prior information" or covariates when calibrating or re-calibrating parameter estimates for active TMFs for test assembly and scoring purposes.

Notes

1 Note that automatic item generation (AIG) implicitly uses composability to assemble items from static and variabilized content at more of surface level of design. AE task modeling goes further by developing a network of constituent complexity components—the complexity design layers or CDLs—that can manipulate complexity in a principled way (see Chapter 3).
2 This is easily generalizable as the item mean for partial-credit and polytomously scored.
3 In fairness, however, it should be noted that most of the linguistic variables computed by CohMetrix are based on a theory of *text coherence* (McNamara & Kintsch, 1996).
4 Although "over-fitting" (i.e., using too many predictors and covariates) is always a concern in statistical modeling, it is not clear that eliminating statistically redundant or nonsignificant predictor variables using iterative methods like stepwise regression is necessarily a good idea from the perspective of statistical quality control over item difficulty. Rather, combining multiple, highly correlated measures into a more reliable composite index may be preferrable.
5 The Drum et al. study was included in the Ferrera et al.'s (2022) meta-analysis.
6 The items were polytomously scored requiring the use of an IRT partial-credit calibration model.
7 The more generic phrase "feature vectors" is often used in the machine learning literature to denote the item feature (independent) variables and covariates.
8 From an engineering perspective, excessive variability in the statistical operating characteristics of items within families is considered to be symptomatic of fundamental task-model or item-model design flaws. That outcome suggests the need to modify or constrain the task design features to significantly reduce the variance.
9 Items showing substantial changes in their statistical item characteristics can either be calibrated as unique items or otherwise excluded from use until their design features can be controlled.
10 In reality, carefully implemented item and test production automation efforts tend to lead to better quality assessments. Test development staff and content experts are then freed up to become more involved in creative task design research rather than just manually writing and editing hundreds of new items per examination cycle.

5 Task Model Mapping

Task model maps (TMMs) are integrated test specifications that serve multiple purposes. First, a TMM is a highly detailed content and cognitive test blueprint. The map aligns to evidence requirements to justify proficiency claims (Chapter 2) and comprises a distribution of complexity-oriented task models that provide that evidence (see Chapter 3). Second, a TMM provides a statistical distribution of task model families (TMFs) based on their difficulties and is proportional to an Item Response Theory (IRT) target test information function (TIF) that designates the required allocation of measurement precision across a score scale. Third, a TMM provides an integrated item bank/inventory specification that documents present and future item production demands in terms of the required content, cognitive, and psychometric characteristics of the items.

5.1 Some Limitations of Traditional Test Blueprints and Test Assembly Methods

Despite sharing a common label, *blueprints* used in testing are nothing like their architectural counterparts used in building or furniture construction, or schematics used in electrical design and industrial manufacturing. The latter are detailed specifications that ensure rather exacting outcomes. In contrast, most test blueprint comprise, at a minimum, allocated counts of items subdomains or content categories to include on each test form. The blueprint may also include content categories, raw-score point targets or ranges, topics or themes, word counts, etc. Ultimately, however, there is no sense of an integrated assembly for most test blueprints. Furthermore, the content and cognitive coding systems used are often very general in nature and rarely checks for integrity or consistency. We all-too-often assume that the human content or subject-matter specialists doing the coding are beyond reproach.

Ignoring, for the moment, the nebulous nature of most test blueprints, we can move on to their use in test assembly. During test assembly, a content blueprint becomes a formal system of constraints on the item selection process. Unfortunately, the constraints may require tradeoffs between choosing the psychometrically optimal items and maintaining the blueprint.

5.1.1 Conditional Measurement Precision in Test Design and Assembly

IRT provides many benefits from a measurement perspective (Hambleton & Swaminathan, 1985; Lord, 1980; van der Linden, 2016). *Conditional measurement functions* are, perhaps, some of the most important benefits of using IRT. That is, we posit an underlying "latent" proficiency trait typically denoted by the Greek letter, θ (theta). An IRT model statistically relates the probability of the (scored) responses to θ for an item, indexed as "*i*." For example, the probability of a correct response to a binary-scored item under the well-known two-parameter logistic (2PL) model can be expressed as:

$$prob\left(x_i = X|\theta\right) \equiv P_i\left(\theta\right) = \left\{1 + exp\left[-a_i\left(\theta - b_i\right)\right]\right\}^{-1}. \quad (6.1)$$

DOI: 10.4324/9781003451051-5

There are two item parameters that characterize the shape of the response probability function: a_i which is a slope parameter denoting the statistical sensitivity of the item to the underlying proficiency—often called the IRT "discrimination" parameter, and b_i representing the item's difficulty (i.e., the item's "location" relative to θ).

The *item information function* (IIF) for the 2PL is

$$I_i(\theta) = a_i^2 P_i(\theta) Q_i(\theta) \tag{6.2}$$

where $Q_i(\theta) = 1 - P_i(\theta)$ as the probability of an incorrect response. The IIF denotes the amount of measurement precision across the proficiency scale. That is, information is conditional on θ. The discrimination parameter, a_i, limits the amount of information. The difficulty parameter, b_i, determines where along the θ-scale each item provides its maximum information (precision).

The IIFs can be summed at a particular value of θ providing a TIF. That is, $TIF = T(\theta) = \Sigma I_i(\theta)$. The conditional nature of the IIFs and TIFs serves two important design functions. First, we can establish a *target* TIF that prioritizes measurement precision relative to key points or regions of the proficiency scale. Second, we can optimize the selection of items to meet a target TIF or some other goal related to measurement precision.

Figure 5.1 presents two target TIFs. The TIF on the right is for a 60-item achievement test with measurement precision optimized near the population mean, that is, the TIF peaks near $\mu(\theta) = 0$. The TIF to the left is for a 60-item certification test with maximum information near an established pass-fail cut score of $\theta_{cut} = -1$.

The TIF priorities relative to the proficiency scale, θ, are largely based on policies. The target merely indicates a plausible demand for measurement precision where it is needed as per policy-based priorities (Luecht, 1998, 2016b).

Target TIFs can even be used for adaptive tests. For example, Figure 5.2 displays three target TIFs for a somewhat more complicated multistage test design (MST) "panel" (i.e., a collection of adaptively administered modules, each consisting of 30 items in this example[1]). The left-hand side of Figure 5.2 depicts how the MST panel works. All examinees assigned this panel would be administered the first-stage module (M1). M1 is scored and, based on an examinee's performance, they are adaptively routed to an easier (E2), moderate difficulty (M2), or harder module

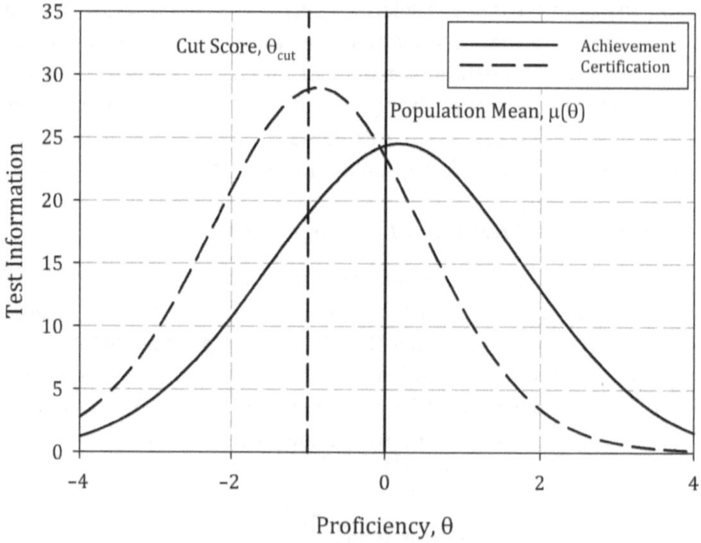

Figure 5.1 TIFs for Two 50-Item Tests with Different Purposes

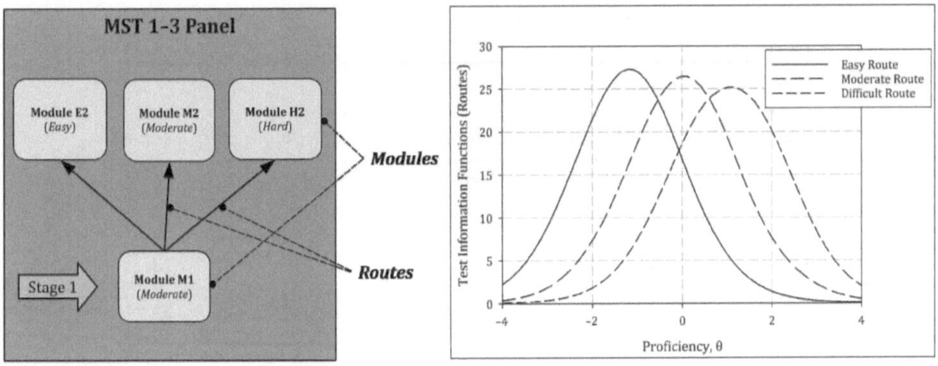

Figure 5.2 Target Route Targets for a 1–3 MST Panel Configuration

(H2) at the second stage. The adaptive nature of an MST provides better measurement precision across the entire proficiency score scale. It also requires a bank of items sufficiently diverse in difficulty to meet the three rather distinct target TIFs at the right—each corresponding to one of the routes through the panel. The important consideration here is that we can actually allocate the test information as a test design strategy so that optimal precision is allocated where it is most needed, given the purpose of our test and subject to practical constraints such as test length.

Given one or more target TIFs, testing organizations often use automated test assembly (ATA) algorithms to optimally select items for one or more test forms that match the target(s) and meet any variety of quantitative or qualitative constraints (e.g., test length, content match counts, a distribution of cognitive levels) (Luecht, 1998; van der Linden, 1998, 2005). As an example, let's consider only the 60-item achievement test from above (see Figure 5.1) and the example Common Core State Standards (CCSS) mathematics test introduced in Chapter 1.

We can create an ATA optimization model by selecting three TIF values as the absolute targets: $T(\theta_1 = -1) = 19.0$, $T(\theta_2 = 0) = 24.4$, and $T(\theta_3 = 1) = 21.4$. Figure 5.3 displays the entire TIF and those three target points.

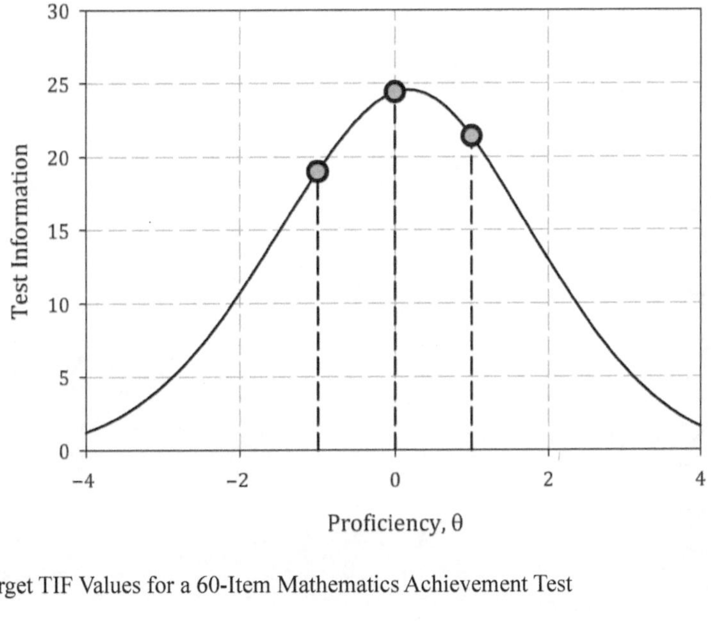

Figure 5.3 Target TIF Values for a 60-Item Mathematics Achievement Test

Table 5.1 CCSS-based Test Content and Cognitive Specifications for a 60-Item Test

CCSS	*Cognitive levels*			
Subdomain	*Conceptual(C)*	*Applied (A)*	*Strategic S)*	*Totals*
NBT	2	5	2	**9**
NF	4	8	3	**15**
OA	3	8	2	**13**
MD	4	7	3	**14**
GEO	2	5	2	**9**
Totals	**15**	**33**	**12**	**60**

Expanding the ATA example introduced in Chapter 1, we can formally add the marginal content and cognitive constraints as shown in Table 5.1. The five subdomains (rows) are from the *CCSS for Mathematics* content areas (National Governors Association Center for Best Practices & Council of Chief State School Officers, 2010): numbers base 10 (NBT), numbers and operations-fractions (NF), operations and algebraic thinking, measurement and data (MD), and geometry (GEO). The centermost columns in the table represent three cognitive categories: conceptual (C), applied knowledge and reasoning (A), and strategic knowledge and thinking (S).

Using a mixed integer programming (MIP) model (see Luo, 2024; van der Linden, 2005), our ATA model can be written as follows:

Minimize y

Subject to $\sum_{i=1}^{I} I_i(\theta) \geq T(\theta) - y, T(\theta) = \{19.0, 24.4, 21.4\}, \boldsymbol{\theta} = \{-1, 0, 1\}$

$$\sum_{i=1}^{I} I_i(\theta) \geq T(\theta) + y$$

$$\sum_{i \in NBT} x_i = 9$$

$$\sum_{i \in NF} x_i = 15$$

$$\sum_{i \in OA} x_i = 13$$

$$\sum_{i \in MD} x_i = 14$$

$$\sum_{i \in GEO} x_i = 9$$

$$\sum_{i \in Cogn.A} x_i = 15$$

$$\sum_{i \in Cogn.C} x_i = 33$$

$$\sum_{i \in Cogn.S} x_i = 12$$

$$\sum_{i=1}^{I} x_i = 60$$

$$x_i \in \{0,1\}$$

$$y \geq 0.$$

The model minimizes a positive "tolerance" value around the target TIF values, subject to simultaneously meeting the five CCSS mathematics content constraints, the three cognitive constraints, and the test length requirement (60 items). Given the model and an item bank, computer software known as an ATA *solver* can optimally choose items for one or more test forms that meet all of the constraints.

ATA is a method of engineering the assembly of test forms. The solver attempts to find a minimum or maximum objective function (like our tolerance value, y under the MIP model), while staying within the mathematically bounded confines of the constraints. There are a number of alternative ATA models and solvers to MIP, but the basic goal is almost always the same. That is, we need to satisfy two separate types of constraints or targets: (1) the psychometric targets or objectives usually related to optimal measurement precision goals and (2) test blueprint requirements reflecting content, cognitive, and other coded or enumerated constraints.

These types of ATA optimization models can be applied to virtually any type of test using Classical Test Theory statistics or IRT (van der Linden, 2005). The constraints represent the test assembly *demands*. The challenge, of course, is having an item bank capable of meeting those specifications rather exactly for a designated number of test forms. When the item bank is hand-crafted, the *supply* side of test assembly may not always be able to meet the above demands. Fortunately, as discussed below, complex ATA models such as the above example and its solution may be unnecessary under a well-implemented Assessment Engineering (AE) paradigm.

5.1.2 The Consequences for Test Assembly of Using Fallible of Content- and Cognitive-Coded Constraints

While ATA has been demonstrated to be a powerful, effective, and efficient way to build multiple test forms—at least in comparison to human-centered test form assembly methods, it often runs into two nontrivial road blocks. The first rather substantial road block is an insufficient item bank—that is, a supply (of items) insufficient to meet the test assembly demands (constraints and statistical targets). Automatic item generation (AIG) may help if the "right" items can be produced, pilot-tested, and calibrated—see Chapter 7. The second road block involves a failure to design and implement an optimal set of targets and constraints for assembling test forms. That is, test developers often create content blueprint and add auxiliary test assembly constraints with little understanding as to whether: (a) those constraints can be met given competing demands and (b) they have substantive value in terms of the quality of the test forms.

To elaborate somewhat, there are at least four issues related to the design of the content or cognitive coding schemes adopted as part of most traditional test blueprint. First, the coding systems rely heavily on human judgment and rarely are the codes authenticated or otherwise checked for veracity. Codes developed from academic standards or from content-discipline frameworks—or generated like a well-organized outline or table of contents—may or may not reflect the evidence we require or its progression along a construct map (see Chapter 2). Second, most content and cognitive coding schemes treat the assigned categories as exchangeable across the scale. That is, easy, moderately difficult, and difficult items are treated as isomorphic from a content balancing perspective. For example, choosing a statistically easy or very difficult geometry item to satisfy a content balancing constraint is seen as acceptable when the items will almost certainly involve differentially complex challenges for the examinees. Third, many auxiliary constraints incorporated into a content blueprint for "face validity" purposes add little to quality of the test forms. Instead, they can act as constraint-based barriers to building more reliable and/or parallel tests (e.g., restricting the number of score points, counts of particular item types, etc.). Finally, most content blueprints have a difficult time contending with item sets or clusters (i.e., two or more items associated with a reading passage or problem-based scenario). The implicit connection among the items within a set can result in non-parallel test forms in terms of their content balance and/or statistical scale properties.

5.2 Building Task Model Maps (TMMs)

A TMM is a complete specification for test assembly, like the ATA model described in Section 5.1. But it is far more than that. TMMs (a) can simultaneously incorporate all relevant statistical, content, and cognitive item characteristics in a single distribution; (b) denote test score accuracy interpretation priorities along the proficiency scale; and (c) provide an unambiguous blueprint for item bank design that is well-aligned to the current and future item inventory production needs. That is, each TMM integrates the required psychometric scale properties as well as all content and cognitive complexity demands that reflect the policy-based priorities for documented measurement evidence aligned to proficiency claims along a construct map (see Chapter 2).

Consider the TMM in Figure 5.4. Overall, this map presents the same distribution of CCSS mathematics content as before. That is, the shading of each dot represents a TMF of items

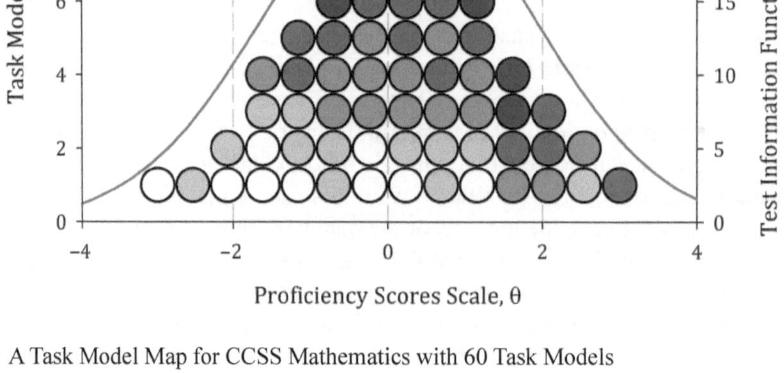

Figure 5.4 A Task Model Map for CCSS Mathematics with 60 Task Models

focused on one of the five content areas. However, the dots in this TMM are not exchangeable in a measurement since each task model has a unique location on the scale and represents different levels of declarative knowledge (concepts, prior knowledge, depth of knowledge, etc.) and procedural knowledge/cognitive skills as discussed in Chapter 4. The curve in Figure 5.4 is the TIF associated with the 60 task models shown in the map. This also matches our psychometric test assembly target.

From a test assembly perspective, we only need to randomly choose one item from each task model to fully achieve our goal of content- and statistically parallel test forms. The key is to ensure that the TMFs are functioning as intended, that is, isomorphically.

5.3 The Alignment of Complexity and Measurement Precision with a TMM

A TMM can truly become a singular test blueprint that specifies the amount of measurement precision, where it is most needed, and the distribution of TMFs needed to simultaneously fulfill that goal as well as satisfying our evidence requirements along the construct. Clear and well-documented alignment can be built into the design process. Figure 5.5 provides a more comprehensive picture of the connections between the TMM and the TMFs.

TMMs can be versioned, like most other components within the AE framework. The modifications may reflect changing priorities or the integration of new knowledge and skills as the construct, itself, evolved.

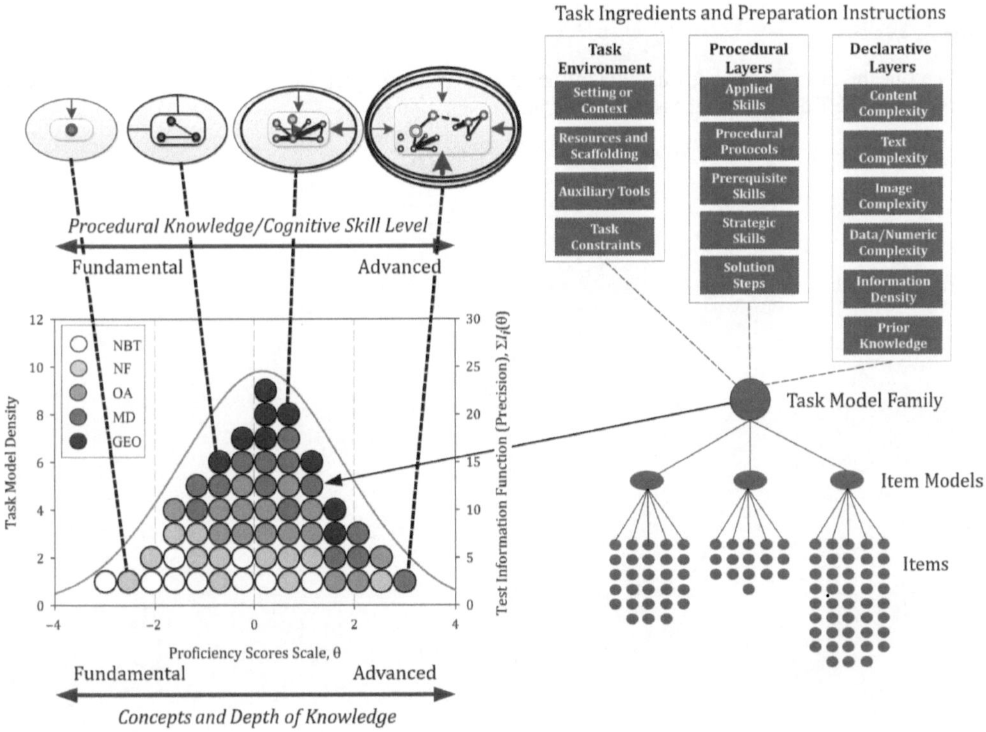

Figure 5.5 Alignment of a TMM with Measurement Precision and TMF Cognitive Specifications

5.4 Chapter Summary

TMMs are meant to alleviate much of the test-assembly *competition* between content and other constrained qualitative test features embodied in a traditional test blueprint and the psychometric priorities established for the statistically derived score scale. That is, a TMM integrates the goals of targeted measurement precision and content coverage. In addition, because TMM can be directly aligned with the distribution of evidence models along a construct map (see Chapter 2), validity-based interpretive argumentation is built into the scale itself.

Ideally, a TMM sustained by isomorphic TMFs makes possible a fairly simple test assembly process. We randomly choose one item per TMF to build our test forms. The exchangeability of items within each TMF ensures a content-balanced test form that is validity-aligned to our construct map and matches our psychometric measurement information target(s).

Functionally, a TMM also serves as a high-level production-control specification that lays out the inventory demands for item production and test assembly. This is all part of the engineering paradigm.

Finally, it should be noted that a TMM does not have to be a static specification. It can be applied with multistage testing "panels" (Luecht, 2014;) as well as item-level computerized adaptive testing. Given appropriate TMMs, we can easily extend this AE idea of task model mapping to adaptive multistage testing designs and even item-level computerized adaptive testing. TMMs can also be developed for almost any IRT model as long as each TMF can be positioned on the underlying proficiency scale relative to its difficulty or point location of maximum precision. Furthermore, practical extensions of TMMs for multidimensional IRT models have been proposed (Ackerman & Luecht, in press).

Note

1 See Luecht, 2014; Luecht & Luo, 2024; Luecht & Nungester, 1998 for more thorough discussions of technical MST design, panel assembly, and implementation issues.

6 Item Model Families and Automatic Item Generation

The idea of using item shells to increase the efficiency of item production and controlling the facets of item difficulty in a principled way has a fairly long history (e.g., see Guttman, 1959; Guttman & Schleisinger, 1966; Bejar & Yocom, 1991; Bormuth, 1969; Embretson, 1999; Finn, 1975; Haladyna & Shindoll, 1989; Hively, Patterson & Page, 1968; Laduca, Staples, Templeton & Holzman, 1986; Meisner, Reckase & Luecht, 1993; Irvine, 2002). The concept is relatively straight-forward. We create a template, shell, or generating algorithm using a *parent item* and then populate variable slots in the shell with designated content (words, phrases, numbers, equations, or images). For example, Figure 6.1 presents a four-option multiple-choice math parent item and template where the total count of the product or material (crayons) is *variabilized.*

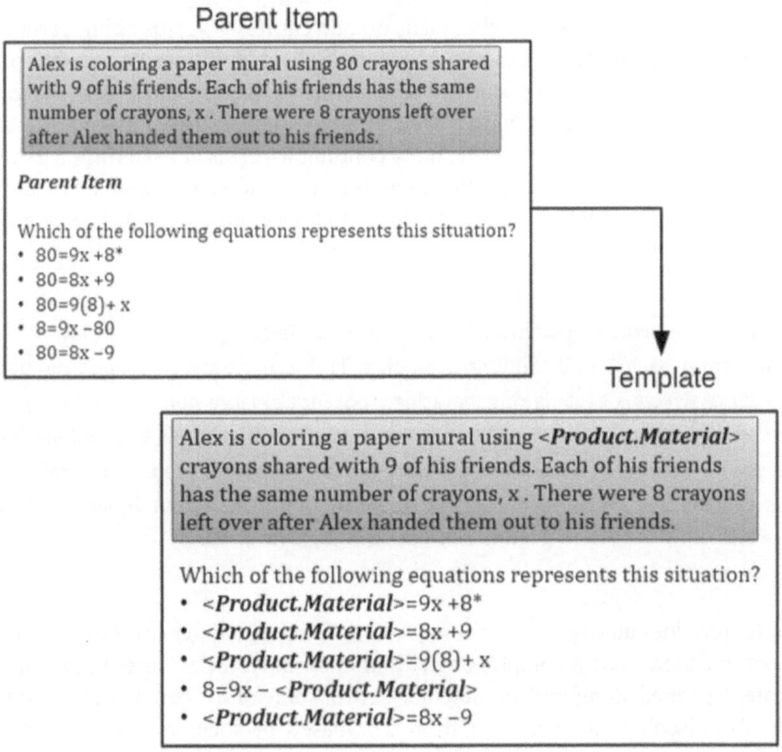

Figure 6.1 A Sample Math Parent Item and Template

DOI: 10.4324/9781003451051-6

Other labels or numeric quantities can also be variabilized with relevant constraints placed on the values used (e.g., replacing the number of products or materials and the corresponding number of friends with a finite number of pairs).

Modern software and massively powerful computing capabilities have more recently made it possible to engage in *automatic item generation*[1] (AIG; see, for example, Drasgow, Luecht & Bennett, 2006; Gierl & Haladyna, 2012; Gierl, Zhou & Alves, 2008; Gierl & Lai, 2018;; Daniel & Embretson, 2010; Embretson & Kingston, 2018). In fact, as discussed further on in this chapter, some recent language and medical education testing programs are even using deep learning, recurrent neural nets, and generative artificial intelligence (AI) models to create completely novel item content on demand from documents and other source materials (Hommel, Wollang, Kotova, Zacher & Schmukle, 2022; von Davier, 2018, 2019).

However, AIG is largely about large-scale item *production*. It has less to do with directly building a construct-relevant score scale. In fact, the vast majority of operational AIG efforts to date have involved the mass production of multiple-choice item types with little to no discussion of the substantive or psychometric properties of those items, much less the relationships between the items and the interpretive qualities of the scale. However, there have been proposed evaluative methods (e.g., Embretson & Kingston, 2018; Pugh, De Champlain, Gierl, Lai &Touchie, 2016) most of which involve qualitative methods using human comparative judgments rather than rigorous quantitative quality control mechanisms.

Under the Assessment Engineering (AE) paradigm, every item corresponds to a designated task model family (TMF). We cannot lose sight of that basic design requirement whether or not we use AIG. Items created without a strong connection to task models may need to undergo *ad hoc* content, cognitive- or standards-based alignment studies to justify their use. Furthermore, they may need to be independently calibrated as unique entities—versus being part of a design-anchored TMF. That is, while AIG can almost assuredly lead to more efficient item production, we cannot ignore the need for statistical and substantive isomorphism in item design and production. As discussed in the next chapter, we can and should empirically monitor and verify statistical isomorphism within each TMF on a continuous basis. Furthermore, because each TMF is located on a task model map (TMM) to provide the evidence demanded by the construct map and evidence models, all item generation needs to flow from those intentional and substantive design specifications.

> AE TMFs are conveniently presented as comprising a hierarchy with three levels: the task model, the item model(s), and the items. A single TMF can, however, include multiple item families, each of which is capable of generating a potentially large quantity of ideally isomorphic items. Furthermore, the hierarchical structure can be readily constructed using deeper layers where TMFs and item families are part of larger design-based object models—not unlike the current crop of powerful large language models used within under the heading of generative AI.

This chapter provides an overview of some AIG and associated generative language technologies. It is not intended to be a comprehensive summary of AIG past, present, or future. Some AIG basics are described along with commentary about some of the benefits and pitfalls of AIG. The chapter also discusses item models from data-based perspective, focusing on rendering models, scoring evaluators, and data models for almost any item type (i.e., selected response items, constructed response items, and even complex performance simulation items).

6.1 Components and Types of Automatic Item Generation

AIG is typically characterized by three steps (Gierl & Haladyna, 2012; Gierl & Lai, 2013). First, an item template or structure is developed by the subject-matter experts (SMEs) and test development specialists to specify the presentational form, shell, or template for the item, including where the variabilized content is placed in each generated item. Second, SMEs variabilize the key content required for the generated items (i.e., they create the structured lists of alternatives for the content variables in the item template). Finally, a computer algorithm or more sophisticated software is used to place the content specified in the second step into the item model developed in the first step.

Figure 6.2 shows what Gierl and Lai (2013) called *n*-layered item model. There are seven actual variables, each with a potential list of values. The variables and their content lists are typically selected by SMEs working with test development specialists to prioritize the content chosen, clarify the appropriate granularity, identify the type(s) of relationships among the variables, and indicate relevant constraints on the numerical or labels used. For example, the "Product Name" (crayons in Figure 6.1) is characterized as an (implicit) three-tier data object, "*Product*" where three different counts (integers) are also shown as properties of the "*Product Counts*" object class. The structured stem and distractors below the item content model constitute a *template.* Additional quality control steps can be added to evaluate the plausibility of the generated content (Embretson & Kingston, 2018; Gierl & Lai, 2013).

Customized software is typically used to apply the variabilized content to the template. For example, the **Item GeneratOR** (IGOR) software system, originally developed at the University

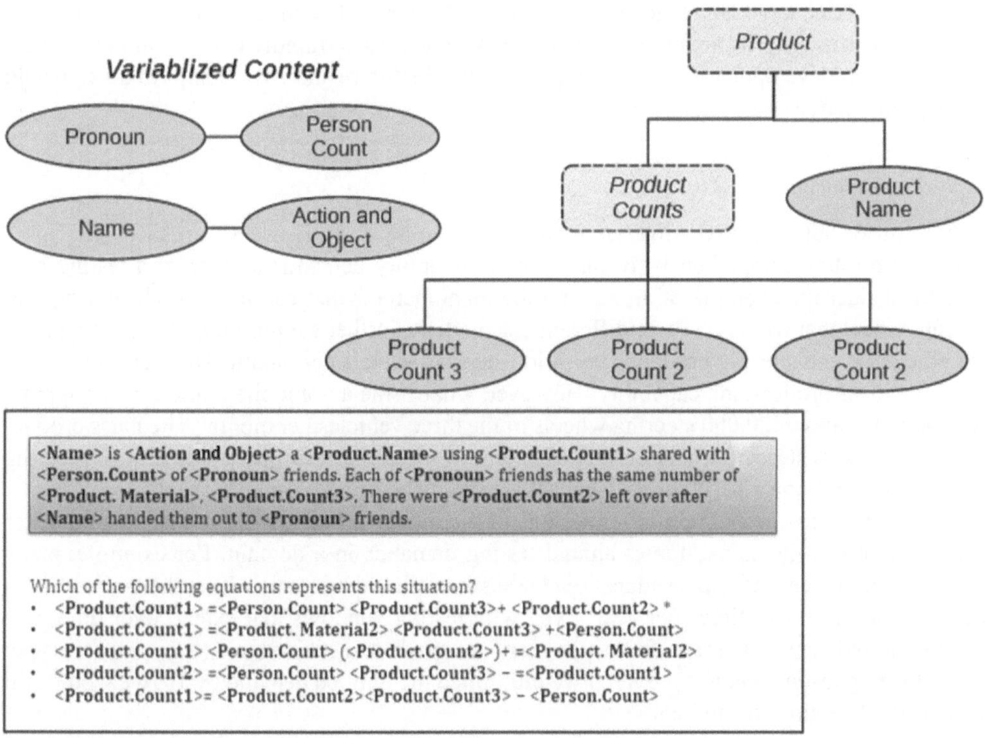

Figure 6.2 An *n*-Layered Item Model

of Alberta, has been widely used for various AIG applications in educational and professional certification and licensure testing (Gierl & Lai, 2013).

6.1.1 AI and GPT Applications for AIG

Some of the recent *generative AI* to AIG involving recurrent neural nets, large language models, and transformer-based architectures like generative pre-trained transformers (GPTs; Radford et al., 2018) and Google's bidirectional encoder representations from transformers (BERT; Devlin, Chang, Lee & Toutanova, 2019) can use unstructured inputs such as text and other source documents to generate questions. BERT, in particular, introduced a significant improvement in natural language processing by removing the typical directional restrictions of processing text based on "masked language models"; that is, text representations modeled loosely on the word-substitution "cloze" item type format originally proposed for measuring the lexical complexity of texts (Taylor, 1953).

Language testing programs like Duolingo are even using GPT architectures to dynamically generate reading passages with academic content and associated selected-response questions as well as for grading of open-ended questions with written student responses (e.g., Attali, et al., 2022; Runge, 2023). In general, GPT architectures depend on a massive and ideally content-relevant corpora for pre-training (i.e., using conditional pre-training and fine tuning). At present, a human-review layer is still incorporated to evaluate the final content from AI-generated items.

Attali, et al. (2022), von Davier (2019), and Hommel, et al. (2022) provide more comprehensive discussions of these technologies with examples. Also see Circi, Hicks, & Sikali (2023) for a brief review of both operational and research-based issues involving AIG. A more in-depth discussion of AIG, large language models, and transformer architectures is beyond the scope or intent of this chapter. The area of generative AI is advancing so rapidly that it is almost impossible to predict developments two or more years into the future and any attempt to do so would be incredibly naïve.

6.1.2 Some Limitations of AIG

There is little doubt that AIG solves an item production problem. However, are they the "right" items and do they comprehensively satisfy item inventory demands to support a testing program? Consider the example of an automobile manufacturer that can mass produce a type of steering wheel that works on three different car models. Further suppose that the manufacturer can efficiently and cheaply produce 10 million steering wheels per month. That certainly qualifies as a "mass production" capability. However, what if the automobile market only supports average joint sales of 20,000 steering wheels of the three vehicles per month? The mass production capability[2] of steering wheels, left unchecked, would create a surplus of 9.8 million steering wheels per month (nearly 120 million excess steering wheels per year).

This leads us to one of the first limitations of AIG: over-production. Many testing agencies only need enough items to support annual testing demands in a domain. For example, many end-of-grade and end-of-course educational assessments used by states within the United States are given, at most, two times per year. Even with testing windows that extend over time, it is common to only create four test forms per year for a grade and subject area (e.g., two forms per fall and spring testing window). Even if we multiplied the implied demand by 10, we would still only need 20 versions on an item.

A second limitation is the restricted scope of item types used. AIG has been almost exclusively applied to one-best-answer multiple-choice questions (MCQs). By some estimates, nearly 99 percent of AIG implementations exclusively use MCQs. If we extend the concept of an MCQ to include any item type that relies on examinee choices from a finite list of alternatives, then the MCQ-based AIG saturation may be greater than 99 percent—especially if we further include some of the so-called technology-enhanced items that amount to selected choice formats with overly elaborate graphical user interfaces and extended interactivity to capture the examinee response (Jodoin, 2006; Luecht, 2017a, 2017b).

Most item types can be characterized as comprising a combination of four classes of components: (a) passive or semi-passive displays of information (question stems, reading passages, etc.); (b) tools or resources such as calculators, formula sheets, highlighters, etc.; (c) response-capturing mechanisms—for example, selections from an MCQ list of options, short-answer or extended response text entries, or even using a software application to generate a complex product such as a graphic or statistical plot; and (d) a scoring mechanism that converts the examinees' responses or actions to a numerical item score (e.g., a binary correct-incorrect score). Much like combining the variables from content lists using AIG, these item components are multi-layered and can be combined to produce hundreds if not thousands of "item types." Given that number of possibilities, our automobile manufacturing analogy might be restated as entailing the mass production of a rather specific, and arguably limited type, of steering wheel.

The third limitation of AIG is more technical in nature. If the generated items are not statistically isomorphic (as discussed in Chapters 4 and 7), they need to be administered as independent items on operational test forms. Assuming Item Response Theory (IRT) calibration and scaling, sufficiently large samples from the target examinee population need to take the items and the responses then need to then be calibrated to obtain the operational item parameter estimates for each item. The calibrated parameter estimates are used both in test assembly and scoring. Now, suppose that we have a relatively large annual test-taker population consisting of 40,000 students. Further suppose that we have AIG models ($m = 1,\dots,5$) that can generate, respectively, $k_m = (200, 500, 1000, 2000, 4000)$ individual items. If those items cannot be empirically verified as statistically isomorphic, they all needed to be pretested using different (ideally random) student samples (Shu et al., 2010; Sinharay & Johnson, 2012). The available *per-item* sample sizes would be $N_m = (2000, 200, 80, 20, 10)$. Unfortunately, the latter four sample sizes are pragmatically insufficient to obtain stable parameter estimates for most IRT models, assuming isomorphism for automatically generated items is never recommended (see Chapter 7).

The final limitation involves data management. In general, AIG creates natural "enemy" items—that is, items that are clones, closely related instantiations or that contain redundant content that precludes letting a given examinee from seeing more than one of the items.[3] If the items are generated from a common parent or item model, constraints on the allowable count of items selectable from a family can be automatically added to the test assembly model. However, where deep-structure generative methods are used, enemies may be more difficult to detect (Weir, 2019).

6.2 AE-Based Item Models

AE does not presume the use of AIG- or generative AI-based item production. It can certainly incorporate those technologies with three important *provisos*. First, every item model should stem from and belong to a task model. That provision serves to ensure validity-based alignment between the generated items and the task model, which is itself aligned to an evidence model (see Chapter 2). Second, statistical and substantive isomorphism must be empirically evaluated and monitored on an ongoing basis. The exchangeability of items within TMFs cannot be a convenient, largely untested, assumption. Third, the conceptualization and implementation of item models should be extendable any item type, as needed. AE can also be effectively used with human item writers or with hybrid item writing where generative AI methods like GPT are used to create draft items and resources that are then modified by human item writers and editors. The provisos apply here, as well.

Regardless of the type of item authoring or production mechanisms used, designing highly structured data systems that can support efficient authoring, data storage, retrieval and composition to help ensure that the above three stipulations can be met. The remainder of this chapter therefore focuses how to think about and build flexible and scalable item model structures and the content stored and manipulated from the content.

6.2.1 Item Model Structures and Content

A common theme in this book has a to visualize and anticipate operational assessment needs—from score-point interpretations to items—and then engineer scalable and efficient solutions to meet those needs. Consider a single task model (see Chapter 3). The TMF can comprise multiple item models and each item model can be used to generate an item family. The data structures and content associated with an AE item model are more elaborate, by necessity, than those incorporated into the design of most "traditional" item banks.

Figure 6.3 shows the underlying data structures and content for an AE item model as part of a TMF. This architecture includes four classes of data structures at the bottom of the figure. The item type structure components extend the notion of an "item type" to include relevant software mechanisms that render the items, control navigation and access to resources or tools, and capture the examinees' response(s). The rendered item data is the visible content (i.e., displayed text, images, exhibits, etc.). Stealth item model data includes all of the behind-the-scenes "metadata" for a family of items such as the complexity design layer (CDL) specifications inherited from the task model. Included are statistical and other psychometric indicators such as IRT item parameter estimates, text or image complexity indices, content codes, topics, etc. (*Note that stealth data can also be generated when items are first created to provide an additional quality control layer for human item writers or AIG.*) Finally, the scoring data and processing mechanisms are used to convert the examinees' response(s) into a numerical value (or ordered classification).

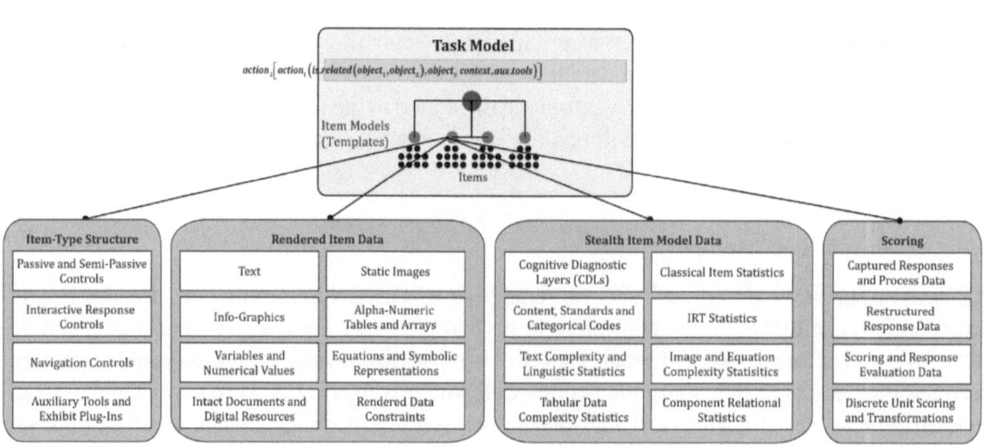

Figure 6.3 Data Structure Architecture for an AE Item Model

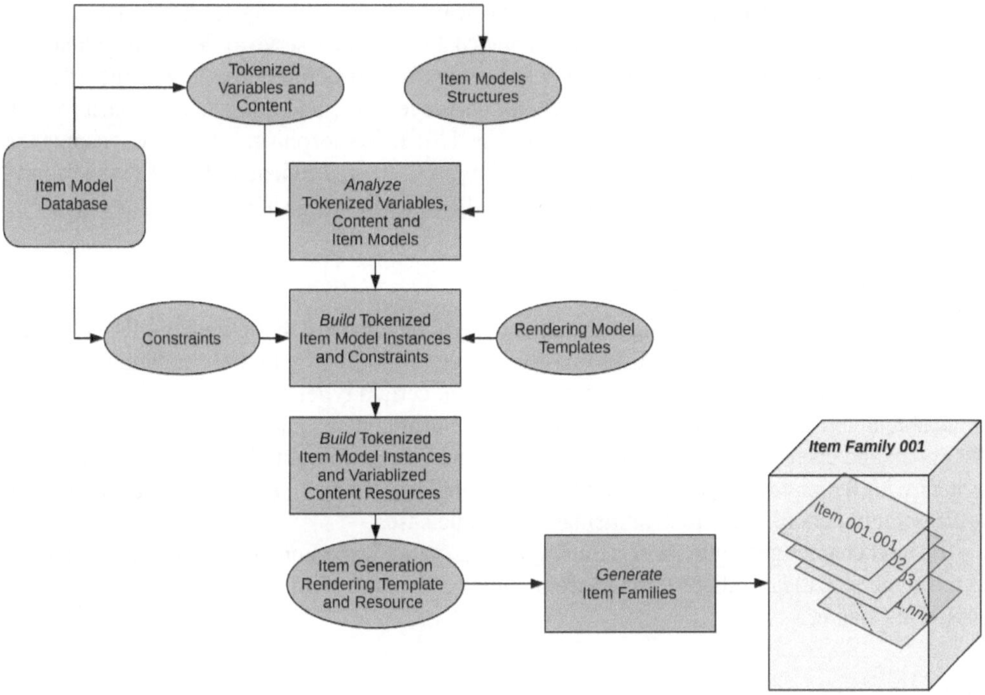

Figure 6.4 A Generic AIG Item Production Architecture

The underlying data structures for an item model need to be efficient and extensible to support enhancements over time and to incorporate new technologies such as the next generation of AIG. An effective item model architectural design recognizes that there is a lot of data and many different software and human-led processing steps between the concept of an item model and the system outputs: the items in a family. For example, Figure 6.4 shows a generic software-based item-production architecture for AIG. The item model database stores and provides the data (tokenized content, structures, templates, and constraints) to an analytical software layer that extracts and then builds a family of items for a given task model during a production cycle.

Also keep in mind that the above type of software architecture merely gets us to the items. The equally important point, however, is these types of carefully designed, comprehensive architectures must manage any and all complexity factors in a consistent and stable manner.

6.2.2 Item Model Quality Control

Quality control (QC) plays a central role in most industrial engineering and manufacturing settings. This is also true for AE. Item models are the design-based realizations of task models. AE is not about processing unstructured, unlabeled content—what is often called *unsupervised learning* with respect to natural language processing technologies. On the contrary, AE is all about alignment, building efficient and reusable data structures and software, creating effective test design targets and constraints, and (always) moving toward isomorphism within TMFs!

Evidence models align proficiency claims with the evidence-based requirements to justify those claims. TMFs are aligned to the evidence models, where a task model map (TMM) lays out the prioritized distribution of evidence. Each task model within a TMM has a location—its *target*—along the construct-focused proficiency scale. The complexity design layers and derived complexity covariates discussed in Chapters 4 and 7 ideally serve as design specifications for the item models. Finally, the item models use carefully structured item type templates and related data structures, consistent item-generation procedures, and constraints to ensure both the statistical and substantive isomorphism of the TMFs. Isomorphism, of course, ensures the exchangeability of items within families, providing us with an efficient and robust way of having sufficient items to meet our measurement needs, whatever those are.

6.3 Chapter Summary

This chapter discussed some of the research and developments involving item models. AIG and generative AI methods were discussed in brief, along with three potential limitations of those highly automated procedures (i.e., over-production of certain types of items, restricted scope of applicable item types, the consequences of non-isomorphic items and having to calibrate every AIG item, and enemy item management). It was noted that a combination of using human item writers with templates and/or very tight item writing constraints may be sufficient to produce sufficient numbers of items to meet demands in some cases.

The next chapter goes into more detail regarding QC and psychometric analytics since many of the same statistical indices derived from and/or applied to item difficulty modeling as discussed in Chapter 4.

Notes

1 AIG is sometimes synonymously referred to as *automatic question generation* (AQG).
2 In practice, manufacturing industries have quite sophisticated ways of optimally controlling production to meet ongoing demands while minimizing excess inventory.
3 There are obvious exceptions for retesting examinees who take different test forms or low-stakes formative tests used for instructional purposes.

7 AE Analytics and Quality Control

This chapter discusses three topics that fall under the general heading of *computational analytics*: (1) object analytic procedures, (2) complexity scoring protocols, and (3) residual analytics. These analytic procedures are meant to provide statistical indicators that can subsequently be used as predictors in item difficulty modeling (IDM) research (Chapter 3) or as part of an automated or semi-automated quality control (QC) system for item production and task model family (TMF) quality assurance. The chapter concludes with a discussion of the types of robust, flexible systems architectures needed to support the breadth and depth of computational analytics described in subsequent text.

7.1 Object Analytics

The phrase *stealth item data* is used here to refer to a myriad of numerical and categorical information associated with an intact item or component parts of the items. Examples include item type codes, Item Response Theory (IRT) item difficulty and discrimination parameter estimates, content topics, cognitive codes, linguistic and psycholinguistic indices, image- and table-analytical indices. IDM, in particular, can require a rather large collection of conditional, predictive, or statistically explanatory variables. Some of those same indicators can also be used for QC and calibration/scoring.

An **object** in this context is consistent with modern database terminology (e.g., object-oriented design). It can refer either to an intact item or its component parts such as text segments such as item stems and multiple-choice distractor option, software control captions/labels, numbers, images, etc. Objects can also be external to individual items. Some examples are text passages referenced by multiple items, statistical plots or infographics used in an item cluster, or a data frame containing multiple variables used in computer-based performance exercise (e.g., working with multiple columns of numbers in a spreadsheet). The term analytics refers to both the statistical analyses used as well as the output indicators—for example, text complexity statistics for a reading passage.

Figure 7.1 repurposes the sample item and item template from Chapter 6 to demonstrate how object analytics work. The "object layer" at the top provides three types of source data: (a) the generated item; (b) relevant item type, response complexity and scoring—where in this example "MCQ_1" denotes a one-best answer multiple-choice item; and (c) the variabilized item model (structure). The data from the object layer is passed to the lower "analytic layer." That layer performs three functions: (1) decomposing the item into its constituent parts in raw form; (2) converting and restructuring those analytical inputs to numeric vectors or arrays and submitting them to the analytic software; and (3) processing and compiling the analytic outputs for IDM, for use as psychometric calibration and/or scoring covariates, or for item production QC purposes.

DOI: 10.4324/9781003451051-7

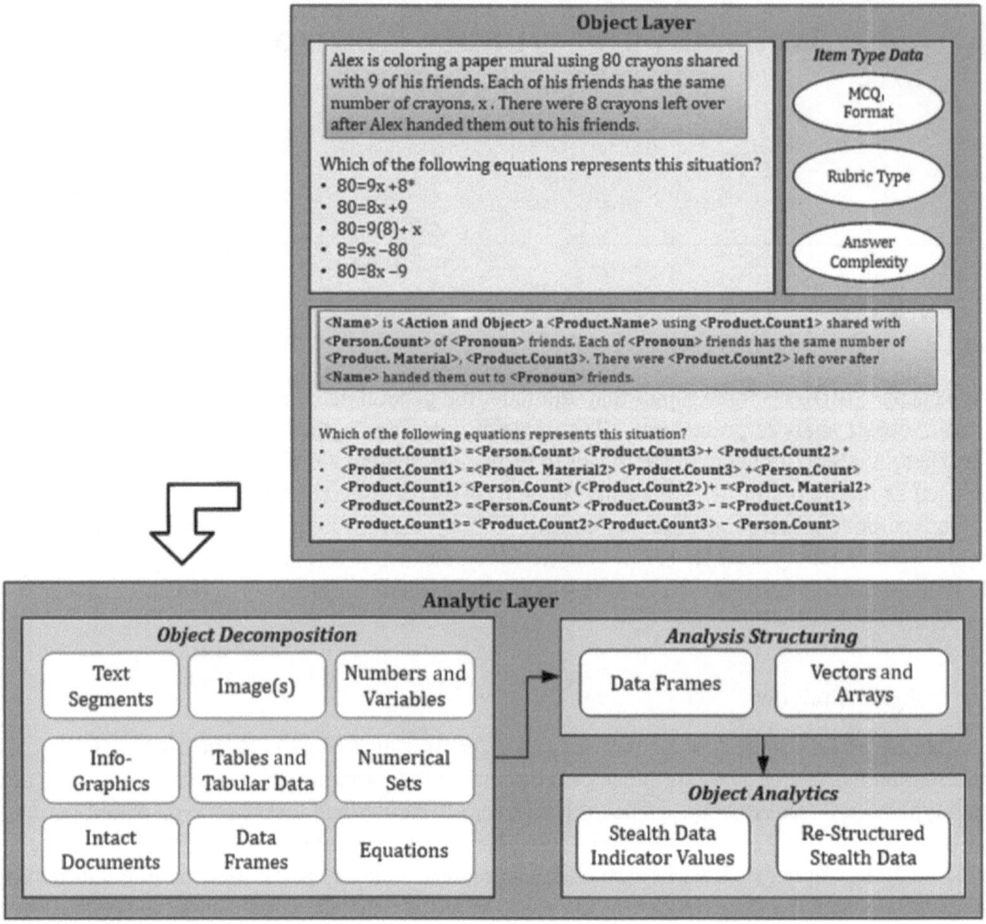

Figure 7.1 Object and Analytic Layers for a Multiple-Choice Question

There are four basic steps in carrying out the analysis of assessment object. First, we need to retrieve the relevant text, images, and other metadata associated with an item, item set, cluster, or performance assessment problem from a database. Second, we have to *decompose* the larger item or item set into the objects of interest (text segments, images, etc.). Those decomposed objects are submitted in the third step of our analysis process where we may be required to reformate/restructure the object for the analysis. Finally, in the fourth step, we can set up and run our analysis using the restricted data as inputs. Selected outputs from the object analysis are then used as inputs to our IDM research or for QC purposes involving TMF functioning.

There are (at least) eight categories of object analytics that can yield IDM-relevant outputs: (1) text analytics; (2) image analytics; (3) mathematical expression and equation analytics; (4) table analytics; (5) numerical analytics; (6) audio and video analytics; (7) item structure analytics; and (8) human-rated complexity scoring protocols (CSPs) applied to evaluate any component or an item, item set/cluster or performance exercise (e.g., critical evaluation of required prior knowledge or the indirect indirect(s) between a multiple-choice item stem and an exhibit or between the correct answer and the other options (distractors). Of these eight types of analytical procedures, text analytics offer the most mature collection of software tools and analysis methods given the proliferation of open-access and open-source software packages in *R* and *Python* for text and natural language processing (NLP), machine learning, and artificial intelligence (AI).

It may seem to be a daunting and complicated endeavor to apply, or in many cases, develop custom analyzers for these object categories. However, careful software system designs that stress agent/function encapsulation, extensibility, scalability, and automation can make even complex analytical tools readily for IDM applications. Furthermore, designing the software to provide flexible and robust decomposition, encoding and analysis, implies these eight categories of analyzers can be combined to provide composite complexity metrics (e.g., combining text analytics, with mathematical expression analytics and image analytics).

7.1.1 Text Analytics

Text analytics are carried out by submitting a text segment (word, phrase, sentence, paragraph, or document) to analysis software that produces one or more output variables. For example, *CohMetrix* (Graesser and McNamara, 2011; McNamara et al., 2010) produces 106 computed features of text. Those include:

- Descriptive indices (e.g., number of paragraphs, sentence count, word count)
- Text easability principal component scores related to linguistic complexity (e.g., word concreteness, syntactic simplicity, verb cohesion)
- Referential cohesion indices related to the overlap in content words between local sentences or co-references within your text (e.g., noun overlap, argument overlap, content word overlap)
- Latent semantic analysis indicators signaling semantic overlap given relationships between word, word phrases and/or concepts
- Lexical diversity (i.e., unique word types and type-token ratios)
- Connectives measures involving organization of the text as well as cohesive links between ideas and clauses within the text segment (e.g., casual connectives, logic connectives, temporal connectives)
- Situation model measures of the level of mental representation for your text beyond the obvious words (e.g., the plot in a narrative)
- Syntactic pattern complexity indicators (e.g., counts of nouns, verbs, non-phrases, verb-phrases)
- Syntactic pattern density variables indicating the frequency of syntactic patterns, word types, and word phrases
- Word information including the syntactic categories of words (nouns, verbs, adjectives, and adverbs) and word functions (e.g., preposition, pronouns)
- Readability indices like Fleisch-Kincaid

To appreciate some of the sophistication of modern NLP and AI applications for text, consider how most text analysis software packages work. After segmenting the target section of text, the software often starts by parsing the text segment in the normal reading/writing direction of the language (e.g., left to right, top-to-bottom for English). Word counts and other descriptive features of the text segment can be directly computed from the parsed text segment. The text analyzer may next apply syntactic checks of the input text structure against formal grammatical structures—possibly forming a syntax tree. The text analyzer may further encode the input data by applying a type of filtering known as "text normalization" (i.e., replacing all punctuation, delimiters, and separators with white spaces, replacing numerical entries with letters that preserve structures like phone numbers, and lower-casing all alpha characters), followed by stemming and lemmatizing the segment (i.e., reducing a word to its root or base form called a "lemma" by removing auxiliary endings such as tense—called stemming). The analyzer may then create a "N-gram" or other representational structure, which is an ordered sequence of tokens (words, subwords and punctuation). The N-gram format is conducive to comparison with other N-grams (e.g., potential overlapping words or identifying common syntactical features of the text). Additional transformations may be applied to matrix representations or to facilitate referential coherence and other types semantic analyses (e.g., Dumais, 2004; McNamara et al., 2010).

A notable exception to the traditional approach to NLP was developed by Google. The *Bidirectional Encoder Representations from Transformers* (BERT) model developed by Devlin, Chang, Lee, and Toutanova (2019) underlies the powerful Google Search engine and is available as an open-access cloud-based analytical engine. BERT and similar transformer architectures, among having other technical and performance advantages over traditional text parsers and preprocessors, consider the text in both a forward and backward manner that takes into account the context in which each word appears in the text segment. These types of transformer architectures replace a recursion approach to processing text with query-based approach called *self-attention* where the queries and keys are generated by the text segment, itself (i.e., contextualizing the query). BERT can further represent text tokens in an extensible, context-dependent, hierarchical way similar to a syntactic tree structure—rather than simply considering word order. This flexible structure of tokens implies that BERT can also capture semantic encodings better than N-grams, for example. Built-in analytic capabilities the quality of the prediction of tokens in a text segment or familiarity/common-use of token structures might also aid in quantifying semantic complexity.

Python is clearly one of the most popular programming environments for researching and developing NLP applications, given its extremely large and growing system of machine-learning packages and applied programming interfaces for deep learning AI. *NLTK* is the primary Python library for NLP, offering multiple preprocessing functions for tagging and segmenting text, parsing, classification, stemming, tokenization and semantic reasoning. The library further provides access to more than 50-word corpora. Another popular Python library is called *TextBlob*. It offers essentially all of the same features as *NLTK*, but is significantly faster and further includes functions for parsing, spelling correction, part-of-speech tagging (including automated noun-phrases), tokenization, word/phrase extraction and frequency analysis, *WordNet*[1] integration, generation of N-grams, and sentiment analysis.

Word frequency-based outcomes like type-token ratios or TTRs (unique item count divided by the total number of words—or averaged across standardized-length segments) are relatively straight-forward to directly use as inputs in an IDM research study or for task and item model family QC (e.g., as crude lexical uniqueness or semantic density indicators). Other syntactic or semantic indicators may require additional, creative and possibly complex analytics. For example, applying classifiers to nested token structures like multi-layered N-grams or syntactic trees to evaluate the familiarity of an item's grammatic structure is not something that a text analyzer would handle directly. Similarly, creating a "propositional text" structure (Kintsch, 1988) to represent, evaluate and compare the semantic complexity of "idea units" is not automatically provided by any text analysis package. Instead, outputs from multiple text analysis functions within the Python library would need to be combined with other statistical functions to provide the outputs that are eventually used for research or operational QC.

The R programming language also provides many text analysis libraries (packages). Many R libraries provide a limited set of functions, implying that end-users may need to work with several R libraries to actually carry out a text analysis. For example, the *Quanteda* package contains functions for converting text to internal analysis structures (e.g., creating tokens from a text segment, reading a formatted document, or creating a corpus from a text collection that holds metadata like word or phrase frequencies and other metadata). Similarly, the *Tidytext* library transforms an input text segment in a unique table-like structure with one token per row. The *WordVec2* library deals with words that take on different meanings in different contexts by using high-dimensional vectors known as word embeddings—conceptually similar to what Google's BERT engine does, albeit in somewhat a less-sophisticated and comprehensive way.

A thorough treatment of text analysis is beyond the scope of this report. Suffice to say, there is a growing body of software tools and libraries offered in languages like R and Python that provide many powerful preprocessing capabilities that can produce the input data for highly sophisticated statistical and/or linguistic analyses carried out using other packages or libraries. The outputs from those analyses may or may not prove empirically useful for TMF QC. That is why IDM research is needed. Clearly, automating the preprocessing and of text segments and providing flexible use of multiple types of analyses is key to ultimately ensuring that more than just the surface features of text can be considered in an efficient manner.

7.1.2 Image Analytics

Image analytics are far less mature than text analytics, especially for assessment applications. From an AE perspective we want to identify and quantify features related to an image's complexity in the context of the problem or task presented. For example, like a passage-based reading comprehension item, we might ask the examinees to consider an image[2] and simply identify or name one or more objects within the image. We might further request that they locate or determine the main idea depicted in a picture or infographic, locate specific information, or make inferences from what they are observing. Images can also serve as tangential resource exhibits or merely as decoration to enhance a text passage.

The label *infographics* refers to charts, plots, maps, and other data visualizations that show patterns between two or more variables, aid in making visual comparisons for grouped data, demonstrate trends, provide profiles across multiple variables, etc. An infographic can plot or display "raw" data, aggregations of the raw data such as group means (averages), or abstract functions of the data such as statistically fitted lines, curves, or surfaces. Infographics also provide an interesting example of how the complexity of a graphic as part of an item model can be manipulated. Consider the various choices of coordinate spaces and scales for locating plotted objects within those spaces (the ranges of values in a rectangular/Cartesian space versus a polar or spherical space—or even the option of using other non-Cartesian geometries or projections). Further think about the choices of axes and their properties (e.g., tick marks, text style and utility of axis labels), use of grid lines, plotting symbols, depth and breadth of layers of information (e.g., adding a smoothing function) and other aesthetic elements such as the appropriateness and clarity of colors, the familiarity or intuitiveness of symbols used, use of meaningful legends, etc. All of these choices can either facilitate or obfuscate the overall message (gist) of the infographic or key details or patterns that a text taker must ascertain.

The density of key information, itself, can also be manipulated. For example, suppose that we have percentages corresponding to four categories of self-reported party affiliation adult voters in the United States: 31% Democrats, 25% Republican, 41% Independent, and 3% unspecified or other. We might simply state those percentages in a sentence (as text), put the values in a table sorted by the percentages/proportions, themselves, or plot them in bar chart or stacked bar chart. We might also convert the stacked bar chart cumulative percentage values to a polar coordinate system and create the ubiquitous pie chart. Pie charts may seem like a simple graphic, but the use of polar coordinates for the percentages, the required relative visual comparisons of the sizes of each slide, and the possible confounding by applying colors, shading or other aesthetics to "separate" the categories—which are already spatially separated by the position of each pie slide—can make a seemingly simple choice in graphic more complicated than needed to interpret or otherwise make use of the data.

What is clear is that images can be far more complicated to work with than text segments given the multitude of image types (photos, drawings, maps, charts, plots and other infographics, schematics, etc.). Images also come in many digital formats at different resolutions and sizes; and they can differ dramatically in terms of other properties (e.g., distortions, two- versus pseudo-three-dimensional depictions, use of black-and-white, color hues and saturation or grayscales, and extent of layering of the image features).

Beyond the obvious need to initially digitize any image or video segment as a preprocessing step, there are at least six image processing technologies that might provide promising outcomes in automated or semi-automated item or task difficulty modeling contexts. The first is *image segmentation* which applies a process of partitioning or cropping a digital image or video frame into multiple image segments called image regions or image objects (e.g., a set of pixels within a grid). The second is *object recognition*, which involves the identification and classification of objects in a digital image, infographic, or video segment. In digital image processing and computer vision. The third technology is *image filtering* which might either isolate key objects in an image or quantify the amount of distractive background noise or otherwise nonessential information in an image. The fourth technology is *layering* which includes slicing and stacking. Slicing refers to the process of segmenting one or more objects or properties in an image as separate layers that can be manipulated independent of other layers. New layers in the image can then be added (stacking) or removed to add clarity or complexity. The fifth technology is *zooming* which increases or decreases the perceived distance between the viewer and the object, up to the resolution of the source image. The sixth is *optical flow*. This technology is typically applied to video segments. However, it could be applied to still images or frames as a way to consider the pattern of relationships of objects within an image (hierarchies, connectives, shared or overlapping surfaces and edges.)

There are three purposes for using image analytics under AE. The first is to help automate the selection (or generation) and screening of graphical exhibits like pictures, charts or graphs, drawings, shapes, etc. The second purpose is to provide ordinal (categorical) or numerical indicators that allow us to quantify image complexity as part of IDM research and applications. The third is to use image analytics to systematically modify or contextualize problem scenarios through the strategic use of images (e.g., adding a photo, flowchart, or map as a type of scaffolding to replace lengthier text narratives describing a scenario, context, or setting).

Current open-source analytical environments like R and Python do offer various image analytic packages. There are also a number of open-source packages like *ImageJ* (https://imagej.net/imaging/) or *ilastik* (https://www.ilastik.org/) that provide somewhat advanced image processing and analytic capabilities.

7.1.3 Analytics for Audio/Visual Segments

Audio/video analytics have much of the complexity as images, with the added complications of play controls, frame-speeds, and overall quality video and/or audio aesthetics. There are numerous commercial and open-source video editing tools, but no complexity-oriented analysis tools. Nonetheless, the CSPs described further on in this chapter may serve as a reasonable interim solution until such analytical tools could be developed.

7.1.4 Analytics for Tables and Tabular Data

Generally speaking, tables use domains or variable labels as column headings and rows (tuples) to represent the values on each of the variables per case or record. A table may also incorporate sub-headings for grouping, grouped subtotal and total rows, etc.). Unfortunately, there are few if any analysis tools that apply to tables.

That said, we might consider decomposing a table into four types of components: (a) an overall table structure represented by quantifiable features such as the number of rows, columns, and grouped or nested subsections; (b) applied tabular functions such as sorting or calculating aggregate values (e.g., row- or column-marginal totals, averages); (c) the nested or embedded data appearing in cells within the table; and (d) aesthetics such as shading, alignment, use of separator lines, etc. If a table is interactive, it is certainly possible that any of these components could be under the control of the test taker (e.g., allowing the examinee to enter a formula to operate on a range of cells or to re-sort the table by one or more columns). However, these components can also take on cumulative complexity values for static tables (non-interactive) tables. Figure 7.2 displays an example of a table that contains seven columns: a row label column on the left followed by five data columns and one "total" column for each row at the far right. There are two groups of data records (rows), A and B, each with column subtotals. The bottom-most total row summarizes either the group A and B subtotal rows or the aggregation of rows 1 to 8 (or both), depending on the type of aggregation function applied (e.g., counts, averages, or other descriptive statistics). (Note: columns containing non-numerical data would likely not have a subtotal or total value.)

Tables are conceptually similar to infographics in that we make choices about the amount and nature of the data displayed. However, we can further consider features of a tabular display such as the use of horizontal and vertical lines and coloring/shading to separate rows and/or columns, the sort variables used and sequencing of the rows or columns (e.g., sorting U.S. states on a

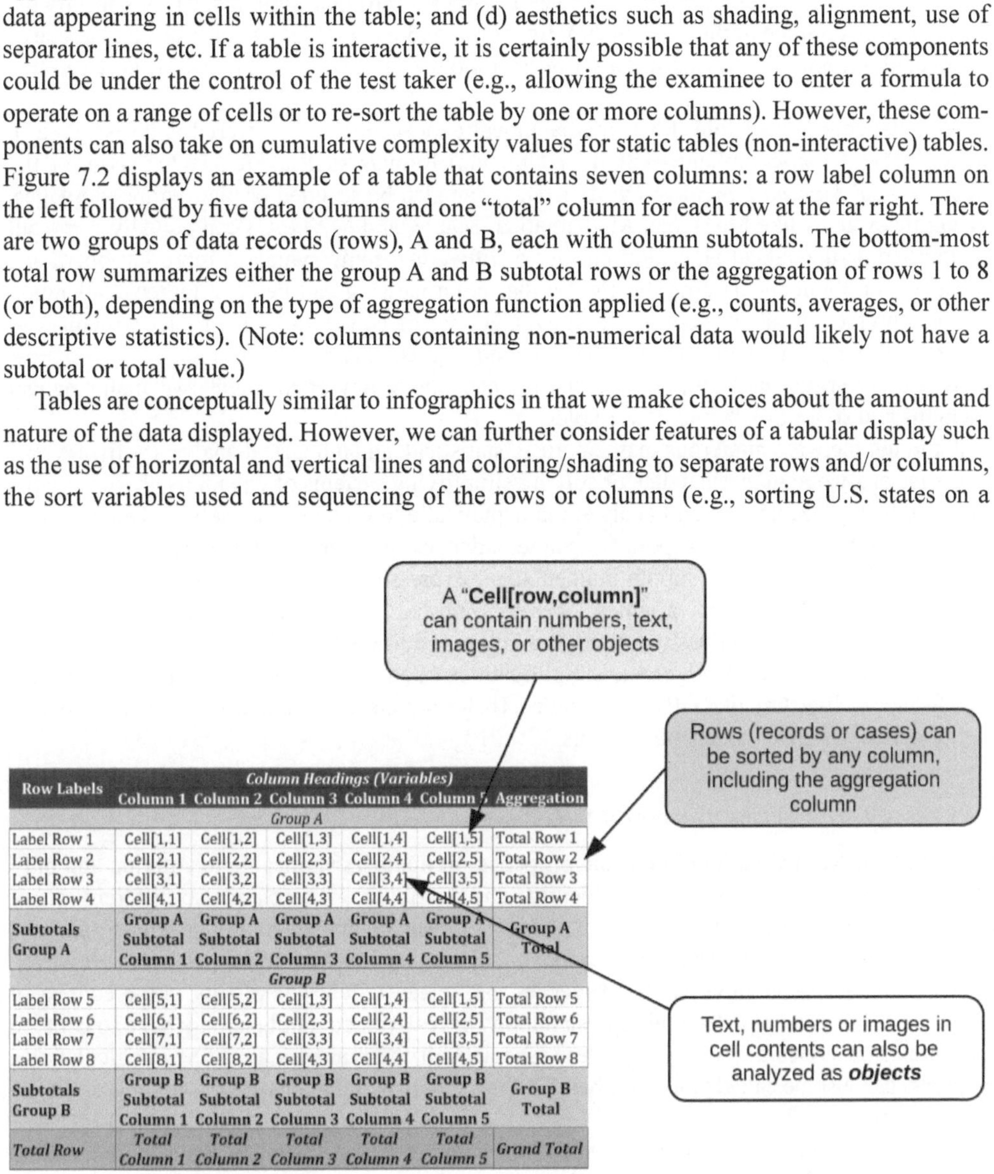

Figure 7.2 A Sample Table Structure with Two Nested Groups (A and B) of 4 Rows Each

value like health care expenditures per capita that might be critical to answering a test question rather than sorting the table alphabetically), text wrapping and value alignments within cells, choices of text fonts and aesthetics, etc.

7.1.5 Analytics for Mathematical Expressions and Equations

Mathematical expressions also present an interesting challenge from the perspective of computational object analyses. A mathematical expression can be any set of variable labels and numbers (arguments) used in conjunction with a set of operators such as addition or summation, multiplication, etc. Equations separate two expressions by an equal sign; inequalities specify the direction or magnitude of the relationship. Equations and inequalities can also serve as a type of compact algorithm for carrying out a set of operations or to specify relationships between two expressions.

The challenge is two-fold. First, mathematical expressions can be stored and displayed in many different text-compliant (ASCII or Unicode) formats such as *TeX/LaTeX*, *eqn*, or the *Mathematical Markup Language* (MML). They can also be scanned or photographed images. Algebraic systems like Macsyma, Mathematica, Maple, and MATLAB can actually carry out the implied mathematical algorithm but use a software-specific syntax to represent operators, variables and numbers. The implication is that preprocessing can become rather challenging without forethought about adopting a convenient set of equation-oriented data structures to facilitate decomposition and analysis. The second challenge is that most mathematical expressions can be written in multiple ways. Different authors may adopt their own mathematical notations and styles of labeling of variables.

Although there are numerous mathematical, statistical, and numerical analysis software programs for analyzing numerical data or solving/simplifying systems of equations, there are none that specifically decompose and analyze mathematical expressions, themselves. There also do not appear to be convenient corpora for mathematical expressions like there are for text (words and phrases). Developing a simple mathematical expression analyzer might include ways to count the number of salient variables, operators, nested operations, and the complexity and properties of numerical values, as discussed below. Additional sophistication could be added by considering the possible algebraic simplifications of an equality or inequality or adopting a transformer architecture like GPTs or Google's BERT architecture for text-based AI preprocessing to represent mathematical expressions.

7.1.6 Analytics for Numbers/Numerical Sets

Most students learn about the four basic properties of numbers applicable to addition and multiplication: commutative, associative, identity, and distributive. There are also different sets or classes of numbers (i.e., natural numbers, prime numbers, composite numbers, whole numbers, integers, rational numbers, irrational numbers, real numbers, and complex numbers). However, numbers can also have more subtle properties that relate to their complexity in the context of task model. For example, decimal representations of real-valued numbers may have to contend with precision issues and rounding rules, especially if the numbers are used in calculations. Numbers can also be called "nice numbers" if they satisfy certain consistent rounding or factoring-by-primes rules[3].

Counts of the number of numbers used, their magnitude, the various types of numbers, and the application of mathematical heuristics (e.g., the "niceness" of a number) have obvious promise when determining the complexity of numbers used in a task model and its associated item models. These could be treated as *properties* of the numbers, conceptually similar to the properties of a word or text phrase. Complexity related to their use would be determined by the mathematical expression/equation analytics.

7.1.7 Analytics for Item Structures

Paper-and-pencil multiple-choice tests with scannable answer sheets are relatively benign when it comes to inter-activity. Examinees page through a test booklet and record their answers by filling in a "bubble" on an answer sheet. In contrast, computer-based testing (CBT) has introduced numerous possibilities when it comes to "item types" (e.g., single- or multiple-option selected-response items, select-from-a-drop-down-list items, drag-and-drop items, etc.). Most CBT item types, however, can be represented as combinations of four types of software controls as shown in Figure 7.3.

Passive controls simply display information with limited to no interactivity (other than scrolling, perhaps). The "stem" of a multiple-choice item that displays a vignette as formatted text with an embedded photo, infographic, equation, or table would be an example of a passive control.

Response capturing components provide the key interactive mechanisms recording examinees selections or constructed-response entries. These components can range from simple to sometimes complex interactions between the examinees and the item. For example, they might select one-or-more options by clicking on a "radio button" control, click one or more checkboxes, select from a drop-down list, or enter a length written response or essay using a text editor. The control might also provide text captions, labels, or images. For example, CBT multiple-choice item types often use grouped radio button control that displays the text for each distractor option. The examinees click on the radio button in the group that corresponds to their answer choice, ◉.

Interactive tools include pop-up calculators, browser text or image search engines, audio-video players, spell-checkers, and other collaborative resources that test takers may use to analyze, evaluate, or otherwise gain insights that might help them respond to each item. Most interactive tools are presented as optional resources, not as an integral and required part of the

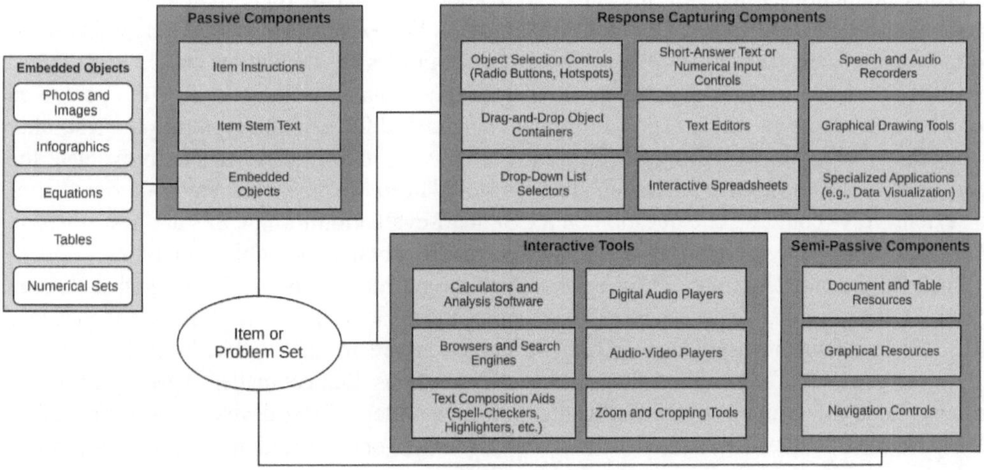

Figure 7.3 Decomposition of Item Types by Four Classes of Components and Tools

problem. Unlike response capturing components, however, these interactive tools rarely provide any responses or data used for scoring[4]. Nonetheless, the design of these tools, the amount of interactivity and intuitive ease-of-use the user interface can add or reduce the complexity of items generated to use each tool.

Semi-passive components are integral to viewing, evaluating and responding to a problem but require more interactivity than simply displaying text or graphical images. For example, an internet browser window containing hyperlinks to additional, critical resources for a constructed-response item in history using document-based materials might be classified as "semi-passive." The associated documents might be too large to display as embedded components and requiring the test takers to locate an evaluate information in multiple documents (text exhibits, graphical timelines, maps, etc.) may be considered essential to providing an "evidence-based" response.

Analytical tools that quantify nature and amount of interactivity within and between each class of components are entirely feasible. For example, by recording time and key actions on a software component, we can develop various normative indicators that can be attached to a designated item structure comprised of two or more of these four component classes.

7.2 Complexity Scoring Protocols

CSPs provide a way to capture fuzzy content or cognitive features of items that are not readily amenable to some of the direct computational OAPs described above. CSPs are rating sheets that trained subject-matter experts (SMEs) or test editors/clerical staff can use to evaluate specific cognitive-oriented, complexity features of individual items (selected-response or open ended), to intact item sets or clusters containing a passage or source material(s) and multiple items, to images or exhibits, or to assessment tools and resources such as calculators or formula sheets). On the surface, CSPs may look similar to an analytical rubric used to score essays. In fact, CSPs can, themselves, be analyzed with respect to within-rater and inter-rater consistency (reliability) similar to any psychometric rating or scoring protocol and subsequently "scaled" to one or more metrics using polytomous IRT modes.

Luecht (2019) devised CSPs for a commissioned empirical IDM study involving evidence-based medicine items used on a large-scale licensing examination (also see Luecht & Burke, 2020). That commissioned study reported significant improvements in the accuracy of item-difficulty predictions when CSP indicators were added to an IDM regression model[5]. Furthermore, the CSPs were shown to be practically efficient. For example, the CSP raters in his study completed more than 25 ratings in only two to three minutes per item, on average.

CSPs are not item-difficulty ratings. Rather, they are quantitative ratings of the perceived complexity of some specified aspect of an item considered for examinees within the test-taker population. For example, asking SMEs like seventh- or eighth-grade teachers to evaluate the amount of "prior knowledge" that their students would need to know, on average—from "none" to "extensive"—could be one question on a CSP item-evaluation form. CSPs are best suited to fuzzy task complexity evaluations that cannot be readily obtained via object analytics.

Table 7.1 presents 25 sample CSP questions. This list is not meant to be exhaustive. Rather, through iterative IDM research, the list can be expanded or contracted to result in an optimal set of questions to use for operational item-production QC. All 25 questions are available to rate for each test item.

An assigned set of items is rated using the CSP questions. Subject matter experts (SMEs) are recommended for evaluating technical content; however, clerical test development staff may be able to handle CSP questions related to the complexity of text or organization of the item as a whole.

Integer rating scales are recommended for CSPs to avoid the complications of relying on verbal descriptors (Luecht, 2019). For example, if we were using a four-point rating scale,

Table 7.1 25 Sample CSP Questions

1	What is the breadth and depth (volume) of PRIOR **[primary content]** knowledge required to correctly answer this item (i.e., information that must be known and understood to answer the question; information that is not explicitly provided as part of the item)?
2	What is the overall breadth and depth (volume) of PRIOR **[auxiliary content]** knowledge required to correctly answer this item (i.e., information that must be known and understood to answer the question; information that is not explicitly provided as part of the item)?
3	On average, how lexically diverse are the KEY IDEAS in the item (e.g., does there appear to be an array or inter-related set of key ideas)?
4	How lexically complex is technical or nuanced terminology in this item (e.g., technical terminology or nuanced vocabulary)?
5	What is the extent and explicitness of any connective information (i.e., words, phrases or concepts that are causally, temporally, logically, incrementally, linearly, or adversatively/competitively linked to each other)?
6	How explicit/clear are the key details/data needed for the solution (e.g., units, clarity of modifying information, etc.)?
7	How dense is the numerical data (if any) embedded in text?
8	How organized is the presentation/display of key information?
9	What is the level of reading comprehension needed to process the stem/instructions?
10	What is the level of reading comprehension needed to process the distractors?
11	What is the nature and extent of explicit calculations/quantitative computations needed?
12	What level of data/concept filtering is needed (i.e., to screen out irrelevant information)?
13	What is the extent and depth of any informational searches needed?
14	What is the overall level of biostatistical reasoning/problem-solving needed to correctly answer this question?
15	How many somewhat distinct (sequential) procedural steps are needed to arrive at the correct solution?
16	How syntactical or grammatically complex is the language used in the stem/instructions (excluding the distractors)?
17	How much textual information is contained in the stem (i.e., what is the information density apparent by the number of noun, verb and propositional phrases, etc.)?
18	How coherent is the correct answer given the details in the stem/instructions?
19	What is the nature and extent of explicit text in the stem/instructions that negates one or more incorrect distractors (e.g., mismatches of terms of the noun or verb phrases used in the stem and incorrect distractors)?
20	How much scaffolding or guidance does the stem provide related to explicitly understanding the procedural steps needed to reach a decision or fully understand problem that needs to be solved?
21	What is the nature and extent of inferred conceptual information (not explicit) in the stem/instructions that negates one or more incorrect distractors (e.g., mismatches of terms of the noun or verb phrases used)?
22	How distinct or separate are the distractors as a collection from the correct answer(s) (i.e., the degree of negative coherence)?
23	How syntactical or grammatically complex is the language used in the distractors (on average)?
24	What is the nature and extent of any interrelationships among the distractors (i.e., connections between explicit surface features versus abstract/deeper/inferred connections)?
25	How complex/dense is the information contained in image(s) and/or data tables?

$X_{qi} = (1,2,3,4)$ for each CSP, q, each of the assigned items, i, would be evaluated and assigned a rating of one to four. The analytical anchor descriptors and annotations for the first question in Table 7.1 might be as follows:

- **Lowest rating** ($X_{1i} = 1$) implies isolated statistical concepts and content that seems very basic/highly familiar/common knowledge.
- **Highest rating** ($X_{1i} = 4$) implies that the [primary content] is networked/integrated and inter-dependent requiring a fairly deep level of prior knowledge/understanding about the interrelationships of the content (i.e., not at all explicit in the item).

- **Further rubric explanation and examples**: A "1" implies that the problem requires very limited, well-known **[primary content]** knowledge. For example, basic concepts like [list of basic concepts] are fairly basic and well-known, even to the lay public and, in isolation, could be rated "1." Less well-known terms like [list of moderate complexity **primary content**] are not intuitive and could easily be misapplied–perhaps earning a rating of "2" or "3." Needing to know two or more highly unfamiliar **[primary content]** concepts (or concepts that have multiple nuanced meanings) would probably be a "4."

When multiple raters are used, we can develop CSP QC analytics based on open-ended and constructed-response scoring models to ensure consistent/reliable ratings across items and occasions (e.g., systematically carrying out inter-rater agreement and reliability analyses. A more complete description of those methods is beyond the scope of this chapter.

The matrix of CSP ratings (rows) by items (columns) presents as a standard response data matrix. Furthermore, we can calibrate the CSP ratings as we would a person-by-item response data matrix. Figure 7.4 shows the basic calibration process. In this example, 10 items are evaluated by the 25 CSPs shown in Table 7.1 using our four-point analytical rubrics. The transposed response data matrix in the center is calibrated using an IRT model of choice. The resulting IRT "scores" are item complexity ratings on the relevant CDL metric used to develop the CSPs.

For example, consider a relatively straightforward re-definition of the parameters for the complex partial-credit model (PCM) for polytomous data (Masters, 1982). The item complexity score on the CDL metric is γ–that is, the model can be used to estimate a complexity score for each evaluated item. The other parameters are the CSP question "difficulty." b_q, and the CSP-specific category threshold parameters, d_{qv}.

$$P_{qk} = exp\left[\sum_{v=1}^{k} \gamma - \left(b_q - d_{qv}\right)\right] \Big/ \sum_{k=1}^{m_q} exp\left[\Sigma_{v=1}^{k} \gamma - \left(b_q - d_{qv}\right)\right] \tag{7.1}$$

Applying an IRT model like the PCM in this context has four important benefits. First, these models can handle a large number of polytomous CSP item-rating categories. Second, the calibration (IRT measurement) model reduces the ratings for—in this case 25 CSP questions—to a single value per item. Those estimated item complexity scores can be used as supplemental OAPs for IDM or TMF calibration purposes. Third, the IRT framework can readily

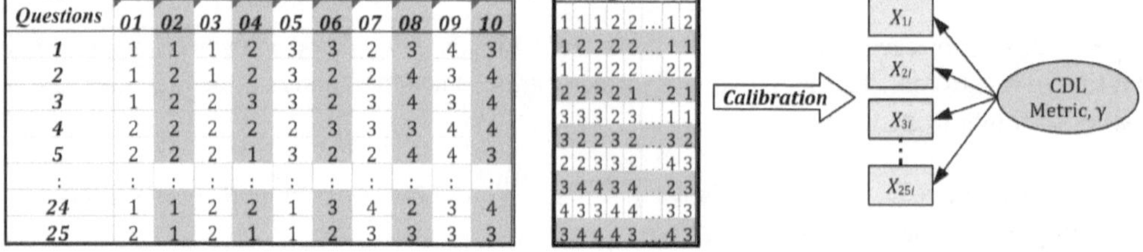

Figure 7.4 From CSP Ratings to Calibrated CDL Item Scores

manage missing CSP responses for some items—subject to certain technical "connectivity" requirements among the rows and columns of the response matrix shown in Figure 7.4. That is essential since some CSP questions may not apply to particular items. Rather than assigning the lowest score to those non-applicable CSP questions, we simply let the responses be coded as "blank" (missing) in the data matrix. Fourth, IRT provides many detailed and useful data-model fit analyses for verifying the psychometric quality of CSP questions or the evaluated items relative to the estimated model parameters (e.g., empirical versus model-based item characteristic plots).

7.3 Psychometric QC Using Conditional Residual Analyses

IRT models are mathematical expressions that denote *response probability functions* (RPFs). The RPFs usually represented as a function of a vector of item parameters, ξ_i, and examinee proficiency scores, θ_j; that is,

$$pr\left(x_i = X_{ik} \mid \theta_j; \xi_i\right) \equiv P_{ijk} \tag{7.2}$$

where i indexes the item and k indexes the scoring category. Common examples used in operational assessment settings are the well-known Rasch model (Rasch, 1960), the two- and three-parameter logistic models (Birnbaum, 1968; Lord, 1980), the rating scale model (Andrich, 1978), the partial-credit model (Masters, 1982—see the modified version above for CSPs), generalized partial-credit model (Muraki, 1992), and the graded response model (Samejima, 1969). Many other IRT models have been suggested (e.g., van der Linden, 2016).

Many IRT research studies and applications focus on data-model fit issues (e.g., finding the best fitting model for various types of response data), calibration and score estimation issues, and item bank maintenance. However, IRT also provides some very powerful and useful statistical methods that can be used for QC purposes. We will concentrate here on the use of conditional residual analyses.

First, we need an IRT model. For convenience, we can use the ubiquitous two-parameter logistic (2PL) model for binary scored data. The 2PL model can be written as

$$P_{i1} = \left\{1 + exp\left[-a_i\left(\theta - b_i\right)\right]\right\}^{-1} \tag{7.3}$$

where θ is the latent proficiency score, a_i is an item discrimination parameter, and b_i is the item-difficulty (response function inflection-point location) parameter—noting that $\xi_i = \left(a_i, b_i\right)$ to connect Equation 7.3 to the more generic Equation 7.2. This is the probability of a correct response, $x_i = 1$. An incorrect response would be modeled as $P_{i0} = Q_i = 1 - P_{i1}$.

The *expected response function* (ERF)—or conditional average score in the population—uses the RPF and can be expressed as:

$$y_{ij} \equiv E\left(x_{ij} \mid \theta_j; \xi_i\right) = \sum_{k=1}^{m} X_{ik} P_{ijk} \tag{7.4}$$

where there are $m \geq 2$ possible categorical scores, $\mathbf{X}_i = \{X_{i1}, X_{i2}, \ldots, X_{im}\}$. [*Note: it is mathematically trivial to show that the ERF simplifies to* P_i *for IRT models that use binary-scored items,* $\mathbf{X}_i = \left(0,1\right)$.]

The ERF is essentially a "model-agnostic" function that also happens to be on the same scale as the observed item-response data. For example, binary-scored items would bind the ERF to a value between zero and one. In contrast, a constructed-response item that employed a four-point rubric such as $\boldsymbol{X}_i = (0,1,2,3)$ would generate a model-based ERF of $0 \le y_{ij} \le 3$.

Denoting item models, *g*, within TMFs, *g:f*, we can rewrite Equation 7.1 to incorporate the TMF, item model, and item layers. That is,

$$pr\left(x_i = X_{ik} | \theta_j; \xi_{i:g:f}\right) \equiv P_{i:g:f,jk}. \tag{7.5}$$

This version of the PRF can represent calibrations at the item, item model, or TMF level. The associated IRT calibrations can employ either data wrangling to collapse the response data from individual items to item models to TMFs or resort to multi-level IRT models. A correspondingly useful conditional residual for QC purposes is:

$$e_{i:g:f,j} = x_{ij} - f_{i:g:f,j}. \tag{7.6}$$

This residual becomes a basic data-model fit variable that represents the difference between the observed item-response scores and the model-predicted item-response scores.

The conditional residuals (Equation 7.6 can be normalized relative to an asymptotic or empirically estimated error variance/standard error or any reasonable baseline variation statistics (see, for example, Wright & Stone, 1979; Yen, 1984). Here, we restrict our discussions and examples to the simple "person-item" residual.

Suppose that we have a task model map (TMM—see Chapter 5) comprised of 60 task models. That TMM represents both our statistical and content/cognitive blueprint for test assembly. Further suppose that we have two item models per task model and are able to manually generate 15 items per item model (30 items per task model). The items are individually administered to N_i=200 examinees producing a total sample size of 6,000 examinees. Capitalizing on our [hopefully solid] cognitive task models and associated item models, we would like to collapse all of the data at the TMF level, $f = 1,\ldots,60$. We calibrate the response data matrix using the 2PL model (Equation 7.3) and obtain 60 task-model estimates of the item parameters, a_f and b_f. We then use the examinees' observed and model-based ERF item scores to compute residuals for every item and every examinee pairing.

Figure 7.5 is a plot of the mean residuals (dots) and associated standard deviations (error bars) of residuals conditional on the task models along the horizontal axis. The dashed horizontal "control lines" set at ± 0.3 are our engineering "tolerances." In words, if the error bars fall outside of those control lines, we would flag that task model for additional psychometric analyses. We could migrate the calibration down to the item-model (g) or item level (i) to perhaps improve the data-model fit. Of course, that would sacrifice some of the stability of the overall IRT calibration—especially at the item level, given those smaller sample sizes.

There are many other conditional and unconditional residual analyses that can and should be added as automatic components of the overall QC system. There are other, more sophisticated alternative IRT calibration or data modeling strategies that could be employed (see, for example, Geerlings et al., 2011; Sinharay & Johnson, 2012). Nonetheless, we need to keep in mind that our AE goal is to ensure that we are improving our designs and item generation constraints to enhance the isomorphic quality of the task models and their corresponding item models. Ultimately, by reducing the within-TMF residuals to relatively small values and monitoring those on an ongoing basis, we can achieve that goal.

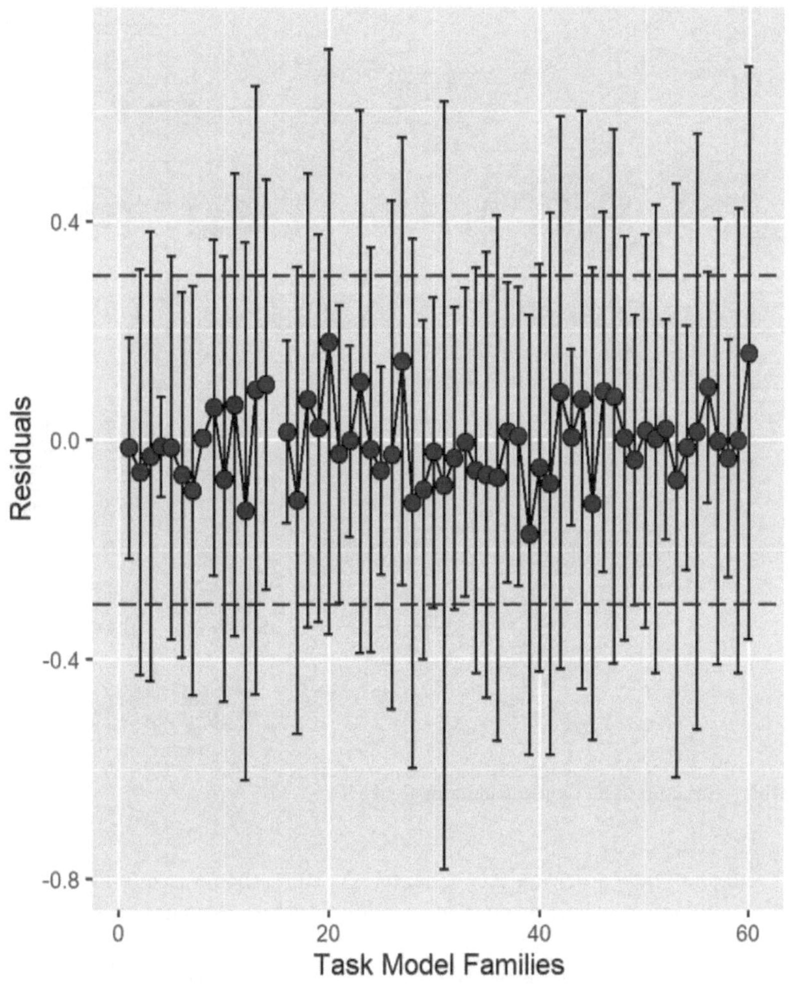

Figure 7.5 A Residual Plot for 60 Task Models

7.4 An Object Analytic Architecture

What does the phrase "quality control system" really mean? It means devising a system comprised of robust data structures, high-integrity data transmission and manipulation, automated and semi-automated software procedures and processing steps, and even a layer of human review—ideally with an eye toward efficiency, cost and value-added of such reviews.

Figure 7.6 provides a fairly comprehensive schema for structuring and carrying out various object analyses of an item's rendered components and content. The data models and normalized data tables used for rendering and scoring items can be readily expanded to likewise provide the inputs needed for carrying out IDM research. The figure also shows the hierarchical relationships between a task model, its associated item models (rendering templates, scoring evaluators, and data structures for rendering and scoring) and the data feeding IDM research, QC procedures, and prediction/calibration for each TMF as well as IDM-related outputs from

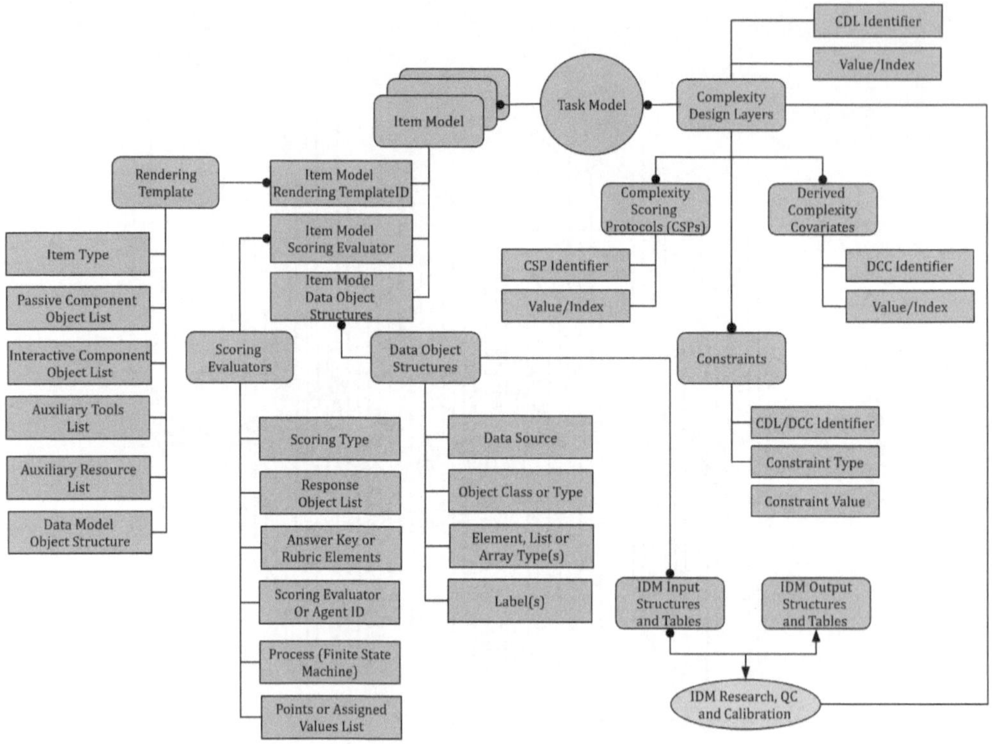

Figure 7.6 Object Structures and Object Relations for TMFs

CSP ratings and analytical software (see Chapter 3). This schema is intended as an example of the types of data objects, their properties, and relationships; it is not an exact specification for an item bank.

The data object structures typically used for rendering and scoring are shown as expanded objects/data structures on the left side of Figure 7.6. The structures to the right support item decomposition and analysis for IDM (see Figure 7.5, shown earlier). As previously noted, the object-analytic outputs from IDM research, QC procedures, and operational calibrations can be fed back into the item bank at the TMF, item model, or item levels.

7.5 Chapter Summary

This chapter discussed the importance of computational analytics for IDM research (Chapter 4) and task/item model family QC and quality assurance. Three types of computational analytics were covered: (1) object analytic procedures for text, images, etc.; (2) CSPs to handle fuzzy complexity evaluations by human raters; and (3) IRT-based residual analytics to evaluate statistical isomorphism within TMFs.

This is not a trivial undertaking. Implementing these technologies requires investments in the needed data infrastructure and analytical architectures. In some cases, open-source solutions in Python or R may be leveraged to avoid creating everything from scratch. The systems architectures also need to be flexible, robust, and sufficiently scalable to support the breadth and depth of computational analytics described in this chapter.

Notes

1 *WordNet* is one of the most popular corpora available for evaluating the familiarity of words relative to frequencies stored in the corpus.
2 Image is used generically here to refer to a photo, drawing, chart, plot, map, schematic, or other infographic.
3 Nice numbers are considered when creating numerical labels for axis tick marks or grid lines in an infographic. They can also be useful when establishing constraints for a set of possible numerical values to specify for the *argument set* of an item model.
4 Given an appropriate design and integration of interactive tools as part of the test delivery software, it is possible to obtain data such as the number of times a component is activated, time spent per access event, etc.
5 Item-level text-complexity indicators obtained from *Coh-Metrix* (Graesser and McNamara, 2011) were included as predictors in the model. Combined almost 90% of the observed variance in the item difficulties was explained by the model ($R^2 = 0.875$).

8 AE Implementation and Future Directions

Assessment Engineering (AE) is about good assessment design. It is neither a cognitive nor psychometric theory. Rather, borrowing proven principles from industrial engineering and manufacturing, AE promotes integration, efficiency, automation (where warranted), continual and iterative improvement through versioning, and strong, empirical quality control across the entire testing enterprise. Isolating item and test development from psychometrics and other *siloed* operational procedures are fair game for change—from human-intensive item writing activities to test assembly to psychometric calibration and scale maintenance strategies over time.

8.1 What Problems Does AE Actually Solve?

AE can solve at least three assessment problems. The first is *validity by design.* Ideally, we can start our test design efforts with more than a content blueprint and then later layer on our score interpretations after the statistical score scale has actually been developed. Chapters 1 and 2 discuss the need to visualize the measurement demands and priorities for a scale and then develop the construct map and evidence models to support well-articulated, proficiency claims along the conceptual scale. Task modeling and empirical item difficulty modeling research (Chapters 3 and 4) help create the empirical connections between ordered content and cognitive complexity and the statistical location of a task model family (TMF) score scale. Ultimately, AE can build fairly strong, empirically supported validity argumentation into the design of every item and into the score scale, itself.

The second problem involves the all-to-common competition between adhering to a traditional content blueprint during test assembly and simultaneously meeting optimal statistical scale properties such as maximizing a scale reliability coefficient or minimizing decision errors near a pass-fail cut score. AE can move us toward a more integrated test blueprinting process where the optimal statistical properties of the scale and the content requirements are aimed at simultaneously meeting intended, well-documented proficiency claims and evidence priorities. Task model maps (TMMs) replace a traditional content blueprints with a single specification that includes content and statistical scale design priorities. A TMM ultimately simplifies both test assembly and inventory control by focusing item-production on the rather exacting demands of building isomorphic TMFs.

The third problem involves costs. Like its parent discipline, industrial engineering, AE is about creating solutions that result in high-quality outputs meeting design specifications. Efficiency, scalability, and robustness are the core principles that permeate all elements of a good engineering design process. For example, a principal goal in developing TMFs is to produce

DOI: 10.4324/9781003451051-8

the high-quality, isomorphic content (items) at the lowest possible cost. Costs can be reduced by using tightly controlled item models and extended to the use of automatic item generation (AIG)—including the growing use of generative artificial intelligence technologies such as large language models and pre-trained generative transformer (GPT) architectures. However, more subtle (and substantial) costs can be reduced by ensuring empirically the isomorphism of items within TMFs.

There are undeniable, potentially large costs upfront associated with moving toward AE. Change takes time and money. There are also undeniable, longer-term cost-reduction benefits that accrue from better and more consistent design processes. One thing is clear, continuing to design items, tests, and score scales the way we do now and expecting a different and improved result is simply wishful thinking. Likewise, adopting partial solutions such as investing in AIG without building the needed infrastructure and without committing to an item-difficulty modeling research agenda that helps ensure the creation of isomorphic content can lead to disenchantment when that type of technology fails to reduce overall costs or creates psychometric analytic bottlenecks (e.g., getting sufficient sample sizes to calibrate every generated item when isomorphism cannot be plausibly assumed).

8.2 Implementing AE: A System of Integrated Systems

As noted above, AE is about *integration.* The four core technologies discussed in Chapter 1 (construct mapping and evidence modeling, task modeling, item-family production, and psychometric and related QC) require robust software and human systems that work together. Drasgow et al. (2006) described a large-scale assessment enterprise as a "system of systems." AE clearly demands a flexible and scalable system of systems comprised of state-of-the-art technologies that work together with highly structured databases and software to automate or at least make more efficient how data are managed and processed. However, it is not all about automation. Human beings will continue to play critical roles in this system of systems. Even semi-automated procedures can help them more efficiently and effectively engage in activities ranging from evidence modeling and the development of TMMs to item writing.

8.2.1 Versioning and Robust Integration

The engineering components and principles making up the AE framework further demand a strong commitment to iterative, versioned design. It simply not infeasible nor plausible to expect to successfully design a construct map, evidence models, complexity design layers and task models, one or more TMMs, and then generate highly isomorphic items for each TMF in "Version 1.0." Rather, iterative design and continuous improvement are hallmarks of good design, where future versions fix bugs in earlier versions, automate or streamline procedures where possible, and successively move the design forward toward seamless integration. Effective versioning strategies should be adopted that focus on prioritizing design modifications that have the most impact on reducing costs while simultaneously improving quality and efficiency.

A cursory consideration of the AE framework may create the impression of a very complicated, resource-intensive, and expensive undertaking. It is certainly not a trivial venture. For example, item writing operations that provide subject-matter experts (SMEs) with limited guidance and then allow them to create items based on their personal interpretations of a content blueprint and cognitive complexity may need to be reconceptualized as *item production* using detailed task model specifications and templates to generate multiple items within an assigned item family.

8.2.2 Quality Improvement Metrics

Almost every aspect of AE is aimed at systematic and verifiable *improvement* along four metrics:

- Better efficiency in item design and production by creating item families based on high-yield task models supported by automated IDM analytics and effective rating mechanisms such as complexity scoring protocols
- Solution scalability implied by the use of robust easily extensible, reusable data structures to represent intact and decomposed item objects—at virtually any level and for any purpose (not just IDM)
- Strong emphasis on proactive planning and iterative design that allows modifications and quality improvements through increasing use of automation and quality control mechanisms to inform system modifications and production controls
- Reduced test-development and pretesting costs through effective IDM research and operational implementation as part of TMF quality assurance.

A commitment to success requires upfront investments in automation, large-scale systems integration, quality control and improvement, sustainability, and procedural efficiencies across an assessment enterprise. Expensive legacy systems may need to be significantly revamped or retired, depending on their overall mission criticality. Lower-cost systems may still need to undergo redesign to allow them to scale up to support higher item and test form productivity.

Ultimately, the AE framework is about designing an assessment program based on integrated enterprise alignment: from the conception of the construct(s) as scales through the use of TMMs tied to evidence models to direct connections between task model specifications and the items within an item family to psychometric modeling as part of the quality-control subsystem to ensure consistent, isomorphic item production matching the content complexity specifications inherent in each TMF.

8.2.3 High-Level Procedures and Systems

Every organization makes its own decisions about system acquisition (e.g., to build system in-house or license externally created applications and tools). Regardless, designing a system of systems needs to start with a vision of the scope of the enterprise. That vision can and should be modified as needed, but it is also important to focus on finishing Version 1.0. Plans for needed design modifications and enhancements can happen concurrently with initial rollout of the current version(s) of the systems. That is all part of iterative design philosophy. It works!

As an example of a systems "vision," Figure 8.1 provides a high-level system architecture showing four functional clusters (subsystems): (1) test design and specifications development; (2) item production or generation; (3) test form production (pre-assembled, fixed-item test forms, linear-on-the-fly test forms, modular adaptive multistage test forms, or item-level computerized adaptive forms); and (4) psychometric calibration and statistical quality control to maintain an item-bank scale over time. The vision lets us understand the design for that robust integration. As noted above, the goal of full integration is essential to the overall alignment of all functional subsystems, data structures, and operational procedures making up an assessment enterprise.

Under AE, it should be apparent that it is almost impossible to avoid also making connections between multiple subsystems within an assessment enterprise. If those subsystems are designed for scalability and to provide consistent messaging/data exchanges using robust, extensible data

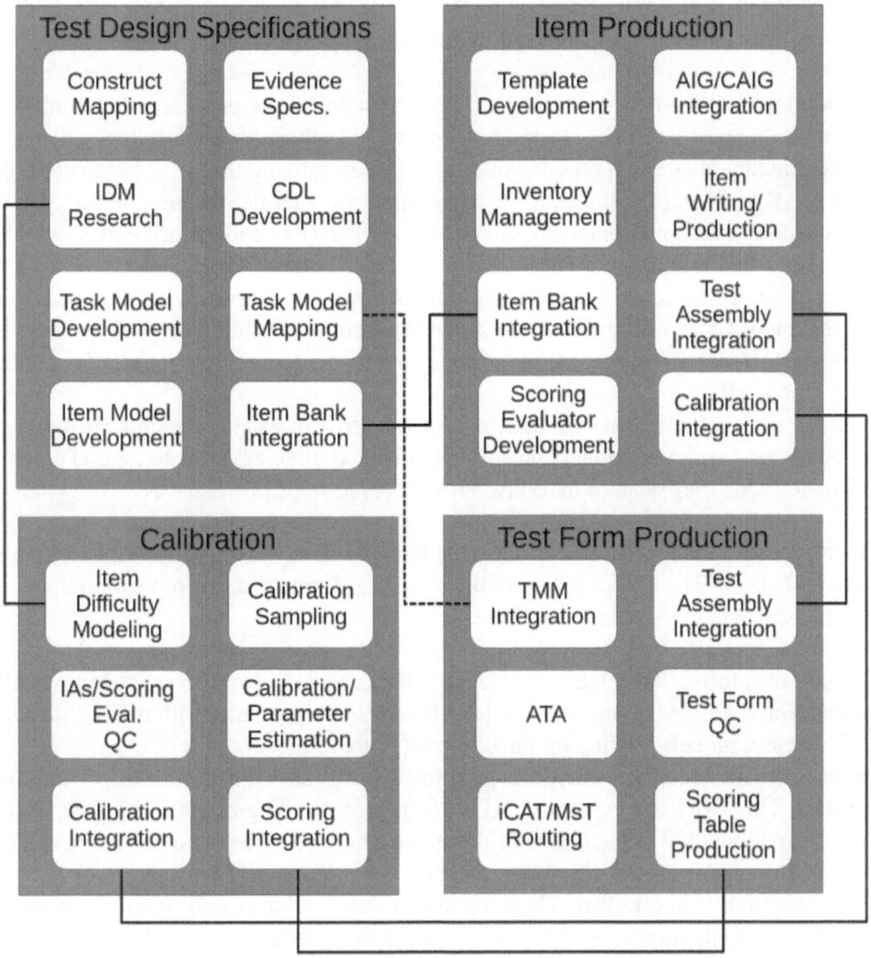

Figure 8.1 AE Systems and Component Technologies

structures, modifications aimed at improvement ought not require continuous redesign or re-engineering. AE can be a complicated, resource-intensive, and expensive undertaking with the need for significant systems development and retooling up-front. However, as already noted earlier in this chapter, the longer-term benefits can include lowered item and test form development costs, improved quality, and built-in score scale validity.

8.3 Future Directions

Item Response Theory was a "new technology" in the late 1970s and early 1980s. Computerized adaptive testing (CAT), multistage testing (MST), and automated test assembly (ATA) were novel technologies introduced in the late 1980s and early-to-mid 1990s. Automated essay scoring has evolved since the late 1990s. Automated item generation (AIG), while first proposed many decades ago, became a high-interest innovation approximately a decade ago. And now, generative AI, large language models (LLMs), and GPT architectures are promising enormous benefits ranging from test content generation to automated scoring and score reporting. It is impossible to predict where these technologies will lead the measurement sciences and operational testing.

This book is not about new technologies. In fact, many of the procedures presented in the previous seven chapters have been around for some time. Rather, this book is intended to change some of the thinking about, and practice of testing by recognizing that we need to change how we design score scale and then design the test content to consistently provide the type of information needed. Traditional practices such as using blueprints with prioritized content topics (constraints) and then expecting test assembly practices to balance those constraints and various statistical properties of a score are often more restrictive than helpful when it comes to good assessment design. Likewise, crafting items as unique content, relying on pilot testing to calibrate every item, building a statistical score scale, and then attempting to layer *ad hoc* interpretations onto the numbers.

Ultimately, a goal of this book was to provide some sense of what is possible. Testing organizations, researchers, and practitioners must think outside of their comfort zones and create their own visions for what they wish to measure. There are five steps to AE:

1 Start with construct mapping; that is, building the proficiency claims and evidence models to achieve that vision. The interpretation of the score scale units in terms of meaningful changes should be part of that visioning process.
2 Creating task models. Task models tell us about the cognitive complexity of the task challenges due to information loads, knowledge demands, etc. Focus on what can actually be measured. Build a TMM to provide a full test blueprint proportionally aligned to the distribution of evidence models making up the construct map.
3 Write or generate items with the clear goal of full substantive and statistical isomorphism within each TMF. AIG and generative AI are exciting technologies but should not be seen as panaceas for solid TMF designs satisfying the design requirements embodied in the TMM. Item difficulty modeling and empirical quality control (QC) mechanisms can be is essential for demonstrating isomorphism. These computational analytics may involve sophisticated statistical and psychometric methods but should still be seen as QC tools and metrics. The same can be said for psychometric models, calibration, fit, and other analysis methods. They are tools that can help achieve the goal of isomorphic items within every TMF and adherence to the intended scale design: the construct and TMMs.

At the very least, considering AE may help organizations realize some basic efficiencies, develop more robust and flexible data structures and software tools for item production and test assembly, and develop better documentation about the intended purposes, use, and interpretation of your score scales. Enjoy the journey!

References

Ackerman, T. A., & Luecht, R. M. (in press). Still interested in multidimensional item response theory modeling? Here are some thoughts on how to make it work in practice. *Educational Measurement: Issues and Practice.*

American Educational Research Association, the American Psychological Association, & National Council on Measurement in Education. (2014). *Standards for educational and psychological testing.* Washington, DC: American Education Research Association.

Anastasi, A. (1988). *Psychological testing.* New York: Macmillan Publishing Co.

Angoff, W. H. (1971). Scales, norms, and equivalent scores. In R. L. Thorndike (Ed.). *Educational measurement*, 2nd edition (pp. 508–600). Washington, DC: American Council on Education.

Andrich, D. (1978). A rating formulation for ordered response categories. *Psychometrika*, *43*, 561–573.

Attali, Y., Runge, A., LaFlair, G. T., Yancey, K., Goodwin, S., Park, Y., & von Davier, A. (2022). The interactive reading task: Transformer-based automatic item generation. *Frontiers in Artificial Intelligence*, *5*, 903077. doi: 10.3389/frai.2022.903077

Bachman, L. F. & Palmer, A. S. (1996). *Language testing in practice: Designing and developing useful language tests.* Oxford: Oxford University Press.

Bejar, I. I. (2002). Generative testing: From conception to implementation. In S. H. Irvine & P. C. Kyllonen (Eds.), *Item generation for test development* (pp. 199–217). Mahwah, NJ: Lawrence Erlbaum.

Bejar, I. I., Lawless, R. R., Morley, M. E., Wagner, M. E., Bennett, R. E., & Revuelta, J. (2003). A feasibility study of on-the-fly item generation in adaptive testing. *The Journal of Technology, Learning, and Assessment*, *2*(3), 1–29.

Bejar, I. I., & Yocom, P. (1991). A generative approach to the modeling of isomorphic hidden-figure items. *Applied Psychological Measurement*, *15*(2), 129–137.

Birnbaum, A. (1968). Some latent trait models. In F. M. Lord & M. R. Novick (Eds.), *Statistical theories of mental test scores (with contributions by A. Birnbaum)* (pp. 397–424). Reading, MA: Addison-Wesley.

Bloom, B. S., Engelhart, M. D., Furst, E. J., Hill, W. H., & Krathwohl, D. R. (1956). *Taxonomy of educational objectives: The classification of educational goals. Handbook I, cognitive domain.* New York: David McKay.

Bock, R. D., & Aitkin, M. (1981). Marginal maximum likelihood estimation of item parameters: application of an EM algorithm. *Psychometrika*, *46*(4), 443–459. doi: 10.1007/BF02293801

Bormuth, J. (1969). *On a theory of achievement test items.* Chicago, IL: University of Chicago Press.

Circi, R., Hicks, J., and Sikali, E. (2023). Automatic item generation: foundations and machine learning-based approaches for assessments. *Frontiers in Education*, *8*, 858273. doi: 10.3389/feduc.2023.858273

Cizek, G. J. (2001). *Setting performance standards: Concepts, methods, and perspectives.* Mahwah, NJ: Lawrence Erlbaum.

Cizek, G. J. (Ed.) (2012). *Setting performance standards: Foundations, methods, and innovations.* New York: Routledge.

Cizek, G. J., & Bunch, M. B. (2007). *Standard setting: A guide to establishing and evaluating performance standards on tests.* Thousand Oaks, CA: SAGE Publications.

Cronbach, L. J., & Meehl, P. E. (1955). Construct validity in psychological tests. *Psychological Bulletin*, *52*(4), 281–302. doi: 10.1037/h0040957

Daniel, R. C., & Embretson, S. E. (2010). Designing cognitive complexity in mathematical problem solving items. *Applied Psychological Measurement*, *34*(5), 348–364.

Devlin, J., Chang, M.-W., Lee, K., & Toutanova, K. (2019). BERT: Pre-training of deep bidirectional transformers for language understanding. arXiv: 1810.04805v2. doi: 10.48550/arXiv.1810.04805

Drasgow, F., Luecht, R. M., & Bennett, R. (2006). Technology and testing. In R. L. Brennan (Ed.), *Educational measurement* (4th ed., pp. 471–515). Washington, DC: American Council on Education/Praeger Publishers.

Drum, P. A., Calfee, R. C., & Cook, L. K. (1981). The effects of surface structure variables on performance in reading comprehension tests. *Reading Research Quarterly*, *16*(4), 486–514. doi: 10.2307/747313

Dumais, S. T. (2005). Latent semantic analysis. *Information Science and Technology*, 38, 188–230. Doi: 10.1002/aris.1440380105

Egan, K. L., Schneider, C., & Ferrara, S. (2012). Performance level descriptors: History, practice and a proposed framework. In G. Cizek (Ed.), *Setting performance standards: Foundations, methods, and innovations* (pp. 79–106). New York, NY: Routledge.

Embretson, S. E. (1998). A cognitive design system approach to generating valid tests: Application to abstract reasoning. *Psychological Methods*, *3*(3), 380–396.

Embretson, S. E. (1999). Generating items during testing: Psychometric issues and models. *Psychometrika*, *64*, 407–433.

Embretson, S. E., & Kingston, N. M. (2018). Automatic item generation: A more efficient process for developing mathematics achievement items. *Journal of Educational Measurement*, *55*(1), 112–131.

Enright, M. K., Morley, M., & Sheehan, K. M. (2002). Items by design: The impact of systematic feature variation on item statistical characteristics. *Applied Measurement in Education*, *15*(1), 49–74.

Ferrara, S., Perie, M., & Johnson, E. (2002). *Matching the judgmental task with standard setting panelist expertise: The item-descriptor (ID) matching method.* Paper presented at the Annual Meeting of the National Council on Measurement in Education, New Orleans, LA.

Ferrara, S., Steedle, J. T., & Frantz, R. S. (2022). Response demands of reading comprehension test items: a review of item difficulty modeling studies. *Applied Measurement in Education*, *35*(3), 237–253. doi: 10.1080/08957347.2022.2103135

Finn, P. J. (1975). A question writing algorithm. *Journal of Reading Behavior*, *4*, 341–367.

Fischer, G. H. (1973). The linear logistic test model as an instrument in educational research. *Acta Psychologica*, *37*, 359–374.

Forte, E. (2017). Evaluating alignment in large-scale standards-based assessment systems (White paper). Washington, DC: Council of Chief State School Officers. https://ccsso.org/sites/default/files/2018-07/TILSA%20Evaluating%20Alignment%20in%20Large-Scale%20Standards-Based%20Assessment%20Systems.pdf

Geerlings, H., Glas, C. A. W., & van der Linden, W. J. (2011). Modeling rule-based item generation. *Psychometrika*, *76*, 337–359.

Gierl, M., & Haladyna, T. (Eds.) (2012). *Automatic item generation.* New York: Taylor & Francis/Routledge.

Gierl, M. J., & Lai, H. (2013). Instructional topics in educational measurement (items) module: Using automated processes to generate test items. *Education Measurement: Issues and Practice*, *32*, 36–50. doi: 10.1111/emip.12018

Gierl, M. J., Zhou, J., & Alves, C. (2008). Developing a taxonomy of item model types to promote assessment engineering. *The Journal of Technology, Learning and Assessment*, *7*(2), 1–51.

Glas, C. A. W., van der Linden, W. J., & Geerlings, H. (2010). Estimation of the parameters in an item-cloning model for adaptive testing. In W. J. van der Linden & C. A. W. Glas (Eds.), *Elements of adaptive testing* (pp. 289–314). New York: Springer.

Glaser, R. (1963). Instructional technology and the measurement of learning outcomes. *American Psychologist*, *18*, 519–521.

Gorin, J. S., & Embretson, S. E. (2006). Item difficulty modeling of paragraph comprehension items. *Applied Psychological Measurement*, *30*(5), 394–411. doi: 10.1177/0146621606288554

Gorin, J. S., & Embretson, S. E. (2012). Using cognitive psychology to generate items and predict item characteristics. In M. J. Gierl & T. M. Haladyna (Eds.), *Automatic item generation* (pp. 131–156). New York: Taylor & Francis.

Graf, E. A., & Fife, J. H. (2012). Difficulty modeling and automatic generation of quantitative items: Recent advances and possible next steps. In M. Gierl & T. Haladyna (Eds.), *Automatic item generation* (pp. 157–179). New York: Taylor & Francis/Routledge.

Graesser, A. C., & McNamara, D. S. (2011). Computational analyses of multilevel discourse comprehension. *Topics in Cognitive Science*, *3*(2), 371–398. doi: 10.1111/j.1756-8765.2010.01081.x

Guttman, L. (1959). Introduction to facet theory and design. *Acta Psychologica*, *15*, 130–138.

Guttman, L., & Schlesinger, I. M. (1966). Development of diagnostic analytical and mechanical ability tests through facet design and analysis (Report Number. CRP-OE-4-21.01). Jerusalem, Israel: Israel Inst. Of Applied Social Research.

Haertel, E. (1985). Construct validity and criterion-referenced testing. *Review of Educational Research, 55*(1), 23–46.

Haladyna, T. M., & Shindoll, R. R. (1989). Item shells: A method of writing effective multiple-choice items. *Evaluation and the Health Professions, 12*, 97–104.

Hambleton, R. K., & Swaminathan, H. (1985). *Item response theory: Principles and applications*. New York: Springer.

Hambleton, R. K., Swaminathan, H., Algina, J., & Coulson, D. B. (1978). Criterion referenced testing and measurement: A review of technical issues and developments. *Review of Educational Research, Winter, 48*(1), 1–47.

Hively, W., Patterson, H. L., & Page, S. H. (1968). A "universe-defined" system of arithmetic achievement tests. *Journal of Educational Measurement, 5*, 275–290.

Hommel, B. E., Wollang, F.-J. M., Kotova, V., Zacher, H., & Schmukle, S. C. (2022). Transformer-based deep neural language modeling for construct-specific automatic item generation. *Psychometrika, 87*, 749–772. doi: 10.1007/s11336-021-09823-9

Horst, P. (1933). The difficulty of a multiple-choice test item. *Journal of Educational Psychology, 24*, 229–232.

Irvine, S. (2002). The foundations of item generation for mass testing. In S. Irvine & P. Kyllonen (Eds.), *Item generation for test development* (pp. 3–34). Mahwah, NJ: Lawrence Erlbaum.

Jodoin, M. (2006). Measurement efficiency of innovative item formats in computer-based testing. *Journal of Educational Measurement, 40*(1), 1–15.

Kane, M. T. (2006). Validation. In R. L. Brennan (Ed.), *Educational measurement* (4th edition, pp. 17–64). Washington, DC: National Council on Measurement in Education and American Council on Education.

Kintsch, W. (1988). The role of knowledge in discourse comprehension: A construction-integration model. *Psychological Review, 95*(2), 13–182.

Kintsch, W., & van Dijk, T. A. (1978). Toward a model of text comprehension and production. *Psychological Review, 85*, 363–394.

Kirsch, I. S., & Mosenthal, P. B. (1990). Exploring document literacy: Variables underlying the performance of young. *Reading Research Quarterly, 25*(1), 5–30.

Kolen, M. J. & Brennen, R. L. (2014). *Test equating, scaling, and linking: Methods and practices*, 3rd edition. New York: Springer.

LaDuca, A., Staples, W. I., Templeton, B., & Holzman, G. B. (1986). Item modelling procedures for constructing content equivalent multiple-choice questions. *Medical Education, 20*, 53–56.

Lord, F. M. (1980). *Applications of item response theory to practical testing problems*. Mahwah, NJ: Lawrence Erlbaum Associates.

Luecht, R. M. (1998). Computer-assisted test assembly using optimization heuristics. *Applied Psychological Measurement, 22*(3), 224–336.

Luecht, R. M. (2006, May). Engineering the test: From principled item design to automated test assembly. Paper presented at the annual meeting of the Society for Industrial and Organizational Psychology, Dallas, TX.

Luecht, R. M. (2007, April). Assessment engineering in language testing: From data models and templates to psychometrics. Invited paper presented at the Annual Meeting of the National Council on Measurement in Education, Chicago, IL.

Luecht, R. M. (2008, October). Assessment Engineering in Test design, development, assembly, and scoring. Invited keynote presented at the Annual Meeting of East Coast Language Testing Organizations (ECOLT), Washington, DC.

Luecht, R. M. (2012). Computer-based and computer-adaptive testing. In K. Ercikan, M. Simon, & M. Rousseau (Eds.), *Improving large scale assessment in education: Theory, issues, and practice* (pp. 91–114). New York: Taylor & Francis/Routledge.

Luecht, R. M. (2012a). An introduction to assessment engineering for automatic item generation. *Automatic item generation*, pp. 59–101. New York: Taylor & Francis/Routledge.

Luecht, R. M. (2012b). Automatic item generation for computerized adaptive testing. In M. Gierl & T. Haladyna (Eds.), *Automatic item generation* (pp. 196–216). New York: Taylor & Francis/Routledge.

Luecht, R. M. (2013). Assessment engineering task model maps, task models and templates as a new way to develop and implement test specifications. *Journal of Applied Testing Technology, 14*. www.testpublishers.org/journal-of-applied-testing-technology

Luecht, R. M. (2014). Adaptive multistage design considerations and operational issues. In D. Yan, A. A. von Davier, & C. Lewis (Eds.), *Computerized multistage testing: Theory and applications* (pp. 69–83). London, UK: CRC Press/Taylor & Francis Group.

Luecht, R. M. (2016a, July). *Engineering design in the assessment world: A new paradigm for test design and development, with psychometric implications*. Invited keynote presented at the International Meeting of the Psychometric Society, Asheville, NC.

Luecht, R. M. (2016b). Applications of item response theory: Item and test information functions for designing and building mastery tests. In S. Lane, M. Raymond, & T. Haladyna (Eds.), *Handbook of test development* (2nd ed., 485–506). New York: Routledge.

Luecht, R. M. (2017a). Data and scale analysis for credentialing examinations. In S. Davis-Becker & C. W. Buckendahl (Eds.), *Testing in the professions* (pp. 123–152). New York: Routledge.

Luecht, R. M. (2017b). Application of assessment engineering design principles to the measurement of clinical decision-making in nursing (Technical report submitted to the National Council of State Boards of Nursing under National Council of State Boards of Nursing (NCSBN) under UNCG Research Agreement 010114). Greensboro, NC: University of North Carolina at Greensboro.

Luecht, R. M. (2019). Feasibility of assessment engineering task modeling for evidence-based medicine items (Unpublished technical report for the National Board of Medical Examiners). Greensboro, NC: University of North Carolina at Greensboro.

Luecht, R. M. (2020a). Generating performance-level descriptors under a principled assessment design paradigm: An example for assessments under the Next-Generation Science Standards. *Educational Measurement Issues and Practice*, *39*(4), 105–115.

Luecht, R. (August, 2020b). The challenges of principled item design. NCME symposium, Principled item design: State-of-the-art. Paper presented at the Annual Meeting of the National Council on Measurement in Measurement (online format for 2020).

Luecht, R. M. (2022, February). Assessment engineering (AE) for improved, lower cost test development. Invited paper presented at the Technical Issues in Large-Scale Assessment (TILSA) Conference (online) conference sponsored by the Center for Assessment and the council of Chief State School Officers.

Luecht, R., & Burke, M. (2020). Reconceptualizing items: From clones and automatic item generation to task model families. In R. Lissitz & H. Jiao (Eds.), *Applications of artificial intelligence to assessment*. Baltimore, MD: Information Age Publishers.

Luecht, R. M., Burke, M., & Devore, R. (2009, April). Task modeling of complex computer-based performance exercises. Paper presented at the Annual Meeting of the National Council on Measurement in Education, San Diego, CA.

Martone, A., & Sireci, S. G. (2009). Evaluating alignment between curriculum, assessment, and instruction. *Review of Educational Research*, *79*(4), 1332–1361.

Masters, G. N. (1982). A Rasch model for partial credit scoring. *Psychometrika*, *47*, 149–174.

McNamara, D. S., Graesser, A. C., McCarthy, P. M., & Cai, Z. (2014). *Automated evaluation of text and discourse with Coh-Metrix*. Cambridge University Press.

McNamara, D. S., & Kintsch, W. (1996). Learning from text: Effects of prior knowledge and text coherence. *Discourse Processes*, *22*, 247–287.

McNamara, D. S., Louwerse, M. M., McCarthy, P. M., & Graesser, A. C. (2010). Coh-Metrix: Capturing linguistic features of cohesion. *Discourse Processes*, *47*, 292–330.

Meisner, R., Luecht, R. M., & Reckase, M. R. (1993). *Statistical characteristics of items generated by computer algorithms*, ACT Research Report Series, RR-93-9. Iowa City, IA: ACT, Inc.

Messick, S. (1994). The interplay of evidence and consequences in the validation of performance assessments. *Educational Researcher*, *32*(2), 13–23.

Mislevy, R. J. (1994). Evidence and inference in educational assessment. *Psychometrika*, *59*, 439–483.

Mislevy, R. J. (2006). Cognitive psychology and educational assessment. In R. L. Brennan (Ed.), *Educational measurement* (pp. 257–305). Washington, DC: National Council on Measurement in Education and American Council on Education.

Mislevy, R. J. & Riconscente, M. M. (2006). Evidence-centered assessment design. In S. M. Downing & T. M. Haladyna (Eds.), *Handbook of test development* (pp. 61–90). Mahwah, NJ: Lawrence Erlbaum Associates.

Mislevy, R. J., Steinberg, L. S., & Almond, R. G. (2003). On the structure of educational assessments. *Measurement: Interdisciplinary Research and Perspectives*, *1*, 3–67.

Mitzel, H. C., Lewis, D. M., Patz, R. J., & Green, D. R. (2001). The bookmark procedure: Psychological perspectives. In G. J. Cizek (Ed.), *Setting performance standards: Concepts, methods, and perspectives* (pp. 249–281). Mahwah, NJ: Lawrence Erlbaum Associates, Inc.

Muraki, E. (1992). A generalized partial credit model: Application of an EM algorithm. *Applied Psychological Measurement, 16*, 159–176.

Nasreddin. (n.d.). AZQuotes.com. Retrieved from https://www.azquotes.com/quote/1120339

National Assessment Governing Board (NAGB). (2024). *Reading Framework for the 2026 National Assessment of Educational Progress*. Washington, DC: Author.

National Governors Association Center for Best Practices & Council of Chief State School Officers. (2010). *Common core state standards for mathematics*. Washington, DC: Authors. Council of Chief State School Officers (2022). learning.ccsso.org/wp-content/uploads/2022/11/Math_Standards1.pdf

National Research Council. (2001). *Knowing what students know: The Science and Design of Educational Assessment*. Washington, DC: The National Academies Press. https://doi.org/10.17226/10019.

Nichols, P. D. (1994). A framework for developing cognitively diagnostic assessments. *Review of Educational Research, 64*(4), 575–603. doi: 10.3102/00346543064004575

Popham, W. J. (1975). *Educational evaluation*. Englewood Cliffs, NJ: Prentice-Hall.

Popham, W. J., & Husek, T. R. (1969). Implications of criterion-referenced measurement. *Journal of Educational Measurement, 6*, 1–9.

Porter, A., Polikoff, M. S., Barghaus, K. M., & Yang, R. (2013). Constructing aligned assessments using automated test construction. *Educational Researcher, 42*(8), 415–423. doi: 10.3102/0013189X13503038

Pugh, D., De Champlain, A., Gierl, M. J., Lai, H., & Touchie, C. (2016). Using cognitive models to develop quality multiple-choice questions. *Medical Teacher, 38*, 838–843. doi: 10.3109/0142159X.2016.1150989

Radford, A., Narasimhan, Salimans, K. T., & Sutskever. I. (2018). *Improving language understanding with unsupervised learning* (Technical report). OpenAI.

Rasch, G. (1960). *Probabilistic models for some intelligence and attainment tests*. Copenhagen: Danish Institute for Educational Research. (Republished in 1980 with Forward and Afterward by Benjamin Wright, Chicago, IL: MESA Press/The University of Chicago).

Raymond, M. R. & Luecht, R. M. (2012). Licensure and certification testing. In K. F. Geisinger (Ed.). *APA handbook of testing and assessment in psychology*. Washington, DC: APA Publications.

Runge, A. (2023, September). Leveraging large-language models (LLMs) for automatic item generation and grading in English language assessment. Online presentation at the Artificial Intelligence in Measurement and Education (AIME) SIG meeting.

Schmeiser, C. B., & Welch, C. J. (2006). Test development. In R. L. Brennan (Ed.), *Educational measurement* (pp. 307–353). Washington, DC: National Council on Measurement in Education and American Council on Education.

Settles, B., LaFlair, G. T., & Hagiwara, M. (2020). Machine learning-driven language assessment. *Transactions of the Association for Computational Linguistics, 8*, 247–263.

Sheehan, K., & Mislevy, R. J. (1990). Integrating cognitive and psychometric models to measure document literacy. *Journal of Educational Measurement, 27*(3), 255–272.

Shu, Z., Burke, M., & Luecht, R. M. (2010, April). *Some quality control results of using a hierarchical Bayesian calibration system for assessment engineering task models, templates, and items*. Paper presented at the Annual Meeting of the National Council on Measurement in Education, Denver, CO.

Sinharay, S., & Johnson, M. S. (2012). Statistical modeling of automatically generated items. In M. J. Gierl & T. M. Haladyna (Eds.), *Automatic item generation* (pp. 183–195). New York, NY: Routledge.

Squire, L. R. (1987). *Memory and brain*. London: Oxford University Press.

Taylor, W. L. (1953). "Cloze procedure": a new tool for measuring readability. *Journalism Quarterly, 30*, 415–433.

ten Barge, T., & van Hezewijk, R. (1999). Procedural and declarative knowledge: An evolutionary perspective. *Theory and Psychology, 9*(5), 605–624.

The College Board. (2023). The SAT Suite of Assessments: Annual Report (Total Group). New York, NY: Author. Retrieved from https://reports.collegeboard.org/sat-suite-program-results, accessed: 07 June 2024.

van der Linden, W. J. (1998). Optimal assembly of psychological and educational tests. *Applied Psychological Measurement, 22*(3), 195–211.

van der Linden, W. J. (2005). *Linear models for optimal test design*. New York: Springer.

van der Linden, W. J. (2016). *Handbook of item response theory: Volume one: Models*. Boca Raton, FL: CRC Press.

van der Linden, W. J., & Luecht, R. M. (1998). Observed-score equating as a test assembly problem. *Psychometrika, 63*, 401–418.
von Davier, M. (2018). Automated item generation with recurrent neural networks. *Psychometrika, 83*, 847–857. doi: 10.1007/s11336-018-9608-y
von Davier, M. (2019). *Training optimus prime, M.D.: Generating medical certification items by fine tuning OpenAI's gpt2 transformer model*. arXiv: 1908.08594v3. doi: 10.48550/arXiv.1908.08594
Webb, N. (November, 2005). Depth-of-knowledge levels for four content areas. Presentation to the Florida Education Research Association, 50th Annual Meeting, Miami, Florida.
Weir, J. B. (2019). Enemy item detection using data mining methods: Latent Dirichlet allocation & random forests (Doctoral dissertation). The University of North Carolina at Greensboro, Greensboro, NC.
Wilson, M. (2005). *Constructing measures: an item response modeling approach*. Mahwah, NJ: Lawrence Erlbaum Associates.
Wright, B. D., & Stone, M. H. (1979). *Best test design: Rasch measurement*. Chicago, IL: Mesa Press.
Yen, W. M. (1984). Effects of local item dependence on the fit and equating performance of the three-parameter logistic model. *Applied Psychological Measurement*, *8*(2), 125–145. Doi: 10.1177/014662168400800201

Index

Note: Page references in *italics* denote figures, in **bold** tables and with "n" endnotes.

achievement-level descriptors (ALDs) 19, 21–23
ACT Assessment Mathematics test 56
ACTFL Performance Descriptors for Language Learners (ACTFL.org) 56
AE analytics: complexity scoring protocols 92–95, **93**, *94*; object analytic architecture 97–98, *98*; object analytics 83–92, *84*; psychometric QC using conditional residual analyses 95–96, *97*; and quality control 83–98
AE-based item models 79–82; data structure architecture for *80*; item model quality control 81–82; item model structures/content *80*, 80–81, *81*
AE task modeling 66n1
alignment of complexity/measurement precision with TMM 73, *73*
analytics: for audio/visual segments 88; image 87–88; for item structures 91–92; for mathematical expressions/equations 90; for numbers/numerical sets 90–91; object 83–92, *84*; for tables and tabular data *89*, 89–90; text 85–87
artificial intelligence (AI) 85; applications for AIG 78
Assessment Engineering (AE): and cognitive complexity 38–39; for comprehensive test design 8–11, *9*, *10*; definitions of 2; design goals 2; future directions 103–104; high-level procedures and systems 102–103; implementation 100–104; overview 1; perspective on test design and specifications 6–7, *7*; problems solved by 100–101; system of integrated systems 101–103
ATA optimization model 4
Attali, Y. 78
audio/visual segments 88
automated test assembly (ATA) 1, 103; algorithms 69–71; Test Information Functions *6*
automatic item generation (AIG) 1, 66n1, 76, 103–104; AE-based item models 79–82; AI and GPT applications for AIG 78; components and types of 77–79; and item model families 75–82; and large-scale item production 76; some limitations of AIG 78–79
automatic question generation (AQG) *see* AIG

Bejar, I. I. 55
Bennett, R. 52, 101
Bidirectional Encoder Representations from Transformers (BERT) 55, 56, 78, 86–87, 90
blueprints 67
Burke, M. 63

Calfee, R. C. 56, 66n5
Chang, M.-W. 86
Classical Test Theory 71
cognitive complexity: and AE 38–39; and task model/modeling 38–47
cognitive construct space 41
CohMetrix 55, 66n3, 85, 99n5
Common Core State Standards (CCSS) for Mathematics 3, 19–20
Common European Framework of Reference (CEFR) 55, 56
complexity design layers (CDLs) 8, *9*, 10, 12, 41, *48*, 48–49, 50n12, 51, 58–61; content-anchored, domain-specific 61
complexity scoring protocols (CSPs) 10, 92–95, **93**, *94*
composability 52; defined 53; in IDM research 52–53
computerized adaptive testing (CAT) 17, 51, 103
conditional measurement functions 67–71
conditional measurement precision: in test assembly 67–71; in test design 67–71
conditional residual analyses: psychometric QC using 95–96, *97*
Constructing Measures (Wilson) 13
construct mapping 13–32; choosing construct trajectory 27–28; creating construct map 30–32, *31*; evidence models 28–30; proficiency claims 28–30, *29*; test score interpretation 15–25

constructs 14–15
content-anchored, domain-specific CDLs 61
content blueprints *19*, 19–20
content domain 16–17
Cook, L. K. 56, 66n5
criterion-referenced tests (CRTs) 18, 23, 33n8
Cronbach, L. J. 14

Daniel, R. C. 56
declarative knowledge 39–40, 50n6
depth of knowledge (DOK) 61
Depth-of-Knowledge (Webb) 39
Devlin, J. 86
Document Literacy scale on the Young Adult Survey 57
domain 16–17
domain-referenced tests *see* criterion-referenced tests (CRTs)
Drasgow, F. 52, 101
Drum, P. A. 56, 66n5
Duolingo 55, 78

Egan, K. L. 8, 12n3, 22
Embretson, S. E. 55, 56
Evidence-Based Reading and Writing (EWR) 15–16
Evidence-Centered Design (ECD) 25–26
evidence models/modeling 8, 13–32
expected response function (ERF) 53, 95–96

"feature vectors" 66n7
Ferrara, S. 8, 12n3, 22, 57–59, 66n5
Fischer, G. H. 55, 62
Frantz, R. S. 57–59

generative AI 78
"generative approaches" 55
generative artificial intelligence (AI) models 76
generative knowledge 50n6
generative pre-trained transformers (GPTs) 78
Gierl, M. J. 77
Google 55, 56, 78, 86–87, 90
GPT applications for AIG 78
Graduate Record Examination (GRE®) 55
Guttman, L. 58

Haertel, E. 18
Hodja, Nasreddin 49
Hommel, B. E. 78
Horst, P. 53

"identical siblings design" 63
IDM research: characterizing statistical item difficulty for 53–54; composability in 52–53; features of reading passages and items **59**; foundations of 54–64; and isomorphism 52–53; item features and complexity design layers 58–61; need for 51–52; statistically modeling item difficulty 61–64
image 99n2
image analytics 87–88
image filtering 88
image segmentation 88
infographics 87
interactive tools 91–92
Interagency Language Roundtable (ILR) 56
Iowa Test of Basic Skills 18
isomorphic items 51
isomorphism 37–38; defined 52; in IDM research 52–53; statistical 52; substantive 52
item difficulty 53–54
item difficulty modeling (IDM) 9–12; composability in IDM research 52–53; foundations of IDM research 54–64; isomorphism in IDM research 52–53; need for IDM research 51–52; phases in implementing IDM 64–65; statistical item difficulty for IDM research 53–54
item features 58–61
item feature variables 58
item generator 50n5
Item GeneratOR (IGOR) software system 77–78
item mapping 19, 23–24, *24*; limitations of 24–25
item models: AE-based 79–82; families and automatic item generation 75–82; quality control 81–82; structures and content *80*, 80–81, *81*
Item Response Theory (IRT) 1, 17, 51, 79, 83, 103
item scale location: and task model/modeling *47*, 47–48

Johnson, M. S. 63

Kintsch, W. 42
Kirsch, I. S. 56–57
knowledge: declarative 39–40, 50n6; generative 50n6; procedural 39–40, 50n6; strategic 50n6

Lai, H. 77
layering 88
Lee, K. 86
Linear Logistic Test Model (LLTM) 55, 56, 62–63
Luecht, R. M. 52, 53, 56, 57, 63, 101

machine learning 85
Macsyma 90
Maple 90
Mathematica 90
mathematical expressions/equations 90
Mathematical Markup Language (MML) 90
MATLAB 90
Meehl, P. E. 14
Meisner, R. 56
Messick, S. 26

Mislevy, R. J. 56–58
mixed integer programming (MIP) 12n1
monotonicity 32
Mosenthal, P. B. 56–57
multiple-choice questions (MCQs) 34, *35*, 40, 43, *44*, 78–79; analytic layers for *84*; object for *84*
multistage testing (MST) 103

National Assessment of Educational Progress (NAEP) 21–22, 57
natural language processing (NLP) 85–86
N-grams 86
nice numbers 99n3
n-layered item model 77, *77*
NLTK 86
nomological net 14
numbers/numerical sets 90–91

object analytic architecture 97–98, *98*
object analytics 83–92, *84*; analytics for audio/visual segments 88; analytics for item structures 91–92; analytics for mathematical expressions and equations 90; analytics for numbers/numerical sets 90–91; analytics for tables and tabular data *89*, 89–90; image analytics 87–88; text analytics 85–87
objectives-referenced tests *see* criterion-referenced tests (CRTs)
object recognition 88
objects 83; and individual items 83; for multiple-choice questions *84*
optical flow 88
"over-fitting" 66n4

passive controls 91
performance level descriptors (PLDs) 21–25, 47
phases in implementing IDM 64–65
policy ALDs 22
procedural knowledge 39–40, 50n6
proficiency claims 28–30, *29*
proof-of-concept investigations 65
Psychological Methods 55
psychometric QC using conditional residual analyses 95–96, *97*
Python 55–56, 85–88

quality control (QC) 1; AE analytics and 83–98
quality improvement metrics 102
Quanteda package 86

range ALDs 22
Raven's Progressive Matrices Test 55
Reckase, M. R. 56
response capturing components 91
response probability functions (RPFs) 95
robust integration 101

schema 36
Schlesinger, I. M. 58
Schneider, C. 8, 12n3, 22
Scholastic Assessment Test (SAT) 15–16
score scale 16–19
semi-passive components 92
Sheehan, K. 56–58
Shu, Z. 63
Sinharay, S. 63
slicing 88
standards-based alignment *19*, 19–20
standard setting 21–23; limitations of 24–25
Standards for Educational and Psychological Testing 14
statistical-control pathway 54
statistical controls 54–55
statistical isomorphism 52
statistically modeling item difficulty 61–64
stealth item data 83
Steedle, J. T. 57–59
strategic knowledge 50n6
strong theory pathway 54
substantive isomorphism 52
system of integrated systems 101–103

tables/tabular data *89*, 89–90
task and item difficulty modeling 51–66
task model families (TMFs) 6–7, 8, 12, 34, 100–101, 104; isomorphism 37–38; location (statistical difficulty) 47–48; schema 36
task model grammars (TMGs) 42–46, 57
task model maps (TMMs) 7, 8, *8*, 11–12, 37, 46, 67–74, 100; building task model maps (TMMs) *72*, 72–73; complexity and measurement precision with TMM 73, *73*; test assembly methods 67–72; traditional test blueprints 67–72
task model/modeling: and cognitive complexity 38–47; complexity *46*, 46–47; data specifications sheet **36**; defined 34; and item scale location *47*, 47–48; multiple-choice question (MCQ) 34, *35*, 40; overview 34–38; structure of 42–46
Taxonomy of Educational Objectives (Bloom) 39
test assembly methods: conditional measurement precision in test design/assembly 67–71; fallible of content- and cognitive-coded constraints 71–72; limitations of 67–72
test characteristic function (TCF) 3, 32
test information function (TIF) 3–5
test score interpretation 15–25; domain-based interpretations 16; normative descriptions 15–16; predictions about future outcomes 15
TeX/LaTeX, eqn 90
text analytics 85–87
text coherence 66n3
threshold ALDs 22

Tidytext library 87
Toutanova, K. 86
traditional blueprints 24–25
traditional test blueprints 67–72
traditional test design: limitations of 2–7; test assembly example *3*, 3–6, **5**

unsupervised learning 81

validity by design 100
van Dijk, T. A. 42
versioning 101
von Davier, M. 78

Webb, N. 61
Wilson, Mark 8, 13
WordNet 99n1
WordVec2 library 87

Yocom, P. 55

zooming 88